500
Workshop
Tips & Jigs

500 Workshop Tips & Jigs

GUILD OF MASTER CRAFTSMAN PUBLICATIONS

First published 2006 by
Guild of Master Craftsman Publications Ltd
Castle Place, 166 High Street,
Lewes, East Sussex BN7 1XU

ISBN-13: 978-1-86108-423-1
ISBN-10: 1-86108-423-4

Production Manager: Hilary MacCallum
Managing Editor: Gerrie Purcell
Project Editor: Stephen Haynes
Chief Photographer: Anthony Bailey
Illustrator: Simon Rodway
Main cover photograph: John Bullar
Additional photography and illustrations by individual contributors
(see page 254)
Managing Art Editor: Gilda Pacitti
Design: Fineline Studios

Set in Neo Tech and Mahsuri Sans

Colour origination by Wyndeham Graphics
Printed and bound by Sino Publishing House Ltd, Hong Kong, China

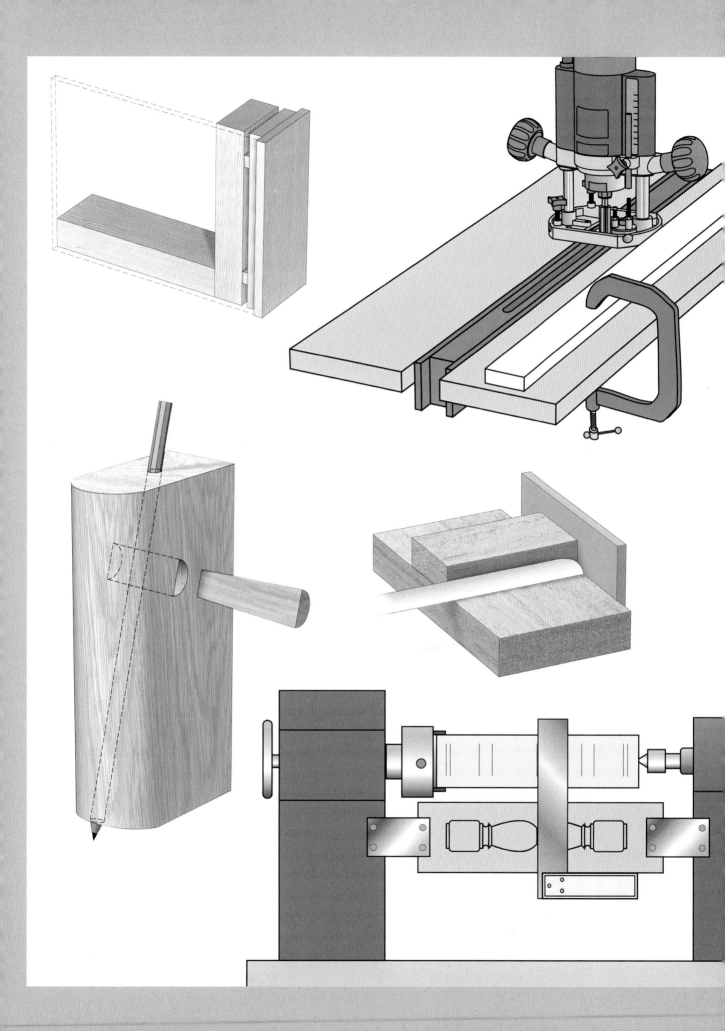

Contents

Health & safety

Woodworking is a potentially dangerous activity unless suitable precautions are taken.

Always ensure that work is securely held in a suitable clamp or other device, and that the workplace lighting is adequate.

Keep tools sharp; blunt tools are dangerous because they require more pressure and may behave unpredictably. Store them so that you, and others, cannot touch their cutting edges accidentally.

Be particular about disposing of shavings, finishing materials, oily rags, etc., which may be a fire hazard.

Do not remove safety guards from power tools. Pay attention to electrical safety, and do not allow leads to trail where you, or others, might trip over them.

Avoid loose clothing or hair which may catch in machinery. Protect your eyes and lungs against dust and flying debris by wearing goggles, dust mask or respirator as necessary, but invest in an efficient dust extractor as well.

When turning, do not use timber which may come apart on the lathe – beware of faults such as dead knots, splits, shakes, loose bark, etc.

Do not work when your concentration is impaired by drugs, alcohol or fatigue.

This book is not intended as a course of instruction. The safety advice in it is meant for your guidance, but cannot cover every eventuality: the safe use of hand and power tools is the responsibility of the user. If you are unhappy with a particular technique or procedure, do not use it – there is always another way.

Measurements

Although care has been taken to ensure that both metric and imperial measurements are sufficiently accurate to be useful, it should be noted that the tips in this book have been taken from a variety of sources; some were originally written in metric and some in imperial units. Conversions have normally been rounded up or down to the nearest whole millimetre or the nearest $\frac{1}{16}$in, or to the nearest convenient equivalent in cases where the measurements given are only intended to be approximate. When following the projects, use either the metric or the imperial measurements; do not mix units.

Key to the symbols used

 Money-saving tip

 Time-saving tip

 Wood-saving tip

 Health & safety tip

 A little extra help for those who need it

Introduction

From the simplest of circle-cutting jigs for the router to the removal of an unfortunate dent from the surface of a piece of timber, this book brings together the very best of advice from magazine readers and stands as a testament to their resourcefulness and enthusiasm for the craft. Many of the tips could be said to represent a significant moment in the development of the contributor's woodworking skills: the moment when they feel confident enough to offer advice to others, and feel that they have something significant to add to the woodworking community.

Although you can buy mass-produced jigs for a multitude of jobs, there is no substitute for designing and making your own - indeed, a great deal of the enjoyment that woodworking has to offer can be derived from making a jig or employing a technique that may have originated thousands of years ago.

The book is also a celebration of the resourceful worker, who prefers thrifty common sense to a quick purchase - not that there's anything wrong with spending money on ready-made products, but adapting the old classics and inventing your own is a rewarding activity in its own right.

Early on in my woodworking career I could never understand how professional makers achieved such perfect results. The truth began to reveal itself when I stopped working in isolation and bought my first book of jigs and techniques. I realized then that much of the hard work had been done before, and that for almost every problem or application there was already a solution. Of course, adapting the hard work of your forebears and contemporaries still requires intelligence and exactitude if you are to get the results you need - nothing can be employed successfully unless it is fully understood first.

Stuart Lawson

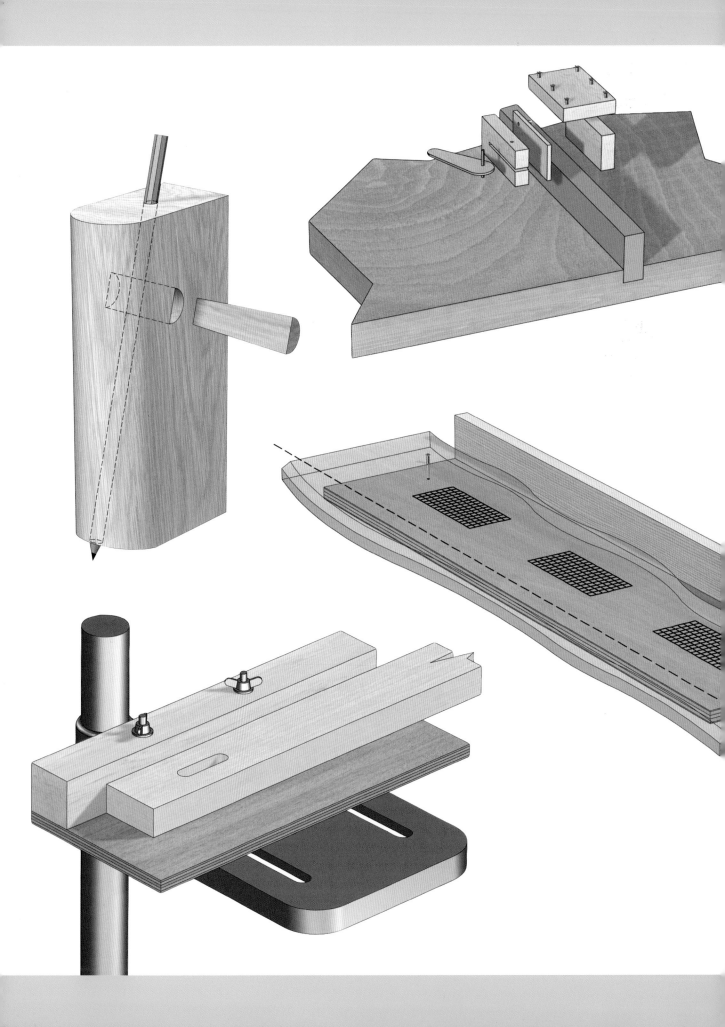

General workshop tips

001-190

Hand tools

001   Lapping planes

If you intend to use a plane for anything other than rough carpentry, first check that the sole is flat and the cheeks are square to the sole. Most planes require some serious but worthwhile attention.

You will need one or two pieces of float glass with wet-and-dry paper stuck onto the surface using spray adhesive. Fix the glass between some battens pinned to your bench top, and begin to flatten the sole. Start with sheets of 80-grit paper, and continue until the surface is flat. This may take an hour or two, but once achieved, you can work your way though the grits to a minimum of 400 grit. This will produce a very satisfying and smooth-running surface.

Once you have flattened this most important part of the plane, it is worthwhile squaring at least one of the cheeks also, if you intend to use the plane with a shooting board.

002   Planing aid

Many beginners find it difficult to true up awkward or irregular edges of timber with a plane. Keeping the plane square and the wood straight is helped a great deal by cramping either one or two of these very simple fences onto the sides of the plane with a G-cramp (C-clamp). The weight of the G-cramp increases the power and momentum of the plane when working on wide edges, like those of a door. Provided your plane iron has a sharp edge, this method will work well for you, but any bluntness will make it skate ineffectually along the surface.

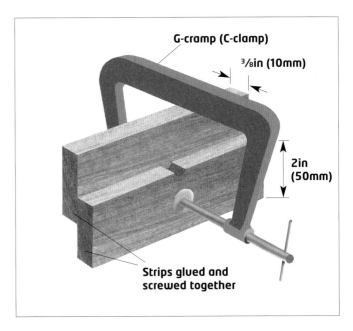

G-cramp (C-clamp)

³⁄₈in (10mm)

2in (50mm)

Strips glued and screwed together

003 Hand router

Using the electric router to level the bottoms of grooves, or the background of relief carvings, can be a daunting task. An alternative is to use an improvised version of the original, non-electric router, consisting of nothing more than a chisel wedged at an angle through a block of wood. This tool is often referred to as the 'old woman's tooth'.

Choose a block of wood large enough to hold comfortably, and drill through its centre at an angle between 30 and 45°. A ½in (13mm) hole will suit a ½in chisel. Finally, with a diagonal cut across a piece of dowel rod, make a wedge to lock the chisel in place.

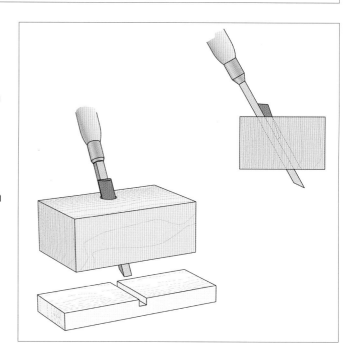

004 Shooting board

Here's a variation on the classic shooting board. It enables the accurate planing of long mitres, for a box or plinth, for example. All the components need to be at exactly 45° for the board to be effective. The V-groove is routed in, and the whole unit rests on a batten which is fixed in the vice when in use.

005 Keeping planes cosy

Keep small tools like block planes in a pair of protective gloves. The tools will be kept safe, and there will be nothing unnecessary in your toolkit.

General workshop tips

006 Scraper holder

A hand scraper is a great tool for smoothing a workpiece, but keeping it flexed is hard work, and the friction from scraping can build up enough heat to make the tool uncomfortable, if not agonizing, to hold.

Eliminate both of these problems with a simple scraper holder. It's just a scrap of ³⁄₄in (19mm) stock with a couple of screws to hold the scraper. To flex the scraper, add a thumbscrew (available at a hardware store).

Start by cutting a blank 2in (50mm) longer than the length of your scraper. Lay your scraper flat on the holder and centre it from side to side. Mark and drill a pilot hole for a screw at each end of the scraper. Drill a hole, centred on the holder, slightly less than the diameter of your thumbscrew. This way the thumbscrew will cut its own threads as it is screwed in. It is threaded through the holder and pushes against the back of the scraper, allowing you to adjust the amount of flex.

To assemble the holder, screw the scraper in place and thread the thumbscrew directly into the holder. Finally, adjust the thumbscrew for the desired amount of flex.

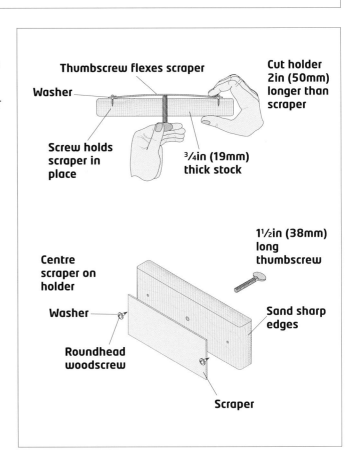

007 Improving a chisel

Manufactured bevel-edge chisels have narrow square edges (A). This may not matter for most woodworking, but when used for trimming the internal corners of hand-cut dovetails, they leave small pieces uncut. Grind the edges of a narrow square-edge chisel at an angle less than that of a dovetail, far enough back to allow for the thickness of the wood you need to cut (B). This gets right into the corners (C). The chisel is still suitable for other work.

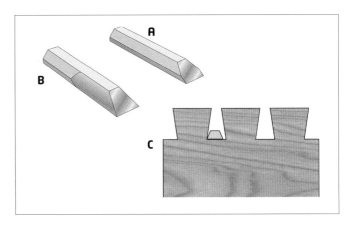

008 Bench hook

This box-shaped bench hook can be made to any suitable size from oddments of wood glued and pinned together. If you want a tapered plug for filling a hole, or a wedge for a hammer handle, take a scrap of suitable wood, hold it in the bench hook against the stop and with the other hand chisel away at the end of the wood to shape as required. Any overcut runs safely into the end block. The bottom of the box section can be flat or concave to suit your type of use. The length is roughly the same as an average chisel blade; this helps prevent damaged knuckles as you push the chisel forward.

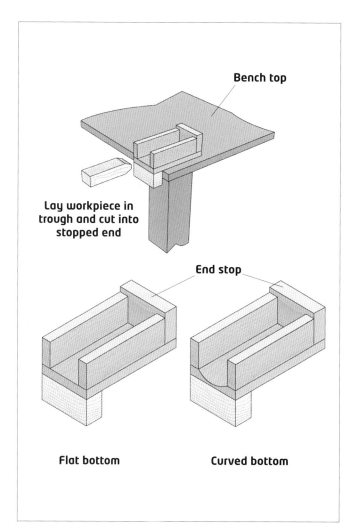

Bench top

Lay workpiece in trough and cut into stopped end

End stop

Flat bottom   **Curved bottom**

009 Short screwdriver

If you need a short screwdriver to work in a tight corner, simply remove the chuck from your electric drill, insert a short screwdriver bit of your choice, and that should solve the problem.

010 Preserving your mallet

A good way of ensuring your new mallet will last for years is to put it in a shallow tray or saucer of linseed oil and leave it overnight to soak in. You'll find it soaks up all of the oil, which also adds a bit more weight to the mallet. Boiled linseed oil is best, but raw is also OK for this sort of thing.

General workshop tips

011 Easier mitres

Many mitre saws consist of three parts: a threaded tensioning rod with wing nut, a hollow tube making up the spine of the saw, and the blade itself.

Dismantle the saw and block off one end of the hollow tube with a small amount of filler, such as plastic padding or similar.

Fill the tube to about ¾in (20mm) from the top with sand, packing it well down. Close the top of the tube with more filler and allow to set. Reassemble the saw.

Now, when cutting with the saw, do not apply any downward force, but allow the weight of the saw to do all the work.

012 Mitre saw adjustment

On some mitre saws it can be difficult to set the depth stop. Two jubilee clips, one on each pillar, are much easier to set, and won't move once tightened.

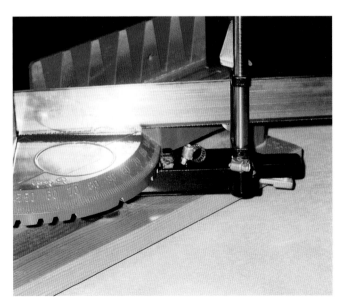

013 Recycled blades

Worn-out hacksaw blades can be made into marking knives. The steel is tempered too brittle for long blades, but they can make long-lasting short blades.

Grind grooves across the blade to help snap it off, then grind the cutting edge to shape and sharpen it. The other end can be left square across, so it can be inserted into a saw cut in a handle and held there with epoxy resin.

014 Straight sawing

If you want to make straight cuts with a handsaw, always use your forefinger to keep the saw in line.

Some modern saws have a handle aperture that is too large for the above method to be applied easily, so check before you buy.

015 Fretwork tips

1 Many writers on fretwork advise gluing your design onto the work. Peeling this off afterwards, however, can be a messy business. The solution is to glue the design onto thin card – a cereal box, for example – and staple it onto the wood. Even the most intricate pieces cut out well, and on completion the design just falls off the wood.

2 When threading a blade through a $\frac{1}{32}$in (1mm) hole, it can be difficult to locate the hole under the wood. Staple a piece of thick card underneath and, using a bradawl, punch a larger hole in the card; this gives you a much easier target to find.

General workshop tips

016 Grinding aid (1)

When sharpening on a small dry grinder, which is really designed for metalworking tools, chisels and plane irons have to be removed frequently and dipped in water to prevent overheating and preserve the temper. Because it is difficult to maintain the same angle each time you return to the grinding wheel, it is worth making a couple of guides, as shown, to bear on the toolrest and maintain the same angle each time. The hardwood guide locks onto the tool and bears on the toolrest. It can be made of beech and held with two brass screws. The thinner, lower piece is rounded where it bears on the toolrest. Have one guide with screws spaced to suit your widest chisel, and this will also hold narrower ones. Make a wider one to fit plane irons.

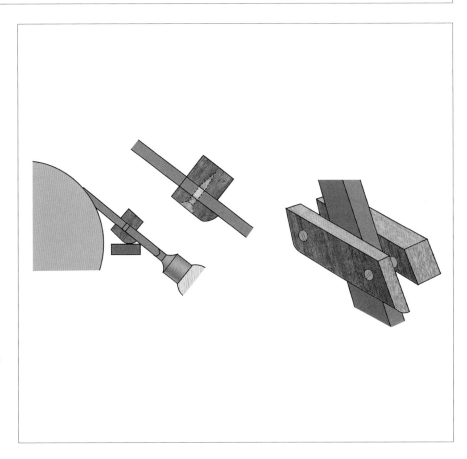

017 Grinding aid (2)

This tip came from a blacksmith's shop in the 1970s. If you are having trouble getting the right angle when grinding your drill bits, just get two steel nuts and weld or glue them together. The angle created at the intersection is 120°, and provides a simple and accurate guide for grinding. Keep them by the grinder at all times for easy reference.

018 Diamond whetstones

Though diamond whetstones are by no means cheap, they are exceptionally effective in honing a fine edge on hand tools. If you do not have the skills to maintain a constant honing angle unaided when sharpening chisels and plane blades, you should use a honing guide; but unfortunately, a benchtop diamond stone large enough to use with a honing guide is expensive.

A much cheaper mini-whetstone, measuring 2³/₄ x 1in (70 x 25mm), is ideal for sharpening small tools such as router cutters; but setting it into a scrap of hardwood measuring around 4³/₄ x 4³/₄ x ³/₄in (120 x 120 x 18mm) enables plane irons to be used across the stone. The honing stroke is of course limited, but as the diamonds cut very fast, a fine edge can be achieved. Leaving one end open allows the backs of chisel blades to be flattened. The stone is secured in the recess using double-sided tape; it can then be removed easily for touching up router cutters, for example.

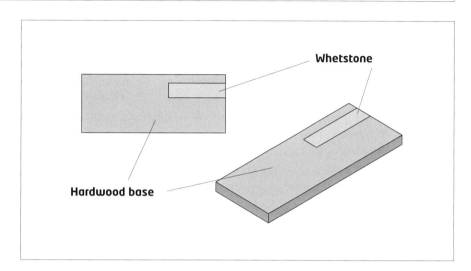

Whetstone

Hardwood base

019 Constant honing

If you don't have a honing guide, try this clever solution to the problem of maintaining a constant angle. As with all honing, a flat stone is an advantage.

Grind the initial bevel on the coarse side of the stone before turning the stone over and honing the second bevel. However, before you do so, lay a piece of ¹/₄in (6mm) MDF under the heel of the plane to raise it up. This will give the correct angle for your cutting edge.

020 Drill press improvements (1)

Most drill presses come without a fence and have a table that is very small. While these drawbacks may not be a problem when metalworking – the primary function of most drill presses – they do limit the woodworking applications. Making the appropriate modifications, however, is easy and inexpensive, and will transform your drill press from a metalworking to a woodworking machine.

The extended table can be made to any size to suit individual needs. Woodworkers who routinely use a drill press for mortising bedposts, for example, will want a long table with additional support legs to the floor. The table featured here is a more modest extension, made from a scrap piece of kitchen counter-top material with a plastic laminate surface. It is mounted on the drill press by screwing from the underside of the standard drill-press table. The only dimensional necessity is that the two holes for carriage bolts match the slots in the fence.

The fence itself is made from a piece of ¼in (6mm) plywood, with a section of hardwood glued to the front edge. A cutout in the centre of the plywood allows the fence to move freely around the drill-press

column. The two slots match those in the extended table. Install by pushing carriage bolts up from the bottom of the extended wooden table through the slots in the plywood, then adding washers and

wing nuts. The fence does not have to square up to the table, as a drill press has only a single cutting position. If a stop block is desired, any block of wood can be clamped to the hardwood portion of the fence.

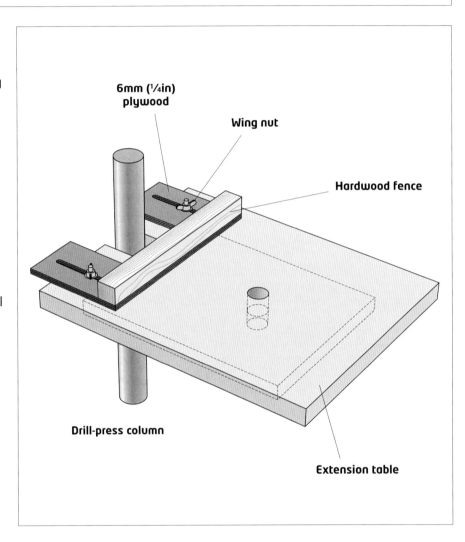

6mm (¼in) plywood

Wing nut

Hardwood fence

Drill-press column

Extension table

021 Drill press improvements (2)

Here is an alternative design for an auxiliary table to give better support for your work. It is a flat ³⁄₄in (18mm) board, wide enough to almost touch the pillar and extend slightly forward of the edge of the iron table. Its length is about three times the width of the original table.

The locating pieces beneath are hardwood, glued and dowelled to the board and cut to fit easily in the slots of the table. The wooden table usually holds firmly under pressure, and the two turn-buttons ensure it stays there.

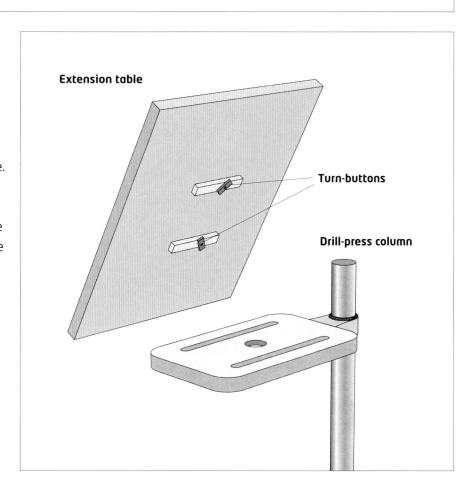

Extension table

Turn-buttons

Drill-press column

022 Truing a drill-press table

Forget messing around with a set square and a long drill bit – here is a simple way to true up the bed of a drill press.

Form two 90° bends in opposite directions in an 8in (200mm) length of coat-hanger wire, 1in (25mm) from one end and 2½in (60mm) from the other. Insert the longer length into the chuck and rotate it through 180°, adjusting the table angle until you achieve consistent contact between the outside tip and the table.

General workshop tips

023 Drilling angled holes

This self-explanatory jig is one of the most straightforward ways of drilling consistently angled holes with a drill press.

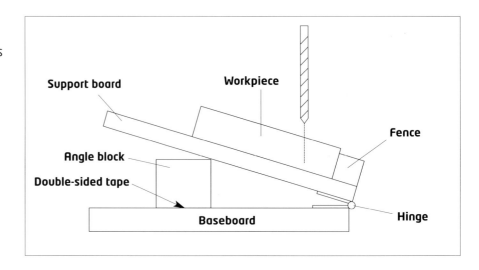

024 Mortising on the drill press

When removing waste from a mortise by drilling a row of overlapping holes, a guide or jig is advisable to keep the holes in line. This one is easy to fit or remove, extending either side of the drill table to give plenty of support.

It consists of a square hardwood strip on a plywood base, kept in place with two coach bolts and wing nuts with washers. Cut the bolt heads in line with the necks so that they become T-heads; they can then be passed through the slots in the drill-press table and turned 90° to grip, without the need to extract them from the wood each time.

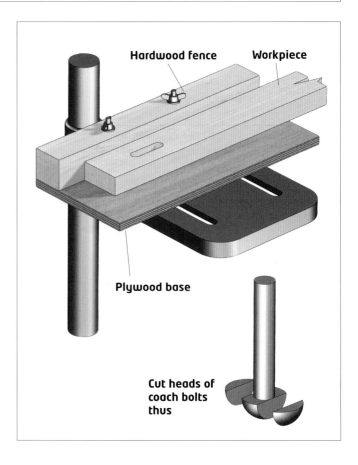

Power tools and machines

025   Drilling small holes

Here is a way of drilling a series of small holes within a number of small frames – too small for an electric drill to fit within them.

Using a flexible drive in an electric drill, preset to the 'on' position and to the desired speed, take the power from the mains plug through a no-volt-release switch. Now, switching on and off only requires one finger, leaving the other hand free to hold the flexible drive securely at all times.

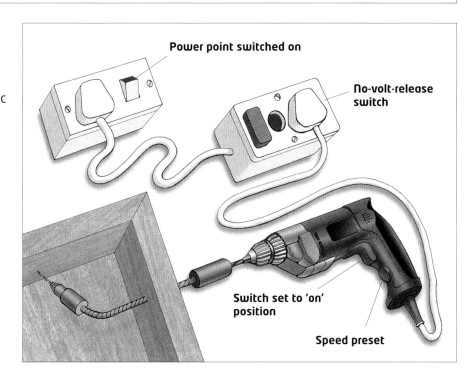

Power point switched on

No-volt-release switch

Switch set to 'on' position

Speed preset

026   Drilling plastic

Drilling perspex and other plastics is not always successful: ragged holes or cracks often result, particularly when the holes are larger than those for screws. This is because a drill sharpened for metalworking tends to snatch plastic. You can prevent this with larger drills by grinding the leading edges vertical, as shown, so a less violent approach is made to the plastic.

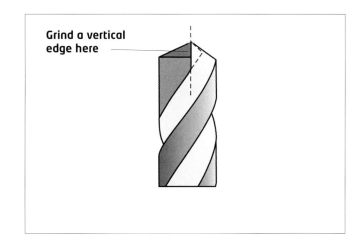

Grind a vertical edge here

General workshop tips

027 Home-made roller stand

Roller stands have always been expensive, and even Far Eastern imports are not cheap. Here is a simple but effective substitute made from offcuts.

Cutting list

Feet (2)	Pine, 19¾ x 3¾ x ⅞in (500 x 94 x 22mm)
Legs (2)	Pine, (height of machine minus foot height) x 3¾ x ⅞in (x 94 x 22mm)
Stretcher rails (2)	Pine, 20 x 3¾ x ⅞in (506 x 94 x 22mm)
Axles (2)	Pine, (internal diameter of plastic pipe) x ⅞in (22mm)
Axle inserts (2)	Hardwood dowel, ⅜in (10mm) diameter x 2in (50mm) dowel
Roller	Plastic waste/soil pipe, 19¾in (500mm) long

End of roller

028 Tablesaw cutting aid

A simple way of marking the position of the saw kerf on a tablesaw is to lightly scratch two lines into the table in front of the blade. First colour in a small area with a permanent marker pen.

Crosscut a piece of timber about ⅜in (10mm) through before moving it along about ⅛in (3mm) and repeating the cut. Continue to do this until you have a notch roughly ⅜in (10mm) wide. Mark a line into the ink with a scribing point against the last shoulder you cut, then shift the workpiece over so that you can make a final cut on the other side of the notch. Scribe a final mark against this shoulder.

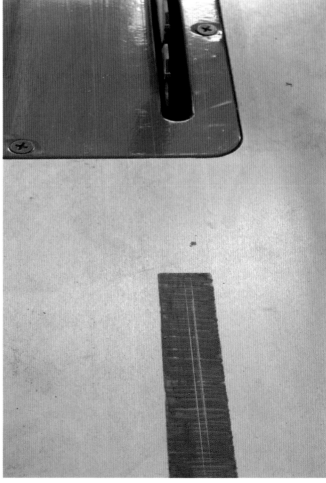

029 | Push stick

There are several variations on this L-shaped type of push stick, but this is a particularly good design. Although ply would probably be stronger, MDF has proved quite adequate.

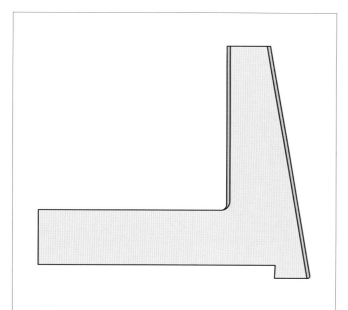

030 | Reversa-stick

The 'reversa-stick' is not just a push stick, but is designed to enable small parts to be withdrawn from, say, the bandsaw, before they jam between blade and table. It guarantees more control where needed, all thanks to a cleverly placed pad of rubber from a puncture-repair kit.

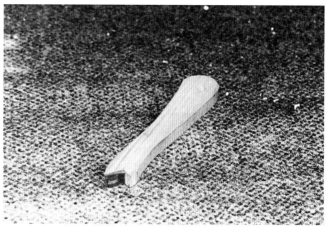

031 | Cleaning saw blades

If you don't clean your tablesaw blades often enough, you will get a build-up of resin and other unknown substances. A last-ditch solution is to remove the blade and use oven cleaner. This seems to have no side effects, and works a treat.

General workshop tips

032 | Improving the mitre gauge

The standard mitre gauge supplied with most router tables and circular saws does not have much surface to press against the work. You can improve it by screwing on a strip of wood, both longer and higher than the metal face. Gluing a piece of fine abrasive paper to the face of the wooden fence will improve its grip against the workpiece.

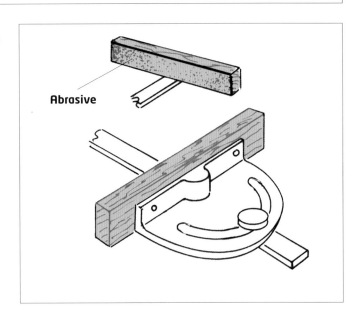

Abrasive

033 | Cutting accurate multiples

It is handy to use an end stop when cutting multiple lengths on the chopsaw, but sawdust can build up if you're not careful, spoiling its accuracy. Here's a simple way to avoid this: just mitre the end of your stop, and you will be all right.

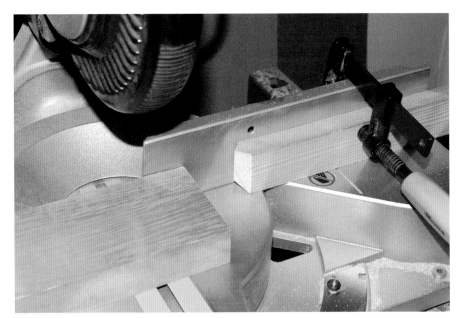

034 Straightening waney-edged boards

Hardwoods can be less expensive if bought from a local sawmill as waney-edged boards. Dimensioning the stock is not too laborious, but if the wood allows it is easier to convert it into planks with a tablesaw rather than a hand-held saw.

This low-tech jig makes the tablesaw method almost a pleasure, and costs very little to make.

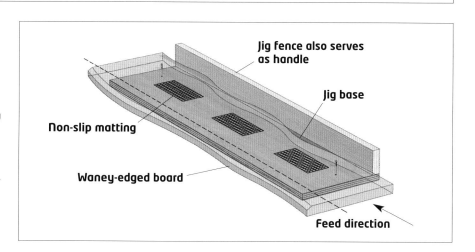

Jig fence also serves as handle

Jig base

Non-slip matting

Waney-edged board

Feed direction

035 Sawing stop

Here's a movable stop for your crosscut saw. No more mucking about with G-cramps (C-clamps) and blocks of wood that foul the saw – this one can be made from hardwood scraps and employs a simple cam lever to hold it firmly in place.

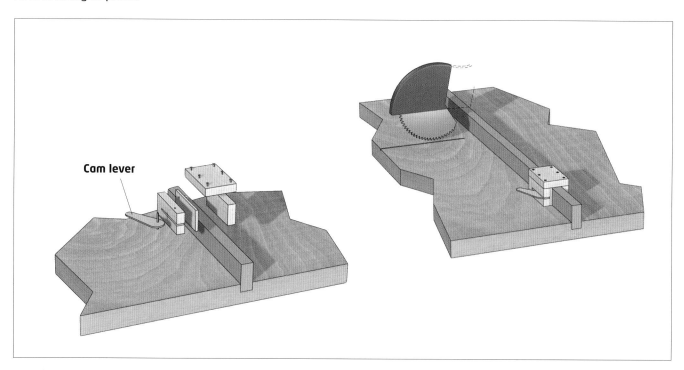

Cam lever

General workshop tips

036 Cutting multiples with the mitre gauge

The tablesaw's mitre gauge or protractor can be very useful for cutting a batch of short pieces of wood to a uniform length.

The sliding block can be adjusted to the required length and tightened up. The sliding block is cut to fit in the recess, to avoid tilting. A measuring scale can also be marked on the 2 x 1in (50 x 25mm) fence if needed;

however, remember to check it for accuracy, taking into account the blade being used and the amount of set on the teeth.

Most protractors supplied with tablesaws already have back fixing points to which the wooden fence can be fixed; all that is required is a suitable ¼in (M6) bolt, washer and locking nut.

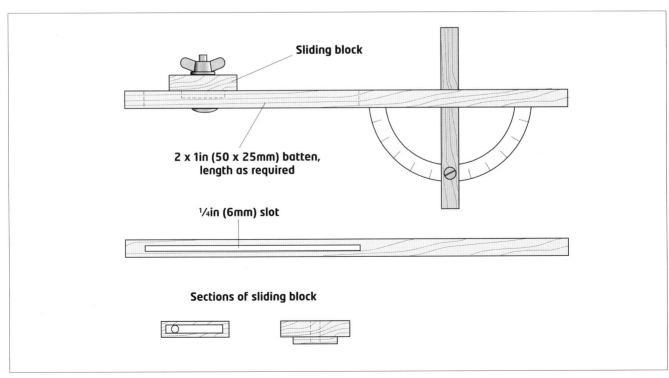

Sliding block

**2 x 1in (50 x 25mm) batten,
length as required**

¼in (6mm) slot

Sections of sliding block

037 | Resawing aid

This simple, spring-loaded feeder is as good as a third hand when resawing stock on the bandsaw. Make the wooden arm and attach it to the bandsaw table with a spring as shown. If you can't find the right kind of spring, substitute an appropriate length of bungee cord.

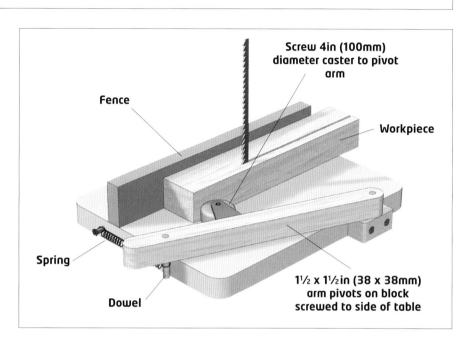

Fence

Screw 4in (100mm) diameter caster to pivot arm

Workpiece

Spring

Dowel

1½ x 1½in (38 x 38mm) arm pivots on block screwed to side of table

038 | Avoiding breakout on the tablesaw

Because of the gap around the saw blade within a table insert, the only sure way to avoid breakout when crosscutting is to construct a jig that supports the workpiece all the way up to the blade.

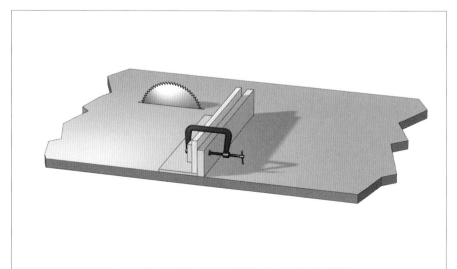

039 | Gaps under fences

Some universal machines use the same fence for the tablesaw as for the surface planer. Because the lead-off part of the fence has a gap under it, this can cause difficulties with thin stock. To fill the gap, simply attach a false fence or fascia made from ³⁄₈in (9mm) MDF, using countersunk machine screws, washers and wing nuts.

General workshop tips

040 Blade storage

When wall space is at a premium, consider using the ceiling to store your bandsaw blades. This simple solution uses two short lengths of plastic cable trunking – use the type that has a snap-on cover, as this will give you a section of channel that has a lip on it. This will ensure that the blade cannot fall out when held in the channel.

Cut two lengths of 1 x ½in (25 x 12mm) trunking approximately 6in (150mm) long, and dispose of the cover strip. Make two brackets approximately 2in (50mm) long from ²³/₃₂in (18mm) aluminium angle.

Attach the brackets to the back of the trunking using two pop rivets, with the heads of the rivets inside the trunking. Drill two holes in the other flange of the aluminium angle, and screw each bandsaw blade support to a suitable roof beam, approximately 4in (100mm) apart.

The supports could just as easily be located on the wall, on a door or even inside a cupboard – in fact anywhere you like.

The natural spring in the blade will ensure it is held firmly in place, and one support will hold three blades if necessary.

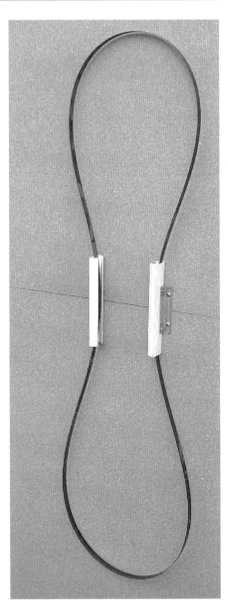

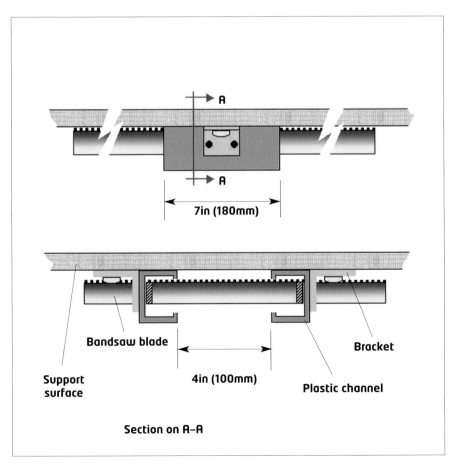

7in (180mm)

Bandsaw blade

Support surface

4in (100mm)

Bracket

Plastic channel

Section on A–A

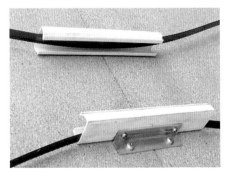

041 Longer life for scrollsaw blades

Most scrollsaws use a 5in (125mm) blade but have a stroke of only ⅝ or ¾in (16 or 19mm). You can get double the life from your blades if you attach a piece of ⅝ or ¾in melamine board to the table with double-sided tape or hot-melt glue.

This lifts the workpiece up by that amount, and uses a higher part of the blade.

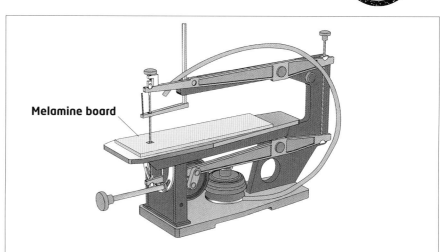

Melamine board

042 Straight cuts with a jigsaw

A jigsaw with a coarse blade is capable of cutting through quite thick wood, though the narrow blade is liable to wander.

To keep the cut straight and square to the edge of the wood, make the guide shown here. It consists of a piece long enough to span the widest wood you expect to cut, and reach back far enough to guide the base of the jigsaw at the start of the cut. The strip fixed squarely below extends each side as far as the cut will come. With one of these ends lined up with the marked cut line, cramp the guide to the wood and then make a straight, true cut. A suitable size might be 12 x 4 x ⅝in (300 x 100 x 15mm), with the crosspiece underneath ⅝in (15mm) square.

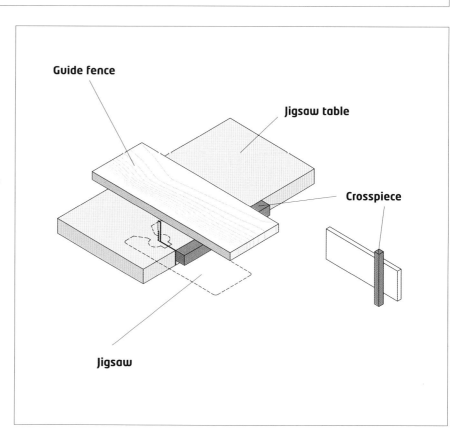

Guide fence

Jigsaw table

Crosspiece

Jigsaw

General workshop tips

043 Door-trimming jig

When hanging new doors, it is not unusual to have to plane a substantial amount from each side. It can be time-consuming to make the cuts on both sides and keep them parallel, but here is a simple way to do it.

First, cut an opening in a piece of ½in (12mm) MDF so that it will fit over the drive section of a hand planer. This becomes a slide, and is firmly secured by a nut and bolt through the body of the planer where the handle is normally fixed. Then cut two full lengths, one 1³/₁₆in (30mm) wide, the other ³/₈in (10mm). The thickness does not matter, as long as all parts are the same.

Screw the two strips together to make an L-shaped section, which forms a one-sided running groove for the slide to travel along. This is temporarily screwed to the side of the door at a calculated distance from the edge, using an engineer's square to set the depth of cut.

Once the runner is secured, it is a good idea to loosen the screws half a turn to let the slide move smoothly. All that needs to be done now is to keep making passes with the planer until all the waste has been removed.

Right: **L-section rail**

Below: **Planer slide located in the jig**

Bottom right: **Planer fixed in the slide**

Power tools and machines

044 | Making spheres

This belt-sander jig for manufacturing wooden spheres works surprisingly well; it might work even better on a sander with a longer bed than that shown here.

Fix your sander upside down in a vice, then construct a box from any suitable material, approximately 4in (100mm) wide with an open top and bottom. The interior length of the box should be a little shorter than the flat bed of the sander. The width should be enough so that the sides rest on the edges of the machine, and the ends should be $\frac{1}{16}$–$\frac{1}{8}$in (2–3mm) short in height, so that they don't touch the belt. At the lead-off end of the box, add a 45° angle strip flush with the bottom edge of the frame; this will stop the cubes getting stuck against the belt. Use a hot-melt glue gun to fix the box to the sander.

Next, cut some wooden cubes, as accurately as you can, which are a little bigger than the desired sphere's diameter. Switch on the sander and drop in the cubes. Sit back and watch a fascinating process in action.

045 | Accurate mortising

When cutting mortises larger than the size of the chisel available on a budget mortiser, the fence must be adjusted to give the required dimension. If there is excessive play in the fence mechanism, when clamped in a new position the chisel may be out of square with the workpiece. To overcome this, cut two slots in the wooden baseplate with a router and fix two hardwood runners to the underside of the fence to eliminate side play, thus maintaining the original squareness of the mortise chisel.

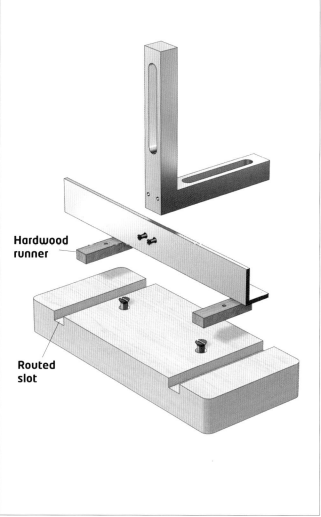

Hardwood runner

Routed slot

General workshop tips

046 Home-made lobe nuts

Here is a cheap way to make lobe nuts for the adjustable fence of a home-made router table. It is not always possible to buy these nuts from your local suppliers, but if you have some appropriately sized T-nuts, you can make your own. Offcuts of ½in (12mm) ply are perfectly adequate, although hardwood would be more aesthetically pleasing. The nuts can be made in whatever size you need, but the drawing and the instructions below are for the ⁵⁄₁₆in (M8) nuts required for the adjustable fence.

For two M8 lobe nuts, cut four discs of ply, 2in (50mm) in diameter, using a holesaw in a drill press. Drill out the centre holes to ¹¹⁄₃₂in (9mm) to give decent clearance for the M8 coach bolt. In one disc, counterbore a hole ²⁵⁄₃₂in (20mm) diameter by ⁵⁄₆₄in (2mm) deep to accept the head (wide end) of the T-nut. In the other disc, drill a counterbore of ²⁵⁄₃₂in (12mm) diameter by ⁵⁄₁₆in (8mm) deep to accommodate the body of the T-nut. (The one disc could be counterbored twice to accommodate all of the T-nut, but sharing the total distance required allows for thinner stock to be used if preferred.)

The T-nut is pulled into place in this second disc using a bolt with a nut and washer (it could also be pressed into position using a vice). Use a ring of PVA adhesive to glue the two discs together; the wide, shallow counterbore for the T-nut head allows the surfaces to contact fully. The assembly can be clamped with an M8 bolt with nuts and washers until the glue is dry. Using a round rasp, file six evenly spaced grooves in the edge of the assembly to create the lobe effect. Keep the clamping bolt and nuts in place to secure the assembled nut in the drill press, and spin it up to sand the rough edges. Finish as required.

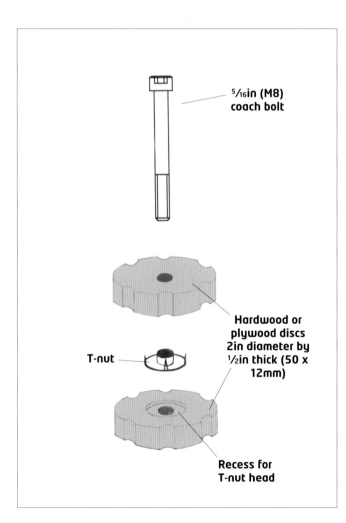

⁵⁄₁₆in (M8) coach bolt

Hardwood or plywood discs 2in diameter by ½in thick (50 x 12mm)

T-nut

Recess for T-nut head

047 PTFE spray

A dry lubricant spray such as PTFE is excellent for improving the slickness of machine surfaces such as planer beds, saw tables and fences. However, if you are prone to asthma you should always wear a mask when applying it.

048 PTFE for saw blades

If you spray PTFE onto your circular saw blade as well as onto the table, your machine's cutting efficiency will be noticeably improved.

049 Easier machine adjustment

How often have you seen a machine with tiny tension knobs that make your fingers ache when you try to tighten them? To avoid this, cut out a hard block and fit it over the knob, making sure its sides are uneven so it won't slip in your hand. This way you will have more comfortable leverage.

050 Cheap alternative

If you would rather not spend your hard-earned cash on PTFE for your machines, use one of those spray-on furniture polishes that contain an all-important ingredient – silicone.

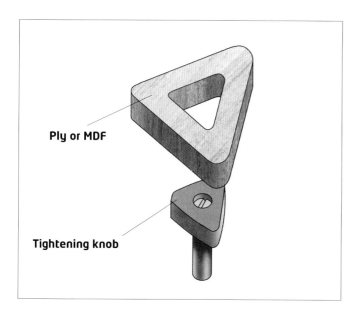

Ply or MDF

Tightening knob

Marking and measuring

051 Making the most of sheet materials

Sheet material is expensive, so plan your cuts on a scaled-down grid to make sure that you use the board as economically as possible. This will also allow you to save time by arranging for same-size cuts to be carried out in one go. Don't forget to allow for the width of the saw kerf.

Draw to scale as many sheets as possible on a gridded pad, keep a master copy and photocopy it to save drawing it out every time. It is now a simple job to draw the components to scale on paper and arrange them on the plan.

In the example shown, the top drawing is what could happen if you started cutting without thinking. Four set-ups and ten cutting operations result in a lot of waste, and component 5 is missing. The second drawing shows only eight cutting operations, resulting in little waste, and leaving enough material for all components.

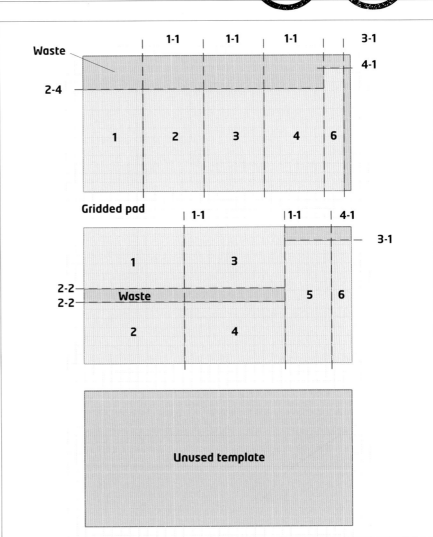

052 Metric conversions (1)

Here's a simple way to convert inches into millimetres.

Example 1

$1^3/_{16}$in = $^{19}/_{16}$in
$^1/_{16}$in = 1.5875mm
19 x 1.5875mm = 30.16mm
Therefore, $1^3/_{16}$in = 30.16mm

Example 2

$5^3/_8$in = $^{43}/_8$in
$^1/_8$in = 3.175mm
43 x 3.175mm = 136.52mm
Therefore, $5^3/_8$in = 136.52mm

053 Using a tape measure

Old pros often advise using the 1in or 1cm mark on a tape measure, rather than the end hook, to ensure accurate measurements, especially when measuring from angled ends.

While this may work for some people, for others it is an excellent way of cutting stock precisely 1in or 1cm short – not good.

A foolproof technique to avoid this possibility is to use the 10in or 10cm mark instead. The chances of a mistake of this magnitude going unnoticed are pretty slim, and the dimensions you work with are still close to the true ones.

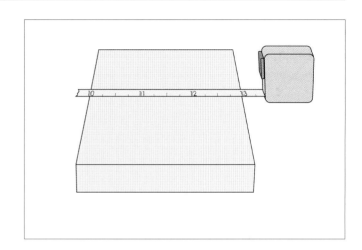

054 Measuring equal intervals

To mark equally spaced divisions across a board, simply mark a length of wood with the number of divisions that you require, using any convenient measurements, provided they add up to more than the width of the board. Lay the marked piece across the board so that its end marks align with the edges of the board, then strike the lines along and they will be perfectly spaced.

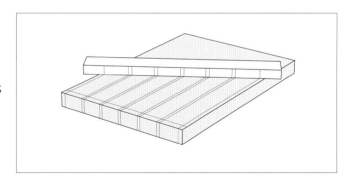

055 Metric conversions (2)

It's not always necessary or useful for conversions to be accurate to several decimal places; there are some approximations which are easy to remember, and near enough for most purposes.

A useful mnemonic is that $1/16$in = 1.6mm, from which you can extrapolate that $1/8$in = 3.2mm, $3/16$in = 4.8mm, $1/4$in = 6.4mm, etc. It's easy to remember $5/16$in, because it comes to a nice round number, 8mm; and from there

you can easily work out that $5/8$in = 16mm, and $1\frac{1}{4}$in ($5/4$in) = 32mm. If you have a need to work on a micro scale, 0.004in (= $4/1000$in or 4 'thou') is, to all intents and purposes, 0.1mm.

You can still buy steel rules that have millimetres on one edge and inches on the other, both running in the same direction, and laying a try square across the rule is a very quick way to convert any measurement.

General workshop tips

056 A fixed marking gauge

Most of us keep our marking gauges at the same setting in the knowledge that any resetting can result in mismatched parts. Making a fixed marking gauge, with four commonly used measurements, is even safer. The example shown is made from a length of hardwood 1³⁄₈in (36mm) square, allowing 2⁵⁄₈in (65mm) for the central grip. The ends are one third the thickness of the central part.

The points are made from fine nails that are driven in and cut off so they protrude about ¹⁄₈in (3mm).

Make a test run and, if any of the lines is not exactly right, correct it by filing a little more off one side of the corresponding point.

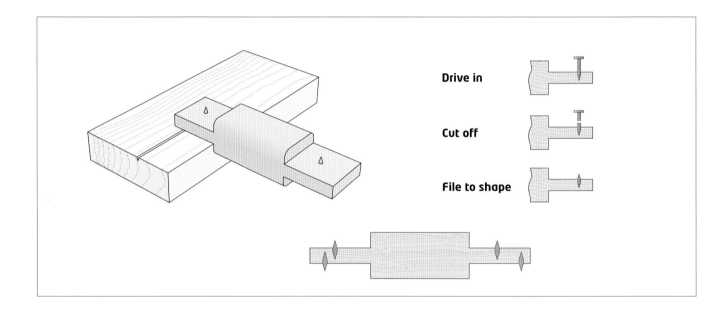

Drive in

Cut off

File to shape

057 Marking gauge and scratch stock

Here's a simple combined marking gauge and scratch stock, easily and cheaply created from a slot-head screw and any small piece of scrap timber. Adjustable when required, it is great for marking out hinges, as you can leave it set up permanently if you only have the one marking gauge.

If you wind the screw out a bit more, you can use it to start off a scratch bead which will only need a bit of handwork with a plane to resemble an authentic antique moulding.

058 | Handy marking gauge

A 4in (100mm) machinist's square can easily be adapted to double as a marking gauge. Use a fine, triangular file to cut a small V-groove in the centre of one end of the sliding rule. Rest a pencil or steel scribe in this notch and, using the square's head as a guide, draw your lines. It really is that simple.

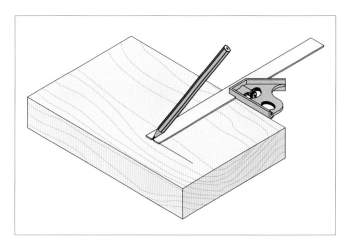

059 | Pencil gauge

A marking gauge is a useful tool, but you do not always want a scratched line – a pencil line may be preferable. Simply cut a notch in the opposite end of the stem to guide a pencil point. Pulling gauge and pencil along together draws a line exactly parallel with the edge of the wood.

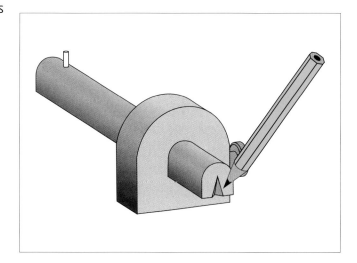

General workshop tips

060 Using dial callipers

One of the handiest things in the workshop is a set of dial callipers (or vernier callipers, if you prefer). Too many workshops lack a set on the grounds that they are too expensive, or somehow unnecessary. The fact is that it's a lot quicker and easier to size drill bits or router cutters with callipers than by reading illegible shank markings. Checking hole or recess depths with the end measuring prong is also better than trying to insert the end of a rule in the hole. Even checking plunge-depth settings on the router is quick and reliable. Checking the thickness of a cabinet hinge before setting in the core diameter of a screw is another example of accurate size checking. A decent pair of callipers is a sound investment.

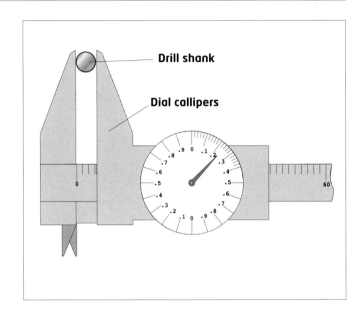

Drill shank

Dial callipers

061 Marking the centre

In most framed construction it is necessary to place mortises centrally in the edges of the wood. You can use a marking gauge, but the little tool shown here will draw a line central on the edge of wood – within its limits – without measuring, so you can set the router fence to bring the cutter down on the line.

Fix two pieces of dowel, say ¼in (6mm) diameter, into holes drilled perpendicularly in a strip of hardwood, a little further apart than the thickest stock you expect to use, and drive a nail centrally between the dowels so that its point projects.

To use the tool, turn it so that both dowels rest against the edges of the wood and move it along so the nail scratches a line. For your initial test, turn the tool round and check that it scratches in the same place; you can correct a slight error by filing the nail point on one side or the other.

062 Home-made marking knife

This marking knife is made from a discarded table knife. It can be sharpened on both sides, but it may be better to make a pair, sharpened on opposite sides; these will work close to a try-square blade, either to right or left. They have an additional use as skew chisels, to remove those annoying bits of fibre which are invariably left clinging to the internal angle when an inside corner is cut, as in a rabbet (rebate).

To make the knife, use the edge of a grinding wheel to cut partly through the blade, and then snap it off. If it snaps cleanly, you know that the steel is tempered hard and will hold an edge for a long time. If you have to waggle very much in order to break it off, it will be softer and will need to be sharpened more often.

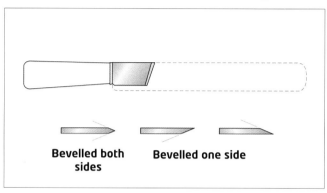

Bevelled both sides **Bevelled one side**

Grind away the original cutting edge, sharpen the new edge to a fairly acute bevel and work down to a fine abrasive stone.

063 Clip-on pencil

You can waste a lot of time looking for a pencil, and once lost it invariably is never to be found again.

All you need to do is get a flat carpenter's pencil and combine it with half of a clothes peg (clothespin). Cut a notch in the pencil to take the spring of the peg, and fit the two parts together – it's that simple.

You now have a pencil that you can clip to your apron, pocket or anywhere else for that matter, and it is always ready to hand.

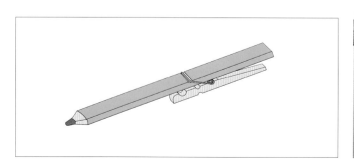

064 Alcove measurer

This alcove measurer is invaluable for fitting shelves. Developed from a simple pair of pinch sticks, it incorporates angle arms to check the out-of-squareness of alcove walls.

General workshop tips

065 Tape around drill bit

This is as simple as they come – use electrical tape wrapped around a drill bit as a depth gauge.

066 Depth gauge

Sets of clip-together building bricks often include flattish rectangular pieces like these. You should find these to be exactly 3mm (1/8in) thick, depending on the manufacturer. Build the bricks into a stair shape – glue them if necessary – and you have a basic but accurate depth-of-cut gauge.

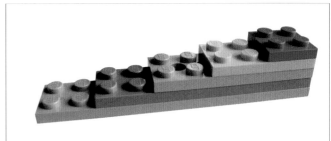

067 Centre punch

When you buy a centre punch it is sharpened at 60°, which is what is needed to mark drilling centres in metal. Most woodworking drill bits have long and fairly slim points, which are better started with a mark made by a more acute centre-punch point. A slenderly ground point is also easier to see when positioning it. It can also be used for marking the centres of wood for turning in the lathe; although the tailstock centre is at 60°, it beds down nicely in the more acute hollow. The headstock spur centre, with its long point, enters more accurately as well.

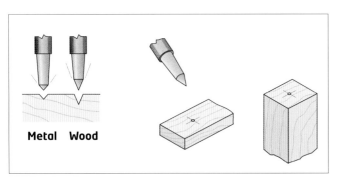

068 Centre punch or screw to locate drill bits

When setting out a workpiece for drilling it is always easier to use a centre punch or screw point to knock in a starter hole. This technique is especially good for the smooth surface of MDF.

069 | Scribing aid (1)

Here's an improvement to the age-old method of scribing with a washer. Use a disc of ⅛in (3mm) thick clear acrylic which has several holes drilled at useful distances from its edge. Requiring only a little practice, this work aid is excellent for scribing curves.

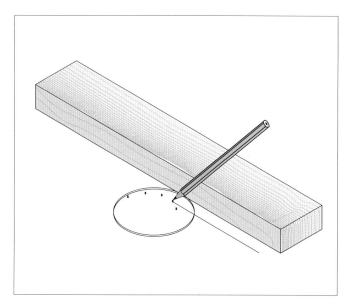

070 | Scribing aid (2)

This device is for tracing around irregular objects, as when making a fitted case for a pistol, for example. If you need more clearance, build up the contact edge with a few layers of masking tape.

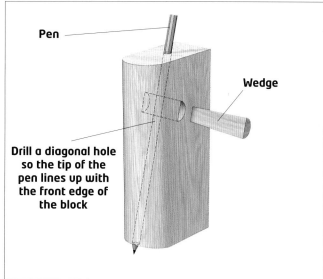

Pen

Wedge

Drill a diagonal hole so the tip of the pen lines up with the front edge of the block

071 | Scribing aid (3)

This is a simpler version of a butt-scribing tool which is sometimes advertised in the catalogues.

You'll need the circular offcut from a holesaw hole, a pencil, a couple of washers and two rubber bands. First enlarge the centre hole in the holesaw offcut to take the pencil, then fit the whole lot together, making sure the rubber bands keep it all pressed tight.

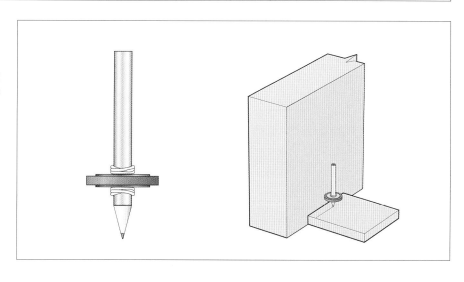

General workshop tips

072 Scribing with a compass

Fitting radiator covers, pieces of furniture and the like is a job made easy by using a pair of compasses with a soft pencil installed. Simply position the piece that needs scribing to a wall or skirting board (baseboard), open the compasses to the distance required, and draw a line. Provided the compasses are held parallel to the floor and the point carefully manoeuvred around the contour, the pencil will mark an exact copy which, when cut, will allow the piece to fit exactly against the wall.

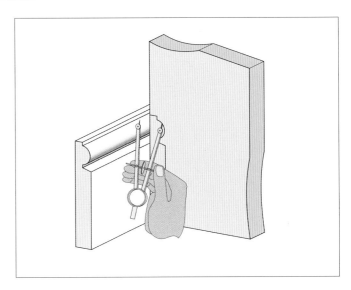

073 Marking out with notelets

The humble sticky notelet can be an invaluable aid to marking out. Simply stick one in the general area of a hole that needs to be drilled, and make the pencil marks on the paper. This avoids spoiling the finish of a piece of furniture with lines that may be in the wrong place.

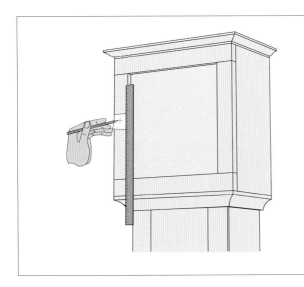

074 Drilling accurate holes in walls

Staying on course and not wandering off when drilling holes in walls can be something of a problem, especially if you hit stone, brick or cement.

Set a target for yourself by marking the position of the hole to be drilled, then drawing a circle larger than the drill bit. Now it will be easier to stay in the original spot after the centre mark has been obliterated.

Draw a circle and think of it as a target

Marking and measuring

075 A non-slip ruler

Drawing straight lines with a ruler is usually easy enough, but there are times when just as you are about to finish, the ruler slips. Using a strip of double-sided sticky tape the same size as the ruler, attach a similar-sized non-slip rubber or foam mat to the underside of the ruler. A very gentle touch will now be enough to hold it quite still. This little tip should be particularly helpful to those who suffer from shaking, as well as the lucky ones who don't.

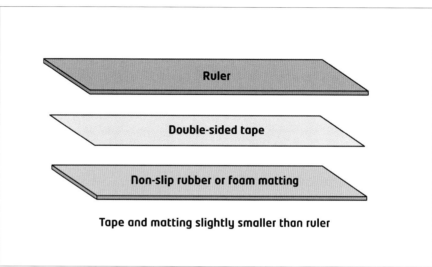

Tape and matting slightly smaller than ruler

076 Colour-coding joints

An easy way to mark matching joint parts, such as mortise-and-tenon or mitre joints, is to use small self-adhesive dots as found in stationery shops. These are highly visible, come in different shapes and colours, and are easily removed and cleaned up afterwards.

General workshop tips

077 Pinch sticks (1)

A really accurate way of checking a frame for square is to use two thin battens, each sharpened to a point at one end. The two battens are held together and their pointed ends slid into diagonally opposite corners. A pencil line is then drawn across the adjacent edges. Remove the sticks as one, place in the other two corners and mark from one of the lines across its adjacent edge. Undoubtedly the frame will not be square at first. To remedy this, draw a third mark between the first two marks on one stick, then adjust the frame until the single mark on one stick lines up with the newly drawn third line. The frame is now square.

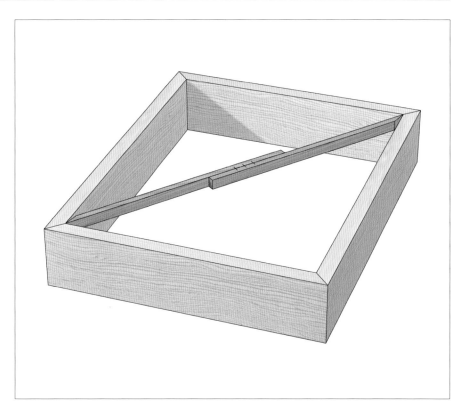

078 Pinch sticks (2)

Pinch sticks or bar gauges can be made in an instant from electrical PVC trunking of 1 x ³⁄₄in (25 x 17mm) section. From a 10ft (3m) length you can make three gauges in these sizes:

Stick length	Maximum opening
5ft (1525mm)	9ft (2745mm)
3ft (915mm)	5ft 6in (1680mm)
1ft 6in (455mm)	2ft 6in (760mm)

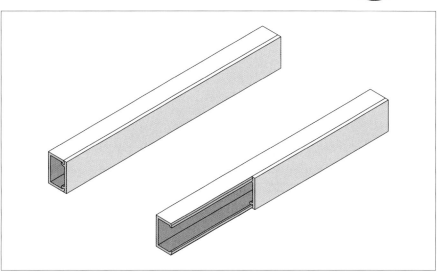

Use them for checking diagonals or for transferring internal dimensions, such as when fitting shelves into a cupboard.

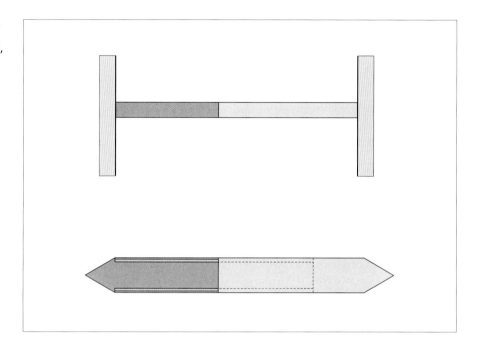

079 Pinch-stick variation

Here is another simple aid to square up a frame. There are several variations on this theme, but this one is good because it is so simple.

Fix a nail into the end of a strip of wood, push it into the corner and mark the opposite corner on the strip. Do the same for the other diagonal, and make a mark between the two original points. This is your 'square point'. Place the stick back in the frame and twist the frame until it lines up. The frame is now square.

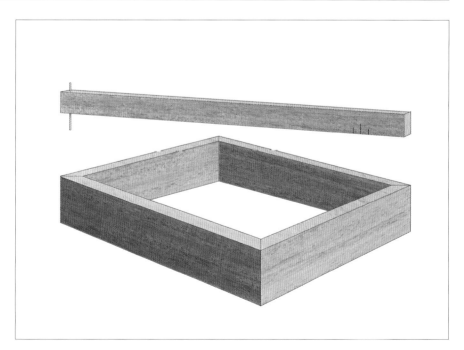

General workshop tips

080 Squaring large boards

If you need to check whether the edges of a large board are square with each other, make a mark along one edge of the board, 3ft out from the corner, then mark 4ft out along the other edge. Now measure diagonally between the two marks. If the boards are square, the diagonal measurement should be exactly 5ft. If you need to check larger boards, just increase the multiples of 3, 4, and 5.

Use metric measurements if you prefer, just so long as you keep the 3 : 4 : 5 proportion.

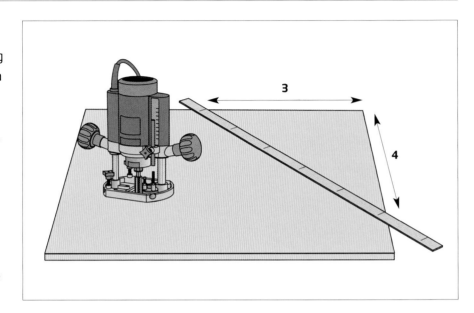

081 Checking a square for square

The simplest way to check if a square is at 90° is to draw a line with it on a flat surface, working from a good straight edge. Flip the square over and mark another line from the same point. If there is a gap between the two lines at the far end, your square is out of true by half that distance.

082 | Custom-made square

Getting frames square is difficult when a corner block or leg interferes with the apex of a traditional square.

The simple way of dealing with this problem is to make your own square. A piece of plywood squared up on a tablesaw or radial-arm saw, or with a router following an accurate template, will do the job. Then simply cut off the corner so the newly made square fits around the obstruction.

A number of these can be made up and stored under the bench for the many jobs that need squaring.

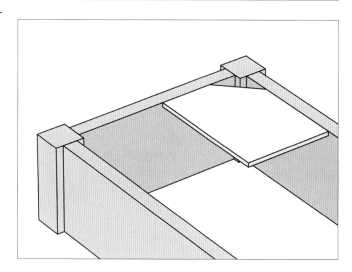

083 | Big bevel

Standard adjustable bevels are not big enough to mark out sheet material accurately. Make your own from a 1½ x ¼in (38 x 6mm) section of any close-grained hardwood. The example shown has a blade 31½in (800mm) long. A coach bolt makes a good pivot, as its square neck prevents it turning when the wing nut is tightened.

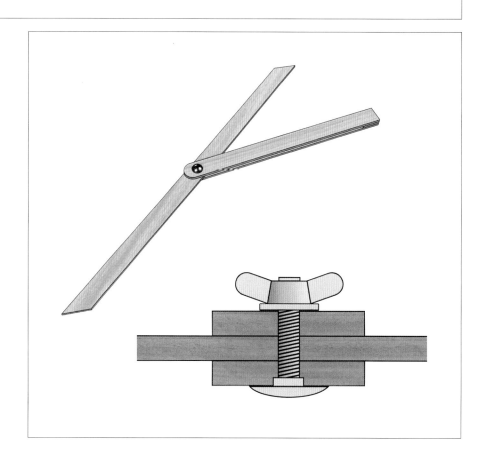

084 Drawing ovals

An ex-maths teacher provided this formula for setting out an accurate oval. All that's needed is a piece of string and a couple of nails.

Once you know the length and breadth you want, make the piece of string – with a loop each end – the same length as the oval (AB). Set a nail where the Y-axis is at its longest (C), put both loops over it and use the string as a compass to make pencil marks at D and E on the X-axis. Drive in your nails at D and E, loop one end of the string over each nail, and the oval can now be drawn with a pencil.

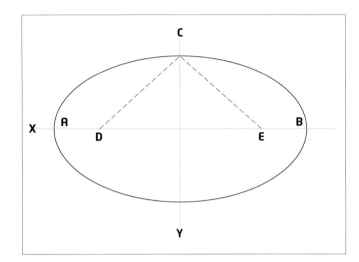

085 Seeking circle centres

To find the centre of a circle, position a postcard or sheet of paper so that one corner touches the circumference (X in the first drawing). Mark the points where the circle crosses the edges of the sheet (A and B in the drawing) and join these points with a straight line. Pick another section of the circle and repeat the process (C and D in the second drawing). The intersection of the two lines always gives the exact centre of the circle.

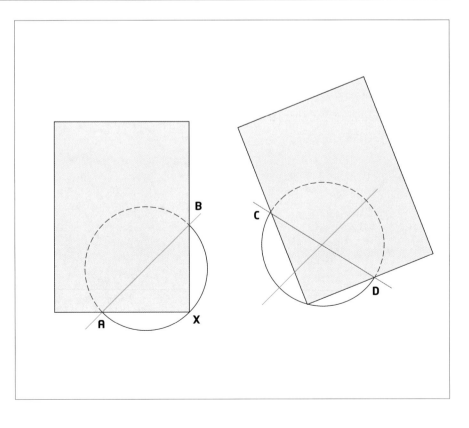

086 | Simple trammel

This spacing stick or trammel is ideal for drawing a parallel path or for marking a circle. The holding knobs can be made from metal or acrylic, and make the device very easy to adjust.

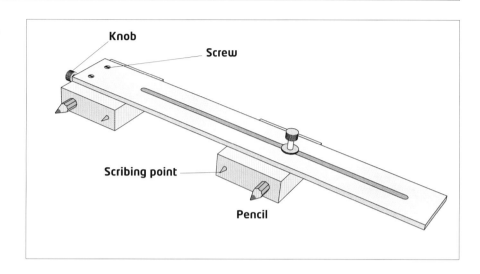

087 | Marking square lines on turned parts

To mark a square line round a curved surface, such as a chair or table leg, use a rectangular piece of stiff paper or card. Simply wrap it round the leg till the edges line up, and there you have it. It might work with tape at a pinch, but stretching might be a problem.

Woodworking materials

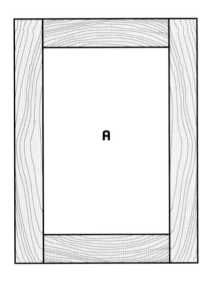

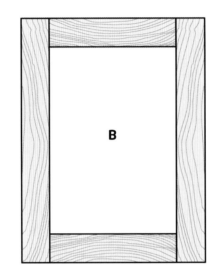

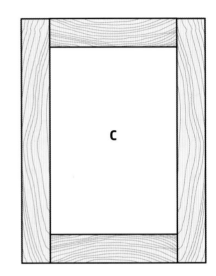

Making framed doors or panels is a great investment in time and wood, so it pays to get it right.

Even the best-made frame can look bowed or twisted if the timber selected has the grain patterns shown in diagrams A–C.

A looks circular because the grain of all the components appears to radiate concentrically.

B appears to have a fat waist because the grain on the side rails curves inwards.

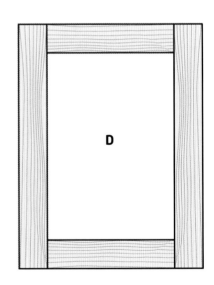

C looks as though the rails bow both ways, because their grain pattern is different on either side.

D looks nice and square, thanks to the use of carefully selected, straight-grained timber.

Timber selection can make all the difference, and it is well worth the effort to get it right.

089 | Rescuing warped wood

This simple device for straightening a warped piece of wood was inspired by the techniques used by the makers of walking sticks and shepherds' crooks, who straighten seasoned hardwood shanks by means of dry heat. The particular arrangement shown here has been used successfully on a piece of 3⅛ x ½in (80 x 12mm) mahogany intended for a shotgun case.

The diagram shows how the jig is set up to apply a countertwist to the warped piece. A heat gun is used carefully to apply heat along the length of the workpiece until the whole piece is warm completely through, and almost uncomfortable to touch. The wedge is then driven through until the twist is beyond straight to allow for a little 'return', and the workpiece is allowed to cool naturally before removing it from the jig.

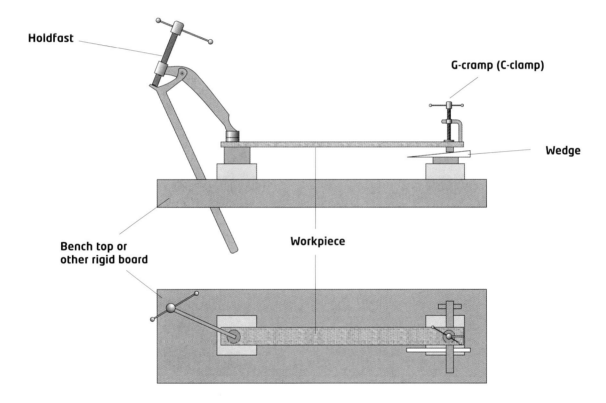

090 | Cross grain

It was my first job, and up until then I had been mainly helping out with making the tea, sanding things up and practising joints with hand tools. I had to make some shelves for a bookcase, and I was allowed to use the tablesaw unsupervised for the first time. I proudly carried the five or six blockboard shelves into the main workshop, only to be sent back to the machine room with my cheeks glowing, to cut them all again – but this time along the grain instead of across it. Those shelves would have started sagging the minute they were up!

General workshop tips

091 Carrying sheet materials

The 8 x 4ft (2440 x 1220mm) size of plywood, MDF and other sheet materials may be useful for many tasks, but makes them difficult to lift on your own.

This neat method of tying a couple of loops in a piece of rope allows one person to carry a full-size sheet on their own. Enough slack is required in the rope to allow the top of the sheet to tuck under your armpit.

Even with this handy lifting device, you should get a mate or two to help when handling 1in (25mm) MDF.

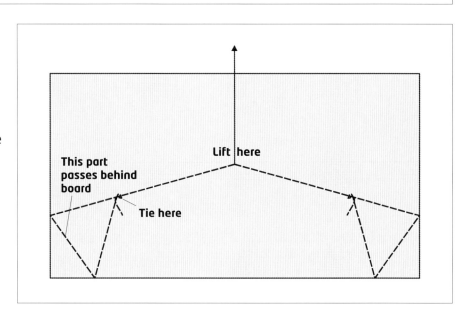

092 Sliding table for cutting sheet materials

The grooved aluminium top found on many of the new-style saw benches can be used as a base for a sliding table for easy handling of sheet materials, laminated worktops and other bulky items.

Take a 2 x 4ft (610 x 1220mm) sheet of ½in (12mm) MDF, then prepare two strips of hardwood, 2ft (610mm) long by the width of the mitre-gauge slot on your saw table. Lower the blade below the top surface, place the two strips of hardwood in the mitre-fence grooves, put some glue on these strips and set the sheet of MDF on top. Align the MDF centrally, square to the front of the table. Panel-pin through the MDF into the hardwood strips and allow to set. It is best at this point to invert the sheet and fix the strips securely with a couple of screws in each.

Now fix a length of ²³/₃₂in (18mm) MDF to the front and back of the MDF sheet with screws, pins and glue, to make an upstand about 4in (100mm) high. Fix a piece of acrylic onto the upstands across the centre

of the MDF and you have a transparent blade guard. Put the sheet of MDF onto your saw bench, gently raise the blade to cut through the full width of the MDF sheet, and your sliding table is ready to use.

093 Storing board materials

It is useful to have sheets of plywood tight-stored ready for when you need them, but it can be difficult to get them out without damaging the edges.

You can improve your plywood storage with the help of some home-made rollers. The storage space shown here is made from a 2 x 4in (50 x 100mm) framework set about 6in (150mm) in front of the wall. Perforated hardboard on the front creates a handy tool holder.

The roller wheels are cut from ¾in (19mm) stock and mounted on wooden axles, but you could use metal axles if you like. Individual sheets can now be slid in and out of the storage slot with no effort at all.

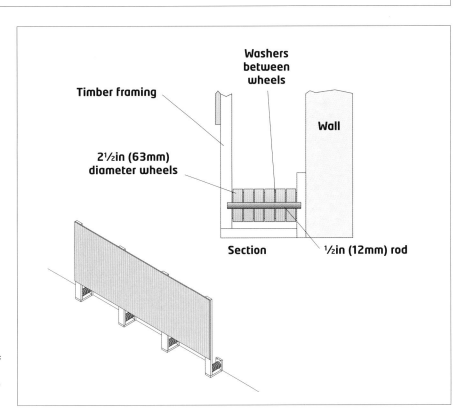

Washers between wheels

Timber framing

Wall

2½in (63mm) diameter wheels

Section   **½in (12mm) rod**

094 Lifting sheet materials

Lifting 8 x 4ft (2440 x 1220mm) sheets onto a bench or tablesaw becomes progressively harder with age. This simple sawhorse makes the whole pivoting and lifting process very much easier.

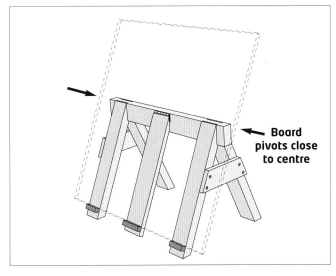

Board pivots close to centre

General workshop tips

095 Removing nails (1)

Recycling used wood often involves removing a lot of nails. Levering with a claw hammer on the surface of the wood does not give sufficient pull on most nails.

This double-edged wedge is a great help. Easy nails are lifted at the short end, but those which have to be pulled in stages are worked up the long slope.

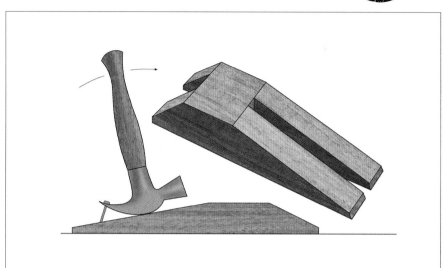

096 Removing nails (2)

To extract deep-set nails so as to cause minimum damage, use a length of steel tube as a punch. The bore of the tube should be a little larger than the diameter of the nailhead. By driving this over the nail you can push the wood down to expose enough of the head for the corners of pincer jaws to grip the nail and withdraw it cleanly.

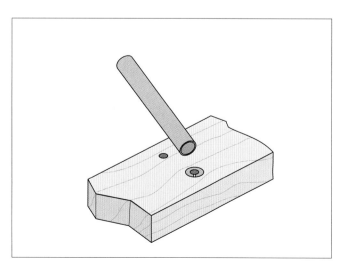

097 Iron-on veneer edging

Iron-on edging can create a very convincing finish to a veneered board, providing it is applied with consistent pressure. This is easy on straight edges, but adding a strip to a round table top can be difficult. The solution is an inexpensive roller of the type used for flattening joins in wallpaper. Work your way around the edge with the iron in one hand and the roller in the other.

098 Plugging screw holes

A neat way to fill old screw holes, especially if they will be visible from both sides, is to drill through the holes to take cross-grain plugs cut from scraps of the same wood. Instead of a long plug going right through, glue in short plugs from opposite sides so that they stand slightly proud of the surface. When planed and sanded level, the surface will be even and the holes will only be visible under close examination.

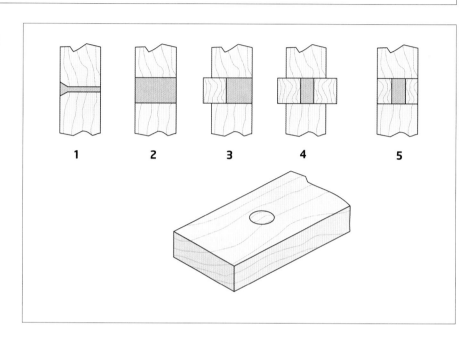

099 Cutting latex foam

The microwave oven is not the only kitchen tool which has other uses. Upholstery suppliers use a tool like a twin-bladed jigsaw on a stand, which glides through latex foam effortlessly. An electric carving knife (carefully cleaned before and after) is just as good, and cuts through foam like butter.

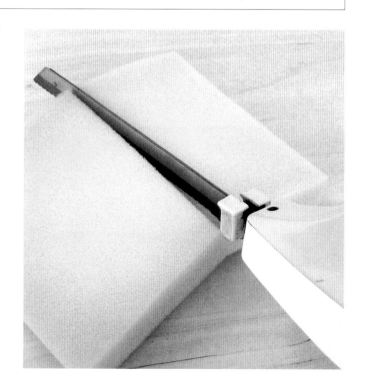

Workholding

100   A traditional sawhorse

The real beauty of this sawhorse is in the simplicity of its design. All of the angles are 4 in 1. To set this out, simply mark out a right-angled triangle with the square sides 1 and 4 units long respectively. The hypotenuse of this triangle gives the angle you require. You will need to set your sliding bevel twice in order to mark the tops of the legs – the angle is the same, but the approach is different.

Mark up the legs in pairs to make sure that you end up with two opposing sets. Check that you have marked the waste clearly, and double-check the splay angle of all four legs. The top of the leg should be cut with $3/8$in (10mm) excess on the 'tenon'. This will be trimmed flush when the horse is assembled.

The saddle is the most straightforward element of the stool. After setting out the leg positions on the face of the saddle, use the bevel to mark the sides. Use a marking gauge to score the chop line in order to start off the laps. Then saw down to the stop line, and with a chisel remove the waste from both sides, leaving the last $1/16$in (2mm) to pare off by hand.

Return to the legs and cut down to the shoulder with a saw, then chop and pare off the waste, working down the grain with a chisel. Apply a little glue to both surfaces of the joint and use a partly driven nail to hold

them in place. Drill the pilot holes for two 2in (50mm) no. 12 screws, countersink and fix. Use the panel saw to trim off the 'ears' at the top. Once these are trimmed, use a plane to make the ends flush with the saddle.

If you initially cut the legs $25^{3}/4$in (650mm) long, this will give you enough spare to set the height at your personal ideal. The main consideration is that you must be able to get above the saw when cutting on the horse. To level and trim the legs, place the horse on a flat surface and, using a scribing block of the height that you want to remove, mark the inward faces and

edges on the legs. Use the bevel to continue the 4 in 1 angle around each one. Double-check that they are correct before you cut them.

The bracing panel at each end can be made from any piece of scrap, such as a floorboard offcut, ply or MDF. Offer it up to the legs and mark the back, then nail or screw into place. It can be difficult to nail through MDF, unless you pre-drill the panel on a solid surface before fixing it to the horse.

101 Three-legged trestle

The tendency of a traditional four-legged trestle to wobble on an uneven floor can be prevented by building a stool with three legs instead. The single leg is half-lapped and bolted to the crossrail, and should be spaced no farther from the pair of legs than a distance one-third more than the overall height of the stool.

The spacing of the pair of legs should be equal to, or greater than, the height of the stool to ensure that it will not tip sideways.

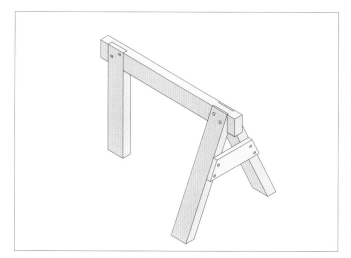

102 Folding sawhorse

These simple folding sawhorses are ideal for a workshop where space is limited. Non-slip matting stapled to the top ridge enables them to be used as trestles to create a secure temporary workbench.

Cutting list

Frame stiles (4)	Pine, 19 x 3³/₄ x ⁷/₈in (740 x 94 x 22mm)
Rails (4)	Pine, 23⁵/₈ x 3³/₄ x ⁷/₈in (600 x 94 x 22mm)
Brass butts (3)	3in (75mm)
Non-slip matting	Oddments
Cord	5ft (1500mm) approx.

General workshop tips

103 | Cramp heads

When using cramp heads on a wooden batten, if the holes become worn, or the original drilling was not very accurate, the heads will tilt backwards, pulling the workpiece out of square.

You can prevent this by screwing a 1in (25mm) no. 10 by each hole, at the back of the 'saddle' of the head. These can be adjusted up or down to keep the heads square.

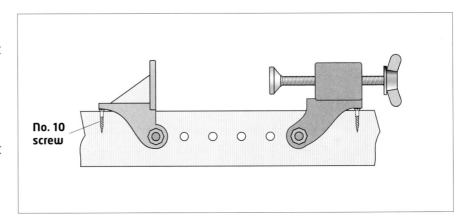

104 | Edge cramping

The best way to hold a veneered edge tight while the glue sets is to use a combination of cramps and wedges. Small fretwork-type cramps are suitable (A), as are G-cramps (C-clamps) and/or sliding cramps (B). A single wedge can put pressure on a strip to spread the load (C). Paired folding wedges (D) give a parallel pressure and are less likely to move the veneer as you tighten them.

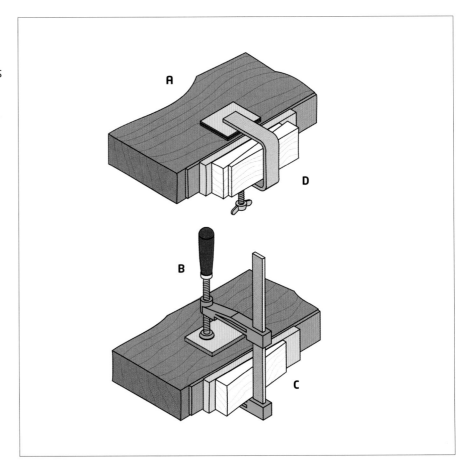

Workholding

105 Lightweight sash cramps

As an alternative to metal bar cramps, this device is concocted from scrap pieces of timber, using two sealant guns to apply the pressure. The end rings are cut off the guns, and their business end is then fixed to the head end of the cramp. The cramp's other end can be moved along the bar and fixed in place with a small bolt and wing nut.

Though these are not as strong as their metal-bar equivalents, provided they are treated with care they can perform a useful job that will repay the effort used to make them.

106 Corner cramp

These natty little devices can be adjusted to any angle you need to cut, making them far more flexible than the standard 45° mitre cramp.

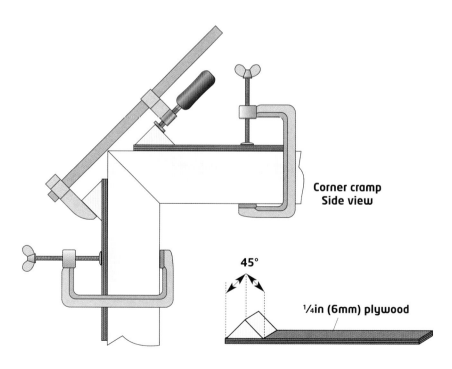

**Corner cramp
Side view**

45°

¼in (6mm) plywood

General workshop tips

107 Cheap holdfast

The screw end of a broken 6in (150mm) G-cramp (C-clamp) makes a useful holdfast. Find a flat piece of mild steel 8in (200mm) long by ¾in (19mm) thick, and simply drill two holes in one end of the steel to take two ¼in (M6) bolts and nuts. Bore matching holes in the cramp, then bolt the two together. The steel fits perfectly between the cast ribs on the cramp. Pushed through a ¾in (19mm) hole in the bench, it makes a perfect bench holdfast.

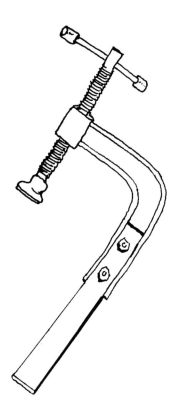

108 Replacing cramp pads

Old G-cramps (C-clamps) can often be found in perfect order, except for a protrusion on the surface of the pressure pad. Here is a way of attaching a replacement pad to the deformed original.

After planing a scrap piece of hardwood to ⅝in (15mm) in thickness, drill a ⅝in (15mm) diameter hole ¼in (6mm) deep into it, and then cut out along a 1in (25mm) diameter circle centred around this hole. Drop a dab of hot-melt glue into the hole to conform to the pressure-pad's protrusion, then press the wooden cylinder onto the metal pad. After screwing the pad down tightly, fill the depression around the top of the wooden pad with more hot-melt glue.

The replacement pad is held to the clamp securely and, despite its ungainly appearance, presses down onto a smooth wood surface with less danger of leaving a depression than a steel pad would do.

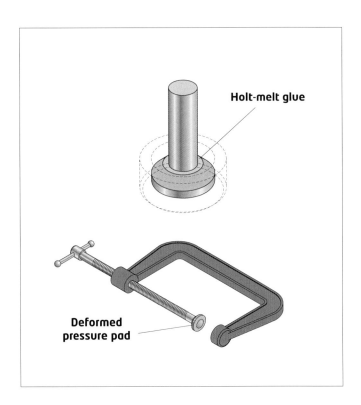

Holt-melt glue

Deformed pressure pad

109 | Banana bars

Cramping shelves into carcass housings is a tricky business at the best of times. Very often the front and back edges of the shelf will pull up satisfactorily, but not the middle.

Curved cauls or cramping blocks, sometimes called 'banana bars', are a perfect solution. Their convex shape means that pressure is applied to the centre, as the ends are forced towards the cabinet by cramps. The curve needs to be the same on all the cauls you are using, to ensure that even pressure is applied. This can be easily achieved by making a template and using a router with a bearing-guided cutter, having first rough-sawn the cauls on the bandsaw.

Don't make the curve too strong, or you may not be able to pull it around at all; it might be worth experimenting with some scrap first.

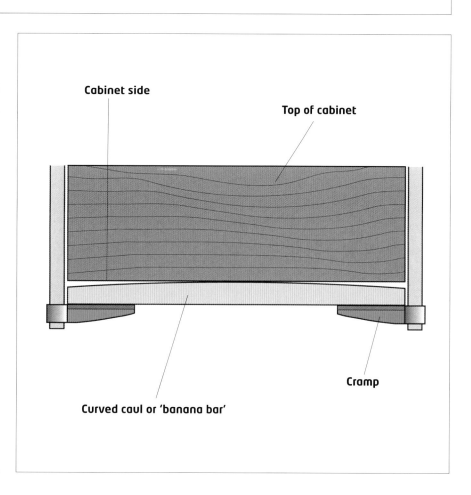

Cabinet side

Top of cabinet

Cramp

Curved caul or 'banana bar'

110 | Bench hook for Workmate

This simple bench hook cramps easily between the jaws of a Workmate and is ideal for cutting timber with a tenon saw.

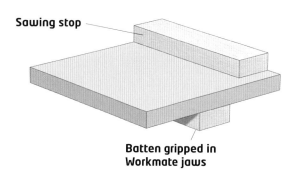

Sawing stop

Batten gripped in Workmate jaws

111 | Pulling a frame into square

If you assemble a frame and it just won't stay square while the glue sets, you can correct this by applying a 'Spanish windlass' to pull the work square. You can do this even while the cramps are in place.

Put on a loop of rope, or several turns of twine, tilted slightly in the direction that needs pulling. The pressure can be considerable, so use blocks of scrap wood under the rope, as shown, to prevent damage to the wood. Twist the loop with a piece of timber until the frame shape is right, then lodge it against the side of the frame. You can use the same technique to correct distortion in a three-dimensional assembly.

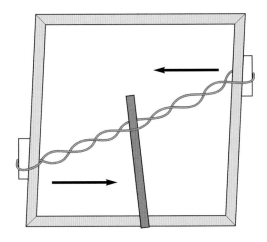

112 | Packing blocks for cramps

To locate and keep packing blocks under cramps and holdfasts, cut shallow recesses in pieces of scrap wood. The pads will then stay in place whilst you attend to other parts of the job. The ones shown are made from 2 x 1in (50 x 25mm) wood, cut to about 4in (100mm)

long. Drill holes about $^5/_{32}$in (4mm) deep, larger than the cramp ends, and then cut into them with several passes of a straight router cutter at the same depth. To give the router fence a good bearing, make several pads together and then cut them apart.

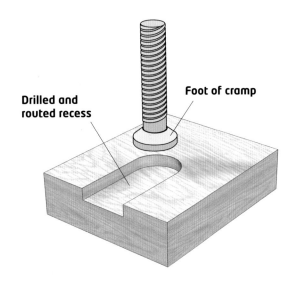

Drilled and routed recess

Foot of cramp

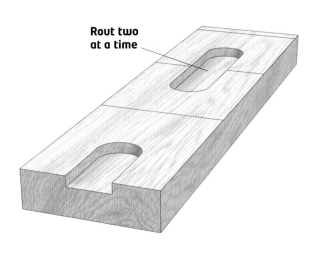

Rout two at a time

113 | Cork clamp cushions

When gluing on edging strips, the simple application of a long piece of cork will distribute the pressure from the clamps more efficiently than a standard block. The cork will also adjust readily to an uneven surface.

114 | Avoiding stains

Sash cramps often leave black marks on the face of the work. This problem is generally the result of the reaction between the steel cramp heads, the adhesive and the wood.

To eliminate this and keep your cramps clean, apply clear plastic lunch wrap (clingfilm) to the cramp heads as a barrier between them and the workpiece. The same material can be used for holding clamping blocks in place on the heads of sash cramps, so eliminating the almost impossible juggling act required when cramping wide boards.

Varnish brushes can be wrapped in clingfilm to keep them clean and in shape.

General workshop tips

115 Fold-down workbench

If your workshop is also your garage, there may be no room for a fixed workbench. One solution is a plywood work table, supported on legs, that folds down against the wall. Stiffen the edges with 2 x 4in (50 x 100mm) battens, as shown, and attach another to the wall with lag bolts. The legs fold up under the bench, and latch with hooks and screw eyes. Tools can be left on the wall, and only the vice has to be dismounted.

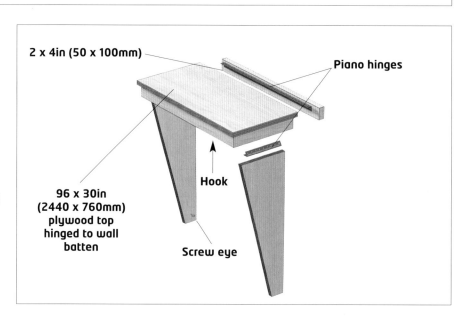

116 Bench-top extension

This improvised 2ft (610mm) extension is useful for planing extra-long stock. It projects far enough for the work to be clamped between the stop on the end of the extension and the dog in the tail vice at the other end of the bench. Smaller extensions can be made by nailing a plywood L to a scrap piece of 2 x 4in (50 x 100mm) softwood.

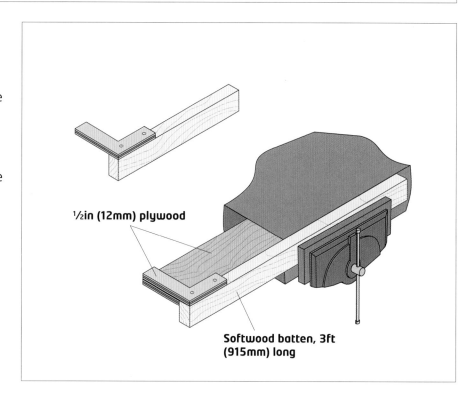

117 Safer chainsawing

This is a safe way to hold a piece of wood to be cut with a chainsaw. You need a Workmate-type bench, a 4ft (1200mm) sash cramp, two small G-cramps (C-clamps) and some scrap wood.

Secure the sash cramp in the Workmate jaws, and fix the bottom of the cramp to the Workmate base with a small clamp. Clamp a piece of sacrificial timber to the Workmate jaws; this piece should suit the size of the timber to be cut. The lower cramp jaw is secured below another piece of timber to stop it rising.

Pressure from the sash cramp holds any shape of timber securely.

118 Clamp blocks

Clamps with deep throats aren't too common, so here is an alternative method of clamping narrow bars that are too far in from the bench edge to be reached with ordinary clamps.

Take a few pieces of 4 x 2in (100 x 50mm) softwood and cut notches in them that are just a tad shorter than the thickness of the bars to be clamped. Set the notched blocks over the bars and clamp anywhere on the block to hold it in place. Usually, two clamps with clamp blocks will ensure that the bar won't move.

119 Lightweight stop

Here's a simple idea for a lightweight holding aid which can be fitted on a portable bench for site work. It can be made of scrap timber or ply around 3/4in (18mm) thick. It's surprisingly strong in use.

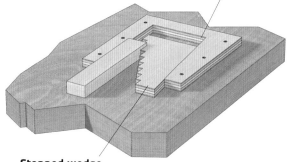

Opening is tapered to provide wedging action

Stepped wedge accommodates different widths of stock

General workshop tips

120 Veneer-cutting table

Many people are put off the use of veneers because of their thinness and delicate nature. The job of trimming veneers is perceived to be difficult, but this table, made from scrap materials, makes the task relatively straightforward.

The base is an offcut of 1in (25mm) blockboard, covered with an offcut of vinyl flooring. There are two clamps to hold the veneer:

one of timber, which has elongated fixing slots to allow coarse adjustments of the veneer, and one of aluminium for final adjustment, against which the cut is made (photo 1). The fence is set to one side, against which the veneer can be butted up (photo 2). The cut can be made against the aluminium, using either a sharp scalpel or a veneer saw (photo 3).

1

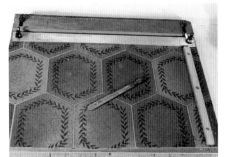

2

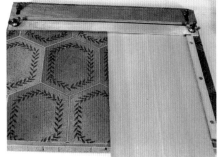

3

121 Grooving dowels

Cutting a groove in a dowel, or sawing a flat on one side of it, can be dangerous, as the dowel has a tendency to spin. A way of overcoming this is to glue square blocks to each end of the dowel. The length of the sides of the block must be the same as the diameter of the dowel, and the two blocks must line up exactly so there is no wobble. You can then go ahead and make your cut in perfect safety.

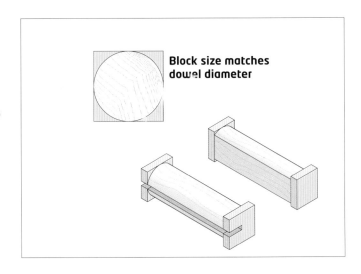

Block size matches dowel diameter

122 | Dovetail jig

It is often difficult to hold the two mating pieces firmly together while marking out the pins of a dovetail joint.

This jig, which can be made in different sizes as required, consists of an accurately squared frame to which each workpiece can be clamped while the marking is carried out in comfort. Fences are fixed to each face so that the workpieces can be butted against them, ensuring squareness.

The jigs are made from scraps, and have a fabricated corner bracket to ensure rigidity and to keep things square. Marking dovetails by knife is more accurate than by pencil.

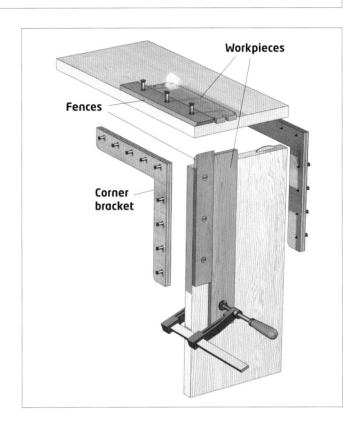

123 | Bench-hook shooting board

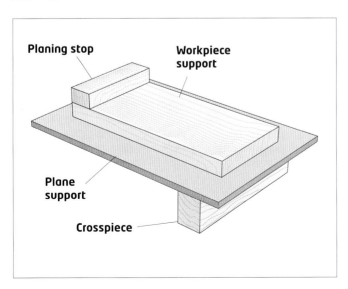

You can plane the edges of small items using a bench hook as a shooting board, by sliding a small plane on its edge on the bench top. To give the work a better grip and the plane a smoother passage, try this modified bench hook. The main part is $^{25}/_{32}$in (20mm) thick, which puts an average piece of wood near the centre of the blade. The extended plywood base provides a good guide and a smooth surface for the plane to slide on. The crosspiece below steadies the hook against the edge of the bench, or alternatively can be gripped in the vice. All parts are glued and dowelled, so there is no metal involved.

General workshop tips

124 Door-machining stand

As anyone who has tried to plane a door to size or cut hinge recesses or mortises will know, when sat on its edge the door suddenly develops a mind of its own and will not stay still.

This simple and portable stand is easily made from a few bits and pieces of 4 x 2in (100 x 50mm) softwood and strips of ½in (12mm) ply.

The stand's carpet-lined uprights pinch the door when the door's weight flexes the plywood strips. Obviously, the heavier the door the better they work, but even the lightest door is held sufficiently.

125 Pivoting stop

This simple holding device was passed on by an elderly craftsman who had learnt it from a German prisoner of World War I. The timber to be held is slid in from the right, where it meets the furthest jaws and pushes them apart. This causes the rear jaws to close up and grip the work securely. If you're stuck without a vice it's worth using, and you can keep the two jaws in your kitbag for emergencies. It's easy to make and should be got out of hardwood for strength and durability.

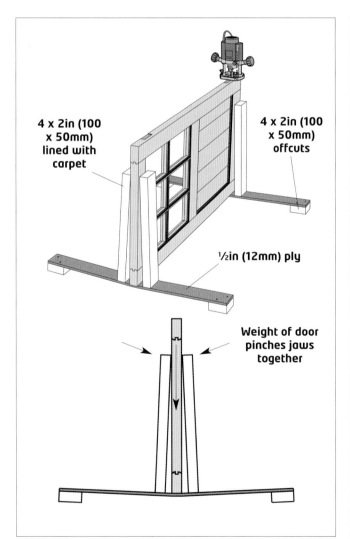

4 x 2in (100 x 50mm) lined with carpet

4 x 2in (100 x 50mm) offcuts

½in (12mm) ply

Weight of door pinches jaws together

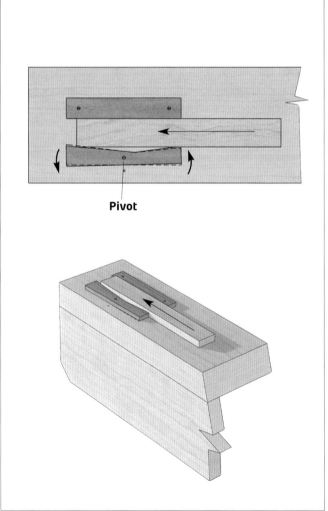

Pivot

126 Planing stop for thin wood

It can be very difficult to hold a very thin piece of wood while planing, but this device makes it easy. The wood block is held in the vice and the thin piece is placed on top, against the wedge, which slides in a carefully prepared housing.

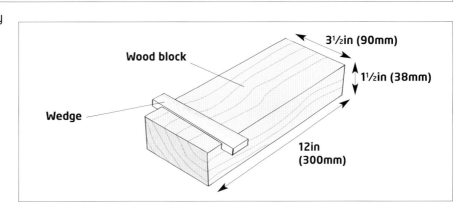

Wood block

Wedge

3½in (90mm)

1½in (38mm)

12in (300mm)

127 Improved folding wedges (1)

It is always worth keeping a variety of wedges with your tools and in your workshop. They are very cheap to make from offcuts, and can often take the place of cramps if used with care. If you find that folding wedges tend to slip apart, try making them with a spline. Biscuits will do, but the spline is much better.

128 Improved folding wedges (2)

A pair of folding wedges is a good way of putting on considerable pressure in an improvised clamp or for lifting something into place, but the usual plain wedges are not always easy to tighten fully and are often difficult to remove.

Try making them with extensions long enough to form handles. These make it easier to position the wedges and to drive them tight, and they provide something to grip for removing the wedges when the job is done.

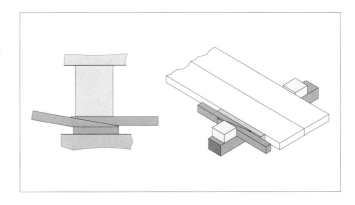

Joints and fixings

129   Correcting loose tenons

A loose tenon can be enlarged with thin strips of veneer sliced from a piece of scrap. Make sure that the grain direction of the veneer matches that of the tenon, and then glue the veneer onto the tenon cheeks and shave or sand the tenon to fit the mortise.

Alternatively, if the tenon will be hidden after assembly, cut a piece of brown parcel paper to fit the tenon, spread the paper with glue and wrap it around the joint. You can add more glued paper if the joint is still slack.

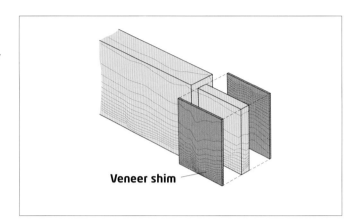

Veneer shim

130   Making round rod

If you need to form a round rod from a square section, first make this simple cradle to hold the work still while you plane it.

True up two pieces of wood and remove a 45° chamfer from one long edge of each piece. Drill and countersink one piece to take the four screws, and rub a flat file over the screw heads and points. Select a piece of ¼in (6mm) dowel to make the stop, and a drill to suit. Fit it about ½in (12mm) from one end, where it can be tapped with a hammer to adjust it to the height required.

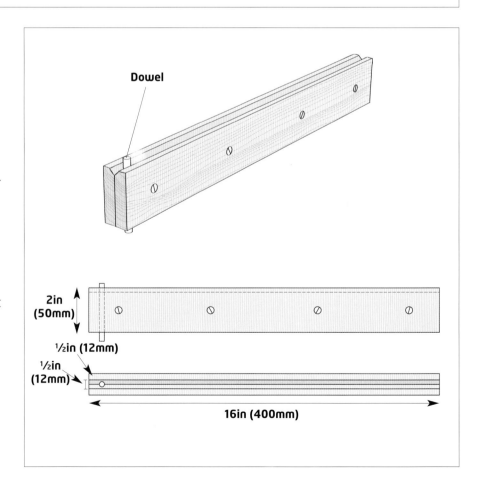

Dowel

2in (50mm)

½in (12mm)

½in (12mm)

16in (400mm)

131 Recycled dowels

Once the sponge bit of a throwaway foam brush is used up or worn out, keep the handle to use as a dowel.

132 Better visibility for joint cutting

When cutting dovetails or tenons by hand, or doing other similar work, it makes life much easier if a mirror is set up behind the workpiece and adjusted so that progress can be monitored without bending or stretching.

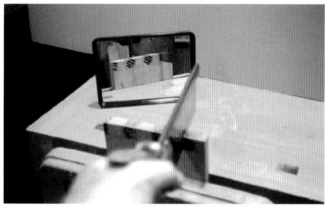

133 Jig for dowel holes

This jig was developed after experiencing much frustration trying to drill holes in dowel sections for toy making. It's really just a strong gripper, but works very well indeed on a drill press.

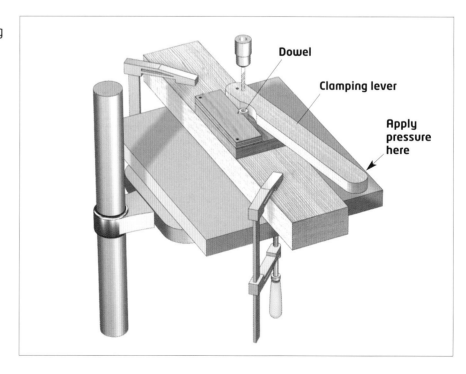

Dowel

Clamping lever

Apply pressure here

General workshop tips

134 Burnishing mitred corners

You can't afford to be off even a little bit when cutting a mitre. Even if the mitre has been cut accurately, a gap can still appear at the corner if the frame is even slightly off-square.

When the mitred pieces fit well to begin with, you can close the gap by 'burnishing' (rolling over) the tips. This means you won't have to recut the mitres. However, if the mitres are too far out to allow this, you'll have no choice but to break the joint and begin all over again.

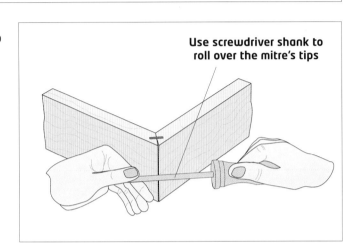

Use screwdriver shank to roll over the mitre's tips

135 Mirror trick

If you want to impress your friends with your mastery of woodwork, then – with a fair amount of practice – the following tip is bound to do the trick.

To cut the perfect mitre, without marking the timber, take a shiny new saw and place it on the workpiece. When the blade is at exactly 45° to the work, the reflection will appear to continue the timber at 90°. Since it is relatively easy to 'eye' a true 90° angle, estimating the mitre becomes almost easy. The photo shows the cutting of a staff bead, which, because of its moulded top edge, is a little more difficult to get right.

Of course, you still have to make a true, vertical cut, and it is probably more worthwhile to learn this first. The only thing to remember is, when you achieve a perfect cut, you must never congratulate yourself too much – this will guarantee a momentary loss of your new-found skill.

136 Taping picture frames

Picture frames are a pain to hold while gluing up, but a simple cramp-free solution for small frames – provided they have a flat on the outside edge, as opposed to a moulding – is to lay the pieces on their backs on a length of masking tape. A touch of PVA glue in the corners of the mitres should provide enough strength for the mitre joints, which can be closed by folding the pieces together and sticking down the end of the tape.

Joint-holding pins can easily be inserted through the tape.

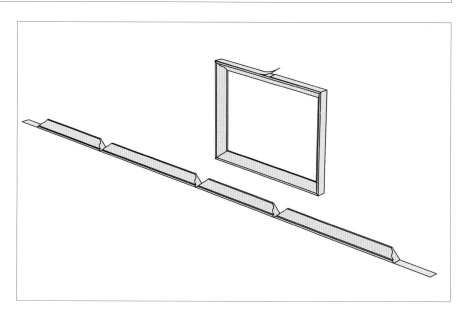

137 Reinforcing large picture frames

The mitre joints of large picture frames are often overstressed by the weight of the glass; this, of course, could be extremely dangerous.

To overcome this problem, and also to make sure you have a good wall fixing, make a square-edged frame so that in profile there is enough space behind the backing board for a ¾in (20mm) or thicker length of timber.

Cut one or more of these timber 'ties' to exactly fit vertically in the back of the frame. Insert them and screw into their ends through the frame. Remove them after marking clearly which is which. Fix the ties to the wall at the exact distance apart and exactly level. Extend some lines onto the wall so that the frame and the screw holes can be located exactly.

Hang the frame and replace the screws. Fill or plug the screw holes.

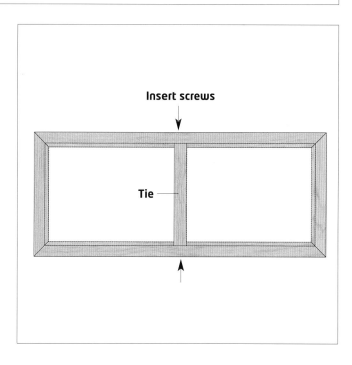

Insert screws

Tie

138 Table-leg connectors

In order to attach a shelf to the turned legs of a hall table, make each leg in two parts, with a reduced-diameter extension at one end for inserting into the shelf. Insert a ¼in (6mm) screw nut in the bottom of the upper section of each leg. In the top and bottom at each corner of the shelf, bore surface holes to the diameter and depth of the leg extensions, with ¼in (6mm) centre holes.

Bore a ¼in (6mm) hole through the entire length of the lower leg section, with a recess in the lower end to take a flanged nut.

When inserting a screw nut into end grain with a screwdriver, the nut has a tendency to be affected by the grain and go off true. To overcome this problem:

1 Bore the insert hole with a $^{23}/_{64}$in (9mm) steel bit.

2 Take a long ¼in (M6) bolt, lock two nuts onto it about $^{5}/_{8}$in (15mm) up, then add an insert nut, with the screwdriver-slot end entered first.

3 Using a spanner (wrench) on the locked nuts, screw the insert into the wood, using the bolt to keep it true.

4 When the nut has been screwed in to the required depth, reverse the spanner action to withdraw the bolt.

The assembled finished article is very solid and does not need gluing.

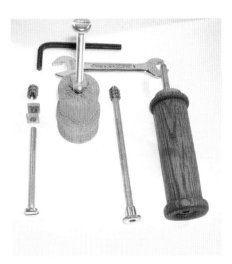

139 Screwing into the edge of MDF (1)

Although not ideal, it is often necessary to screw into the 'end grain' of MDF. If undertaken with care, using the correct sizes of tools, this jointing method can produce a moderately strong fixing whilst an adhesive is drying. Always avoid drilling less than 2³/₈in (60mm) from the ends of a board, and make sure you use the correct size of drill bit for the screw:

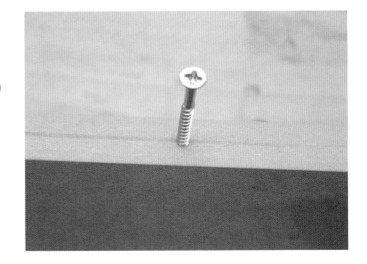

Screw size	Drill size
No. 6	$^{9}/_{64}$in (3.5mm)
No. 8	$^{5}/_{32}$in (4mm)
No. 10	$^{3}/_{16}$in (5mm)
No. 12	¼in (6mm)

140 | Screwing into the edge of MDF (2)

One way to avoid screwing into the edge of manufactured boards when assembling a carcass is to drill a hole in the side of one of the carcass boards to take a short length of dowel. This then gives you a strong anchor to screw into, and effectively reinforces the whole job.

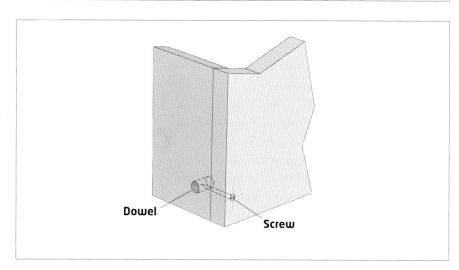

Dowel

Screw

141 | Button biscuits

The traditional way of securing a table top to its frame so it can expand and contract is with buttons screwed to the top which engage with slots in the rails.

You can get the same effect with less trouble and more accuracy by using biscuits. All you need is a biscuit jointer or a suitable router cutter. You can make enough of the buttons in a long length and cut them off. If you plane a shaving or two off the top surfaces of the buttons after cutting their recesses, they will pull the table top down tightly. Leave the buttons without glue to allow for movement.

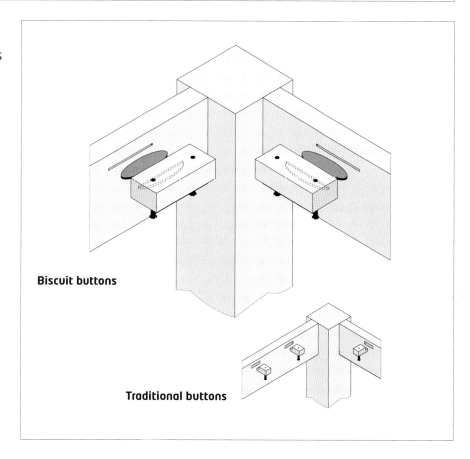

Biscuit buttons

Traditional buttons

General workshop tips

142 End-grain solution

Another way of inserting screws securely into end grain is to drill a hole to take a plastic wall plug as a really tight fit, then tap in the plug. This gives a sound fixing, as the plug responds in just the same way as if the hole were in brick, stone or block. As extra security, use a bit of glue on the plug as well.

 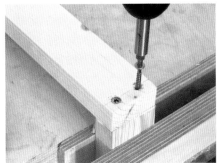

143 Better plugs

When using a plug cutter to make cross-grain plugs to cover screw heads, most of us tweak the plugs out with a narrow screwdriver, which sometimes damages the plugs or causes them to break off short – in either case, the plug is left with one rough end.

It is better to make a cut with a circular saw or bandsaw through the bottoms of the plugs, so they all come out cleanly and undamaged.

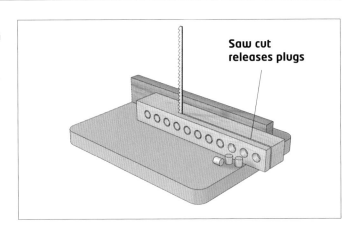

Saw cut releases plugs

144 Allowing for movement (1)

When joining cross-battens to the underside of solid wood table tops, accommodation for any timber movement needs to be made. This solution provides just the right amount of play for any normal changes in humidity.

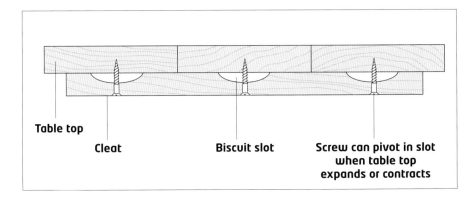

Table top

Cleat

Biscuit slot

Screw can pivot in slot when table top expands or contracts

145 | Allowing for movement (2)

When two pieces of wood have to be attached to each other and their grains cross, as with a batten under a table top, there has to be an allowance for expansion and contraction of the wider piece. One way of dealing with the problem is slot-screwing, but a simpler way is shown here.

Drill the screw holes and countersink them normally in the batten. Then drill back from the other side to enlarge the holes for most of their depth. This allows the screws to bend slightly with wood movement.

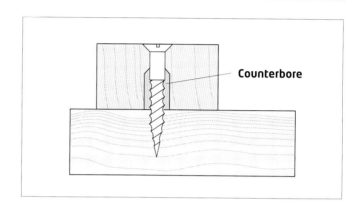

Counterbore

146 | Pocket screws (1)

Here's a cheap and fairly easy way to make your own pocket-hole jig. You could use softwood offcuts, but it would probably be best to use hardwood. Drill an $^{11}/_{32}$in (9mm) hole into the block as far as it will go, cut the end off at an angle of about 25° and glue the offcut bit to the side of the main block as a support. The guide is simply clamped to the workpiece when needed. You could make two or three in one go, for when one gets worn out or lost.

147 | Pocket screws (2)

One of the traditional ways of attaching a table top to its rails is with pocket screws (A) inserted upwards into the rails. This involves some careful work with the chisel and gouge, or the use of a special jig.

Instead, use a Forstner bit at an angle (B). Unlike the long point of an ordinary bit, it will not break through the wood. This is an accurate and much quicker method.

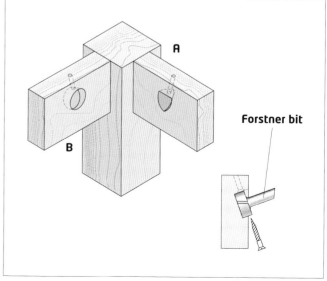

Forstner bit

General workshop tips

148 Nail alignment

If plywood has to be fastened to framing with nails or panel pins, it is advisable to cut the wood oversize and true it after fixing, particularly if it is curved or irregular in shape. The nails should be set at regular intervals and at the same distance from the finished edge. This helpful gauge made from scrap wood ensures accurate distance from the edge, and the extension at the side gives even spacing.

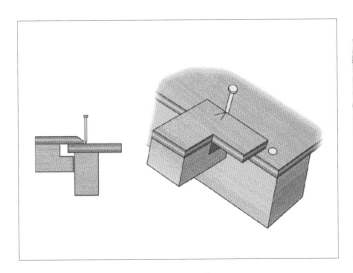

149 Inserting small pins

Holding small pins in your fingers can be extremely difficult, but here is an easy way.

Cut a strip of reasonably thick card (the type found in quality chocolate bars is good) and insert a line of pins so that they almost break through the other side. The strip can be held over the workpiece and the pin struck with a hammer before the strip is lifted off and the slightly protruding pinhead driven home.

150 Sanding a hammer head

Rub your hammer's head in circular motions over the surface of a coarse abrasive for a few seconds. The circular scratches on the surface help to stop the hammer head from skidding and mis-hitting the nail.

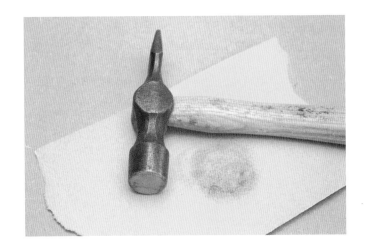

151 Bed brackets

It is often difficult for small-scale makers to obtain hardware items at reasonable prices. Fittings for making beds are an example.

The solution: use shelf brackets. These are readily available from all DIY shops, can be fitted in a similar way to the purpose-built bed fittings, and, like them, become tighter when more weight is applied.

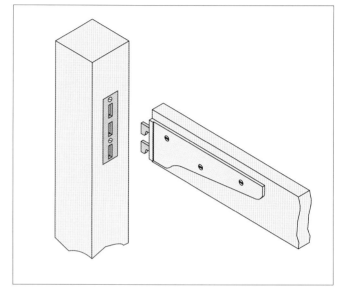

152 Keyhole escutcheons

You've made the cabinet doors, or restored the same, and you have misplaced the escutcheons for the locks. Well, it's time to call in the plumber or go looking through the pigeonholes for old brass compression rings (olives) – the same as used for copper pipe joints. A ⅝in (15mm) ring will cover many key sizes for small locks, and olives are available up to ⅞in (22mm).

File up and polish one edge, then press the ring into shape with the use of an engineer's vice, drill shank and old plough-plane blade or similar piece of metal. You can now sharply tap the other edge of your escutcheon into the wood to mark out the position of the keyhole.

Abrasives

153   Superior sanding block

If you are tired of ordinary sanding blocks, try cutting a piece of wood to fit tightly inside a sanding-machine belt. You can use whatever scrap pieces of wood you can muster up. The main thing is to radius the ends and make it a tight fit into the belt. You will then have the best sanding block ever, and will never want to be without it. Make several for different grades; you could even try different shapes.

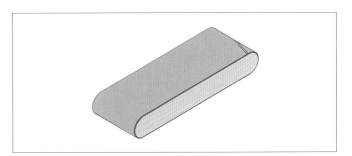

154   Making the most of sandpaper

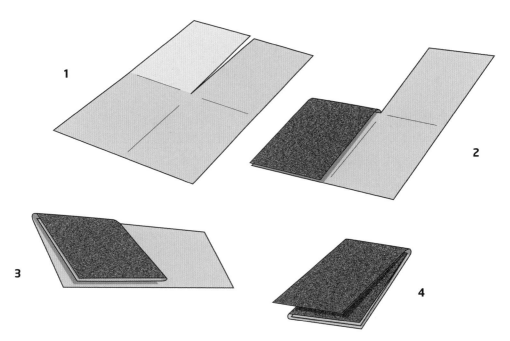

Here is a way of using a sheet of abrasive paper economically for hand-sanding, either freehand or wrapped round a block, without tearing it into pieces.

The sheet folds into a comfortable pad with the working grit sides outwards, yet the grit sides within the pad do not touch each other. When the original outer surfaces are worn out, the paper can be refolded to expose new working surfaces.

1 Mark a sheet into four and cut or tear down one of these lines to the centre.

2 With the grit side down, fold down one of the cut quarters.

3 Turn this folded part over to the other side...

4 ...and bring the remaining flap over it.

155 Contour sander

This simple contour sander, made from a hardwood offcut and a strip from a sanding belt, is ideal for working compound curves, as on a curved handrail. Work patiently so as to not mess up your carving.

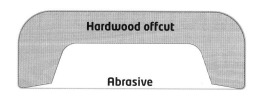

156 Sandpaper dispenser

Here is a simple tip to store 3ft or 1m lengths of abrasive neatly. Acquire a length of plastic drainpipe – the 2½in (65mm) diameter is ideal. Cut the pipe into a number of 5in (125mm) lengths, then make a cut along the length of each piece.

Simply screw these to a suitable backing board and hang in a convenient place in your workshop. Roll up your lengths of abrasive paper and insert them into the drainpipe so that one end comes through the slot you have cut.

Just pull the abrasive through the slot and tear off strips as you need them. If you roll the abrasive paper cloth-side-out, this reduces the friction and allows it to unroll through the slot more easily.

General workshop tips

157 Cutting sandpaper (1)

This simple fixture for cutting sandpaper (or emery cloth) has been in use for a number of years. The hacksaw blade was already old when the fixture was built, yet shows no sign of wearing out.

Cut the base – an offcut of plywood or MDF will suffice – to accommodate the size of your most frequently used paper. Nail or screw the blade in place, with thin washers beneath, and you're up and running.

As this device uses recycled materials and is very cheap to make, there is nothing to stop you keeping several different sizes to hand for whenever they are needed.

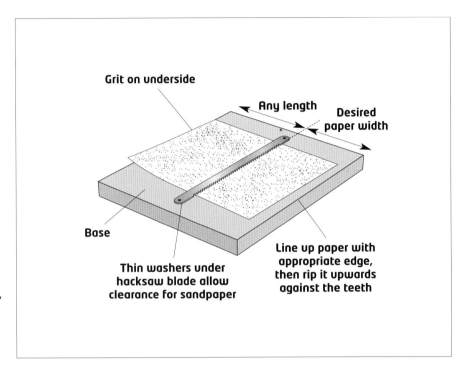

Grit on underside

Any length

Desired paper width

Base

Thin washers under hacksaw blade allow clearance for sandpaper

Line up paper with appropriate edge, then rip it upwards against the teeth

158 Cutting sandpaper (2)

Here's an even simpler way of tearing sandpaper off the roll, utilizing the teeth of a handsaw. It doesn't include a measuring device like the previous tip, but it does avoid ragged and wasted edges.

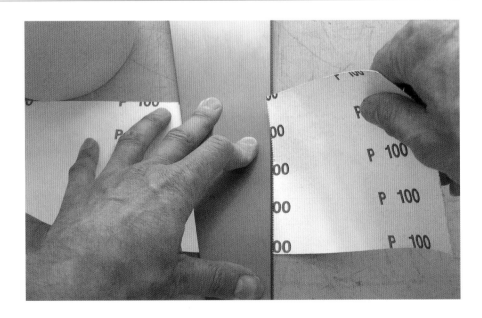

159 Cleaning abrasives

If the sealant in your silicone sealant gun has gone hard through non-use, don't throw it away: it does a fair job of cleaning sanding belts and discs.

160 Heavyweight sanding block

If you don't own a belt sander, try this method of sanding wide boards such as timber worktops. It is possible to build up a rhythm that produces very decent and consistent results. A small chamfer around the edges of the timber offcut prolongs the life of the abrasive sheet significantly.

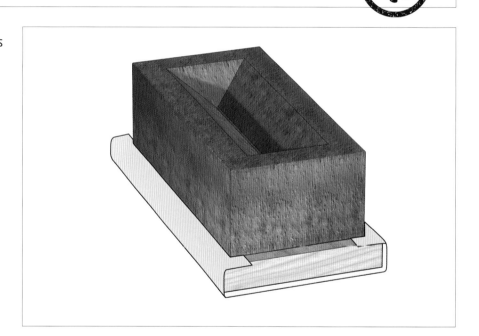

161 Making sandpaper last

The life of sandpaper can be extended by applying duct tape to the back of the sheet when cutting it to fit an electric sander, sanding blocks, or hand-sanding strips. The duct tape keeps the sandpaper from ripping, and consequently each piece will last much longer. This is particularly handy when working with long, narrow strips to sand chair rungs, dowels, and the like. Make up a number of sheets for your sander in various grits, and write the grit size on the back of the duct tape with a grease pencil or crayon.

162 Improved drum sander

If you don't have a dedicated drum sander, and instead use a drill press, this jig will help you optimize its performance. It makes the height of the drum adjustable, so that it is possible for the entire surface height to be used.

Once you have made the basic structure, cramp it to the drill-press table and drill out the centre point of the drum aperture before finishing it to size with a holesaw. If you have more than one size of drum, it would be a good idea to make a dedicated table top or an entire new jig for each one.

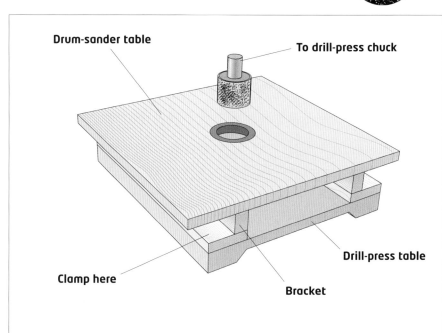

163 Reviving a palm sander

This self-adhesive Velcro roll allows you to continue using your palm sander even if the retaining clip is broken. What's even better is that you can use all the old semi-worn discs from your random-orbit sander, so making a double saving.

164 Cheap belts for Powerfiles

Powerfiles and similar tools are indispensable in the workshop and on site: nothing is better for cleaning up letterbox openings and lock mortises. The only drawback is the cost of the belts.

The belts for some belt sanders are approximately the right length, but much too wide. An easy way to cut the belts to fit is to fasten an offcut of 6 x 1in (150 x 25mm) timber to the bench, leaving about 4in (100mm) overhanging. Turn the sander belt inside out and put it over the scrap timber. With the belt almost flush with the projecting edge, use a cutting gauge to score through the cloth backing ½in (13mm) in from the side. The secret is to run the fence of the gauge along the timber, as opposed to the belt. Score only about 2in (50mm) at a time, then reposition the belt. Keep the cutting gauge sharp; a utility knife is required once you get to the overlap. Holding the belt with one hand and the gauge in the other is a good technique – the sanded side stops the belt slipping on the offcut with only moderate pressure. All that is necessary now is to part the ½in (13mm) belt from the remainder and start on the next one.

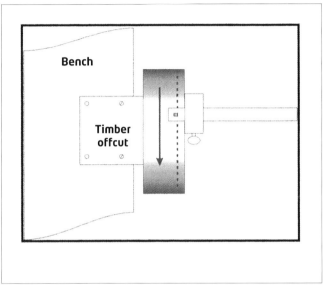

Bench

Timber offcut

You should be able to get five Powerfile belts from each sander belt. Keep the small leftover belt, as it makes an excellent pull-through for cleaning up inside angles on fine work.

165 Making a drum sander

If you don't have a drum sander you can make one easily enough. Turn a scrap piece of wood into a cylinder and then glue sandpaper onto it, holding it in place with rubber bands or string. With the cylinder still centred on the lathe, this makes an excellent drum sander for small work where fine control is required.

By drilling a hole through the centre and securing a bolt through the hole, you can mount the sander on a drill press. If you countersink the head of the bolt, it will not interfere with the base of the drill.

For both variations you can either use a single grade of sandpaper or vary the grades to give a multi-purpose device.

One word of warning, though: do make sure that the drum is correctly centred – otherwise the vibration can be annoying, and may possibly damage your work.

General workshop tips

166 Sandpaper storage

Not really ground-shaking this one, but it's a fine example of recycling, and makes maximum use of valuable worktop real estate by storing sufficient sandpaper (in mixed grades) rolled up for all immediate needs.

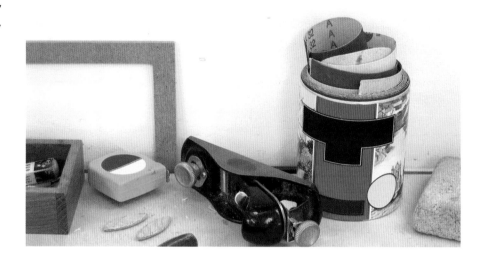

167 Colour-coding sandpaper (1)

As manufacturers do not always print the grade at sufficiently frequent intervals on the back, you often have to unroll your rolls of abrasive quite a long way to find the grade you need. Sifting through part-used scraps can also be a trial. You can save a lot of time by colour-coding.

First write down your 'key': a distinctive colour for each of the grades you are likely to use – red-60, white-80, and so on – missing out the colour of the abrasive itself. Then, using cheap coloured crayons or felt-tip pens, mark each new roll of abrasive. Unroll them, and on the back scribble a zigzag of colour, full width along the whole length. This ensures that future scraps are also marked. Spraying or stippling with quick-drying car paint is an alternative. Find a colour-coding technique that meets your needs, but don't lose your key card!

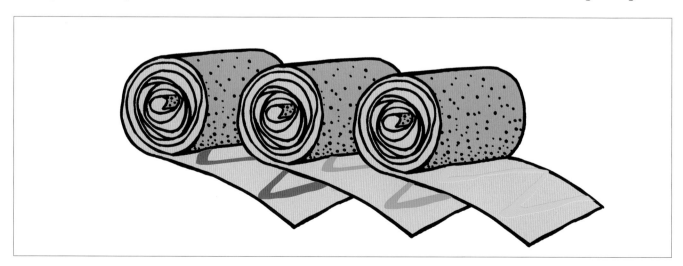

168 Wire-wool dispenser

Buying wire wool in 1kg rolls works out cheaper, but protecting the wool from chippings, dust and grit is a problem. This simple dispenser is the solution.

The box is made out of butt-joined ½in (12.5mm) MDF with hardboard sides. Three of the pieces of MDF are glued at the corners, and the hardboard is glued and pinned onto this framework. The top piece is not glued, so it can be removed in order to replace the roll.

The roll of wire wool rotates on a spindle, which could be a length of old copper tubing that fits snugly into the cardboard tube the wire wool is supplied on. This spindle rotates on a bolt passing through the middle of it. It is much easier to drill the hole for the spindle before assembling the box.

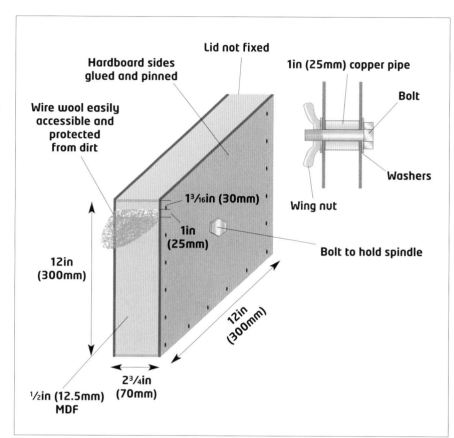

Lid not fixed
Hardboard sides glued and pinned
1in (25mm) copper pipe
Bolt
Wire wool easily accessible and protected from dirt
Washers
1³⁄₁₆in (30mm)
Wing nut
1in (25mm)
Bolt to hold spindle
12in (300mm)
12in (300mm)
2³⁄₄in (70mm)
½in (12.5mm) MDF

169 Colour-coding sandpaper (2)

Buying sandpaper grades in different colours is even easier than marking them or keeping them in separate holders.

Finishing

170 | Finishing stands

When it comes to painting, staining or varnishing a piece of furniture all over, it is usual to reach for a couple of pieces of scrap wood and drive nails through them, so the job can be supported on their points.

It is better to make permanent finishing stands, with nails both ways at different spacings, and with folding feet to provide stability. Make them from pieces of 2in (50mm) square wood, with feet about 6in (150mm) long, pivoted on countersunk screws. Use 4in (100mm) nails. Making one block with a single nail enables awkward jobs to be supported on three nails – anything on a three-point support can't wobble.

171 | Instant filler knife

Any leftover ends of mitred wood are perfect for accurate and economical application of wood filler. Two-part filler can be mixed and applied with the same piece of wood. The mitred face is ideal for filling screw or plug holes, leaving the filler perfectly flush to the surface, as it doesn't flex like a metal filling knife or spatula. The narrow edge of the mitred face is great for pushing filler into thin gaps, and the corners can be used to get into tight right angles.

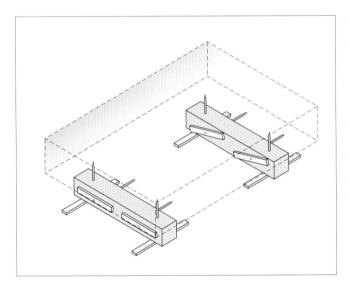

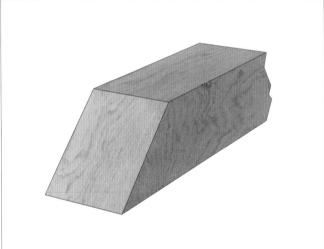

172 | Preparing MDF for finishing

It takes copious amounts of sanding sealer to prepare the edges of MDF for painting, and the sides of a sheet can be problematic too. In order to get the paint to key into the smooth surface with sufficient strength, it is always worth lightly rubbing over the area first with a 100-grit abrasive. Then apply a thinned brush-coat of sanding sealer before rubbing this back lightly with the same abrasive. This method takes longer than simply applying paint to the manufactured surface, but it does produce a superior, longer-lasting finish.

173 Good results from varnishing

It is possible to achieve superb results using polyurethane varnish and this simple tip.

Once the slightly thinned first coat is dry, use 0000-grade wire wool dipped in white spirit (mineral spirit) to wipe over the surface thoroughly with light hand pressure. This will de-nib the slightly rough surface of the varnish. Once finished, wipe over the surface with a lint-free cloth and some more spirit. When the surface is dry it will feel glass-smooth – providing your timber was properly sanded. For the best finish, apply a second coat before repeating the process, then leave the third coat to dry and be left *au naturel*.

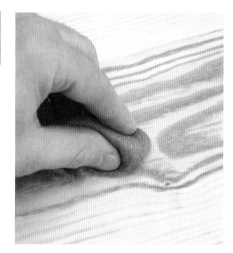

174 Recycling spirits

Tip the used white spirit (mineral spirit) from washing brushes into a 1-gallon or 5-litre clear plastic container. Over a few weeks, all the solids will fall to the bottom and a clear liquid will be left on top. You can pour off the clear fluid and use it again for cleaning more brushes. Then put it back into the 'used' container and the process can begin again. Keep one container for used spirit and another for recycled.

From time to time, refill the recycled container from the used container. If need be, you could always start a second container for used spirit while the first one settles out.

175 Van Dyke crystals

Try Van Dyke crystals for general staining. This traditional pigment dissolves in warm water to your required strength, giving greater flexibility than, say, a spirit stain. This type of stain can be re-applied if necessary to achieve a darker finish – something which is hard to achieve with an oil stain.

Traditionally used on oak and walnut, the Van Dyke crystal stain is equally effective on pine and similar softwoods, and is comparatively cheap compared with stains of the ready-made variety.

It does need a light rub-down when dry to clean up the raised grain caused by the water.

Workshop storage

176 | Revolving tool holder

This revolving tool rack utilizes various odds and ends from around the workshop. A simple turntable has been made from a length of 2in (50mm) plastic waste pipe, additional sections of which are used to house individual tools.

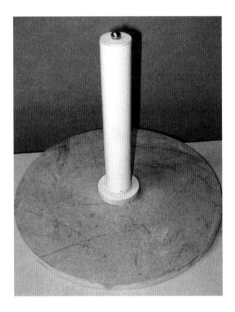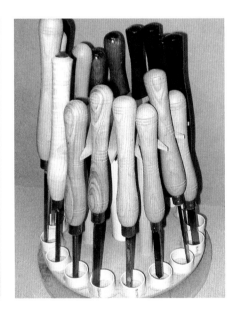

177 | Fold-down shelf

This folding shelf allows you to keep the tools you know you will need away from the rest of the clutter, and within arm's reach. When the job is completed, the shelf simply folds flat.

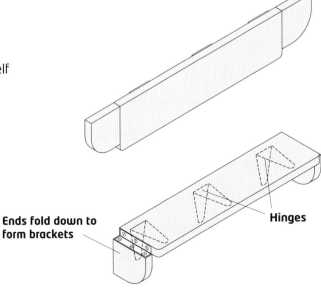

Ends fold down to form brackets

Hinges

178 | Itemized storage

The photograph on the right shows offcuts of pipe set up to to store different types of saw blades. The shelves in the photo below can be made from ply or MDF offcuts, with holes and slots to provide a variety of storage solutions for individual items. It may look disorganized to the uninitiated, but everything is visible and easily to hand.

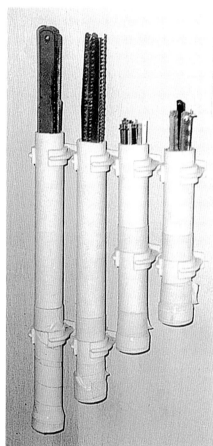

179 | Stacking storage

Instead of the usual assortment of tins and jars, stack your sundries neatly in matching containers. These are discarded measuring containers provided by the local vet's surgery.

General workshop tips

180 Safer shelves

Certain things tend to roll off ordinary shelves. In this design, supporting brackets extend against the backboard to rest against the wall and tilt upwards slightly, to stop things rolling forward. A few degrees here and there are not noticeable. A groove near the front also helps to discourage anything from rolling off.

Weight is best taken at the top, so the only screws to the wall are above shelf level; brackets are only screwed through the backboard and not to the wall or shelf. The bracket angle keeps the joint to the shelf tight, but you could also use glue.

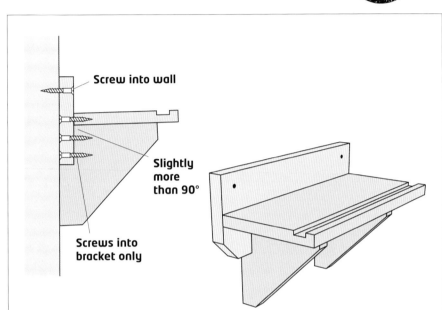

Screw into wall

Slightly more than 90°

Screws into bracket only

181 Keeping knives safe

Plastic wine-bottle corks fit tightly into ³/₄in (20mm) holes drilled into a block of MDF. Trim them flush with the surface using a saw, and they make safe storage for fine knives like these scalpels. The cut closes up as the knife is withdrawn, as the cork is held in constant compression by the MDF. You can also use it to store awls or any other slender, sharp tool.

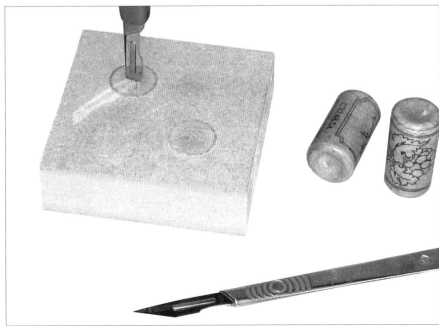

182 | New uses for old bottles

There are a number of woodworking uses for the humble squeezy bottle.

1 Fill one with water to lubricate waterstones. The water supply is controllable and the cap on the end eliminates spillage.

2 Cut the bottom end off and use the remaining top part as an ideal funnel for filling fine-necked containers such as oilcans.

3 Use the bottom end for mixing glue such as urea-formaldehyde. Two V-cuts in the rim give a secure parking place for the glue brush. Dunk the glue brush in a second container, filled with water, as soon as gluing is complete, to save it from going hard.

4 The middle section can be cut into rings to hold drawings, sketches and charts.

You might even be able to think of a use for the little cap on the top.

183 | Storing biscuits

The safest way to keep biscuits dry is to use baby-formula tins, which have really good airtight plastic lids.

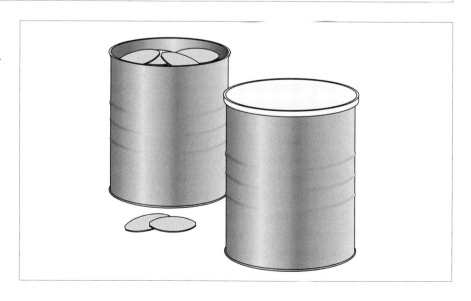

General workshop tips

184 Glue storage (1)

A small block of wood bored to receive the inverted neck of a glue tube or bottle prevents air bubbles in the neck. You know the problem: you press harder, nothing happens, until suddenly a huge dollop comes out. Take care not to bore right through the block.

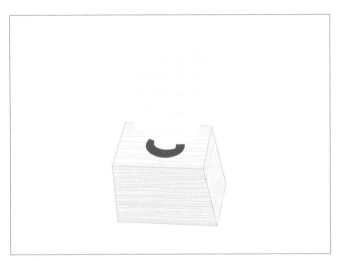

185 Glue storage (2)

It's much cheaper buying wood glue in bulk than in small bottles. Decant it into smaller, more manageable containers like the sauce bottles you can buy for a pittance at the local supermarket, or into empty washing-up liquid containers. Cut a small hole in the cap to allow easy and clean pouring.

186 Glue storage (3)

Use a cup hook to hang your glue in a handy place. The shank of the hook keeps the nozzle open, so the glue never dries out.

187 Sealed environment

A calculator often helps with the workshop maths, but may quickly become clogged with wood dust, moisture, and the odd tea spillage.

Place it inside a resealable sandwich bag; you can still use it and read the results, without having to worry about your tea.

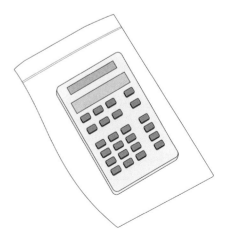

Workshop health & safety

188 Dust control (1)

The system shown here addresses two safety issues. It is all very well having an extraction system fitted to your power tools and machinery, but how often have you used the machinery and failed to turn on the extractor? If you connect the extractor through a double-pole ceiling switch in a central part of the workshop, the equipment cannot be used unless the extractor is running.

Secondly, the switch is an excellent emergency isolator in the event of any mishap.

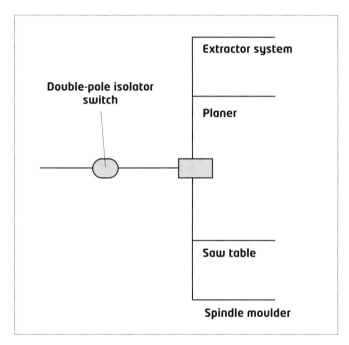

189 Dust control (2)

This adaptation makes it easier and cleaner to empty your dust extractor, but it does involve cutting the bottom out of your extractor – it won't lose any rigidity, but it will invalidate the manufacturer's warranty.

Two pieces of ³⁄₈in (10mm) MDF are fixed to the wall, supported by a cleat and a leg resting on the floor. The size of the two boards depends on how big your machine is.

The top board has a hole in it exactly the same size as the machine, and the bottom of the machine sits exactly flush with the underside of the top board. If the machine has a flange on the underside, this can be fixed to the board with screws, using silicone sealant for an airtight seal.

The bottom board also has a hole, about 1in (25mm) smaller than the other, and a ¹⁄₁₆in (1mm or so) rebate which allows a thin sheet of metal to be slid in and out between the two boards.

Simply place a dustbin (trash can) underneath, with a plastic liner inside. When you think the machine is full, just pull out the sheet metal and all your shavings will drop into the bin.

Don't worry about losing suction power: when the machine is on it actually sucks the sheet metal up to it as though you had never taken the bottom off.

190 Electrical safety

To improve safety in a garage workshop, plug an RCD (residual current device) adaptor into the main power socket. Into this you can plug a four-way trailing socket which is then fixed to the wall. You can now plug in up to three power tools, leaving one socket for your dust-extraction system.

Obviously you will only be using one tool at a time – plus the extractor – but the extra sockets save any fiddling around.

The electrical loading should be quite within safety limits, but in any case the RCD adaptor will trip if there is an overload or imbalance, or a short circuit.

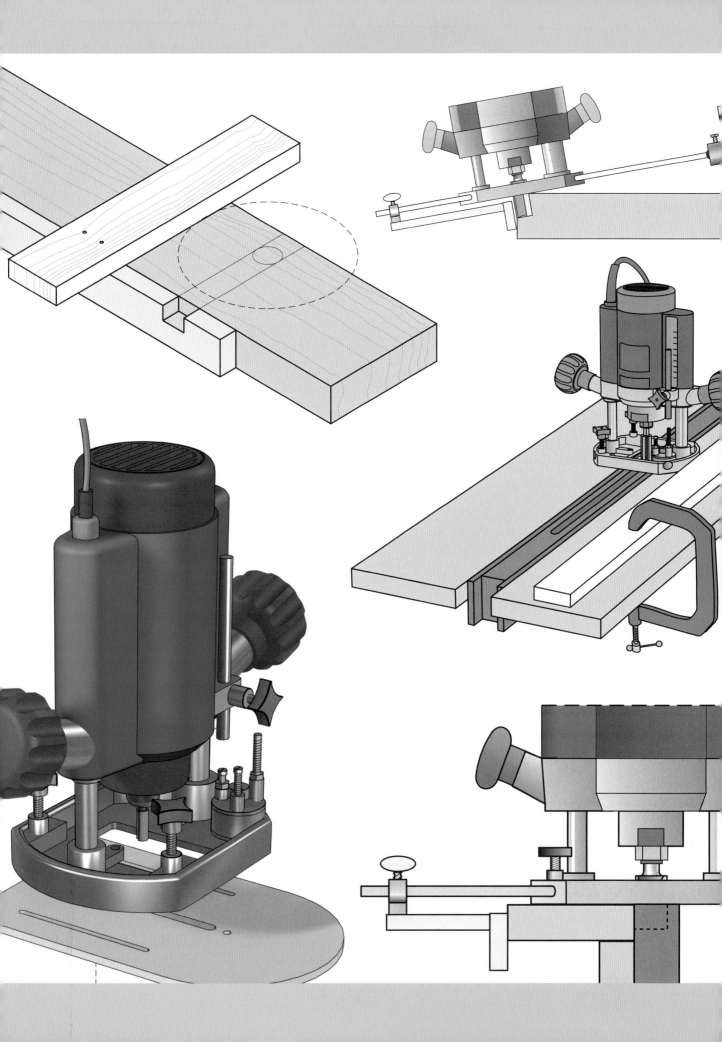

Routing tips

191–362

Router techniques

191   Direction of cut

The feed direction is the direction in which the cutter is fed into the material, or – in the case of table-mounted or fixed routers – the material into the cutter.

Following the right feed direction will ensure safer and easier working, allowing the cutter to cut efficiently. The correct feed direction is always *against* the rotation of the cutter. This can be deduced by looking at the cutter itself. Routers generally rotate in a clockwise direction (looking down from above), and this determines the feed direction. If the feed direction is incorrect, the forces involved will cause the cutter to push itself away from the guiding edge of the work or template, spoiling the work.

When the router is inverted in a table, the feed direction is from right to left. If the material is fed in the wrong direction the material could be ripped away from the operator.

It is good practice to mark the direction of feed (right to left) on the work-table back fence when using your router inverted on a table. With portable routers the rotational direction of the cutter can be marked on the top of the machine, although with experience this will become obvious.

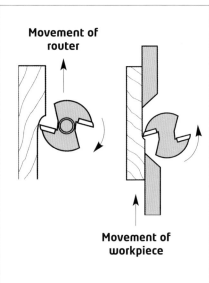

Correct direction of cut for portable (*left*) and overhead routers

192   Fine adjustment

Here is a system of fine adjustment which requires no expenditure at all. Make sure the plunge depth is locked at the last cut you made, then raise the depth stop. Insert one or two thicknesses of paper or thin card, lower the depth stop onto this, hold firmly and lock it. Release the plunge lock, allowing the router to rise, and remove the paper. Now plunge the router down to the depth stop and lock it. You have increased the depth of cut by the thickness of the paper.

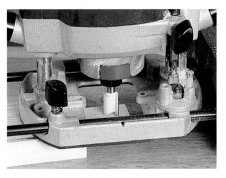

Top: **The router as set after the last cut when forming a tenon**

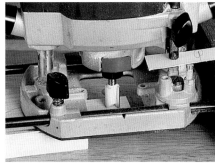

Top right: **Depth stop raised and paper strip inserted**

Right: **Paper removed: cut depth increased by thickness of paper**

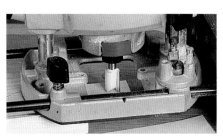

193 | Right-hand rule

Working out which direction to move a router along the edge of a workpiece is often confusing to the newcomer. A simple way to help you to remember which direction to rout is the 'right-hand rule'.

When routing hand-held along the edge of a workpiece, the only equipment required for working out the routing direction is your own right hand.

Hold it as shown, with your index finger pointing and the rest of your fingers curled up. Line up your hand so the knuckles are at right angles to the edge of the workpiece. Your thumb is now curled in the direction of the cutter's rotation, and your extended finger points in the direction in which the router should be fed along the edge of the workpiece.

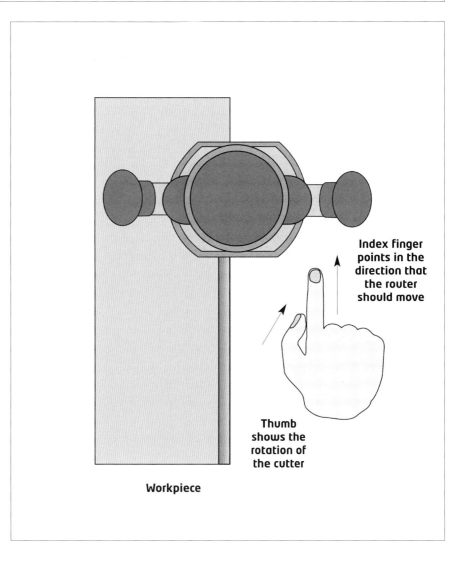

Index finger points in the direction that the router should move

Thumb shows the rotation of the cutter

Workpiece

194 | Lubricating plunge rods

All plunge routers need to have their plunge rods lubricated from time to time in order to avoid the risk of sticking during the plunge. Opinions vary over what sort of lubricant to use; spray-on penetrating oil, dry lubricant spray, etc. Oil in any form can pick up dust, and it may also drip onto the work and be impossible to remove. It can also prevent certain finishes or dyes from taking properly. An excellent alternative is a good-quality clear wax polish, which has a microcrystalline structure (that is, no lumps) and doesn't contain water. Once applied, the wax dries hard and gives the rods a lasting shine.

Routing tips

195 Drawer-bottom grooves

A router table makes it easy to cut a slot for a plywood drawer bottom. First, assemble the drawer without using glue and hold it together using either masking tape or a web cramp tightly wound around the drawer.

Fit a bearing-guided slotting cutter into the router and set the height of cut by means of a trial piece of wood; the depth of cut can be altered by using bearings of different diameters.

The drawer is placed on the router table with the cutter inside. The groove is cut on all four sides of the drawer, moving it in the opposite direction to the rotation of the cutter. At the corners, either square up the groove with a chisel or round over the corners of the drawer bottom. Finally, the whole drawer is glued, reassembled and cramped together.

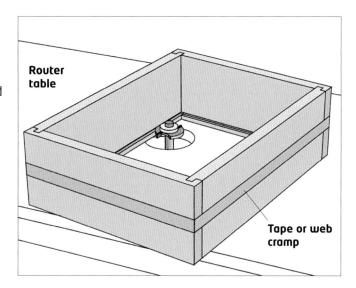

Router table

Tape or web cramp

196 Routing tongue grooves for mitres

When routing grooves for tongues in mitres, clamp all four sides together in sequence as shown. This creates a square shoulder for the router fence, and at the same time a good bearing face for the router base. It also aligns the grooves from the outside, rather than the inside of the mitres, so that the carcass sides will line up even if there is a difference in thickness.

When clamping, make sure you line up the two centre boards carefully, as any misalignment will affect the accuracy of the grooves. Place your clamps as close as possible to the ends of the boards without getting in the way of the passage of the router. Once clamped together, put the whole assembly into a vice.

Set up the router fence so that the bit cuts a groove nearer the inside edge of the mitre than the outside.

Once the first grooves are cut, line up the opposite ends and rout those. Unclamp, place the uncut ends between the routed ones and repeat the process.

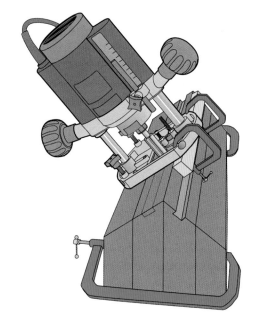

197 Better finish on cross grain

When cutting cross grain, burning and generally poor finish can result. Router expert Ron Fox recommends making a finishing pass at exactly the same settings, but in the reverse or 'wrong' direction. Rather like the pile on a velvet cushion, which in one direction stands up and feels rough to the touch, but in the other lies down and feels smooth and soft, wood grain is often better for gently cleaning up going the wrong way. In most cases this is inadvisable, but in this example you are removing very little wood at all – just enough to give a cleaner result.

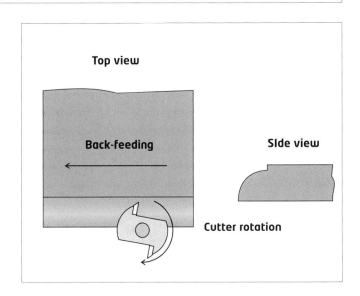

Top view

Back-feeding

Side view

Cutter rotation

198 Ramp-cutting

When making mortise slots or deep grooves, instead of setting intermediate cut depths with the three-stage turret, try 'ramping down' instead.

Simply plunge the router slowly as you move along the workpiece. It is quite an easy action, which allows the cutter to reach full depth gradually without straining the cutter. More importantly, it avoids heat build-up and charring of stuck-on wood-dust and resin that would otherwise damage your cutter. Repeat the process back and forth till full depth has been reached.

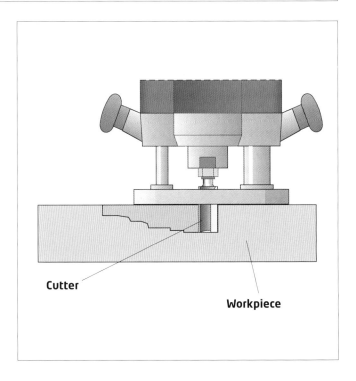

Cutter

Workpiece

Routing tips

199 Attaching and removing patterns

A simple way to separate the pattern and workpiece when they are held together with double-sided tape is to chamfer the pattern locally when you make it, so that a knife blade or chisel can be inserted to part them. The chamfer should be small enough not to interfere with the path of the guide or ballrace, and care should be taken not to damage the faces when inserting the blade.

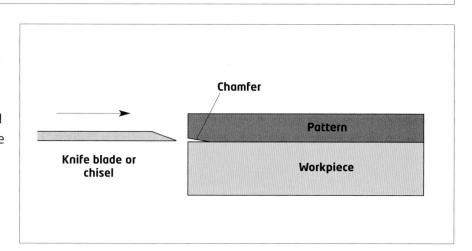

Knife blade or chisel

Chamfer

Pattern

Workpiece

200 Steaming out depressions in wood

Bearing-guided cutters are quick to set up, but there is a slight drawback: the bearing leaves a track, particularly in softwood, where the fibres of the wood have been compressed. It is not so noticeable on other materials – until a finish is applied, when it sticks out like a sore thumb.

Rather than spend a lot of time sanding, lay a damp cloth along the damaged piece of wood and apply an iron, set to a medium heat, to the affected area. Like magic, the compressed fibres swell back to their original size, and only a light sanding is then required. Take care to check while ironing that the wood isn't scorching.

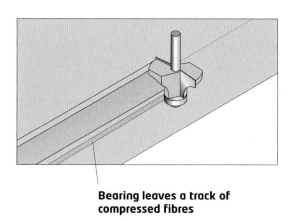

Bearing leaves a track of compressed fibres

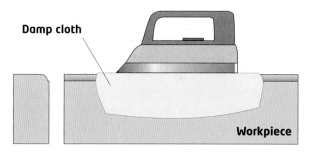

Damp cloth

Workpiece

Router techniques

201 Panel-raising

It is not always necessary to have the right router cutter for every job. Here is an improvised solution to the problem of making raised panels without a dedicated panel-raising cutter. It gives pretty good results, although the panels will need a fair amount of cleaning up.

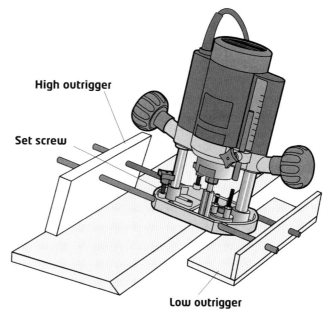

High outrigger

Set screw

Low outrigger

202 There and back

When cutting a groove with a straight cutter, one side of it is cut against the direction of rotation and finishes smooth. The other side, being cut with the direction of rotation, could well be rough, particularly if it is a large diameter cutter working on softwood.

When both edges of a groove are important, it's better to use a smaller cutter – a ½in (12mm) in a ¾in (19mm) groove, for example – and make two passes in opposite directions. This ensures that the final edges cut are both against the direction of the cutter rotation and should finish smooth, whether across or with the grain, on either hard or soft wood.

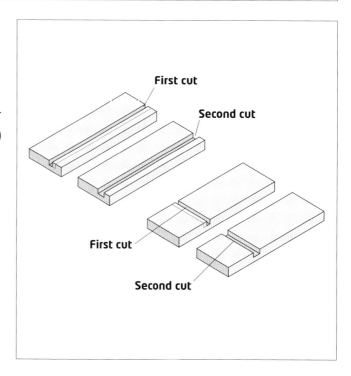

First cut

Second cut

First cut

Second cut

Routing tips

203 Routing on a curved edge

Routing an ovolo or other shaped moulding on items ranging from a 42in (1066mm) diameter circular table top to a disc only 10 to 12in (250 to 300mm) across is not a straightforward operation unless you have the correct cutter for the job, fitted with a bearing.

Mounting a couple of blocks on the faces of the straight guide overcomes the problem, allowing the router to be slid securely along the workpiece. The two wood blocks permit the router cutter to follow the circumference exactly.

To ensure that the router does not tip out of vertical, fit a sub-base and proceed in an anticlockwise direction.

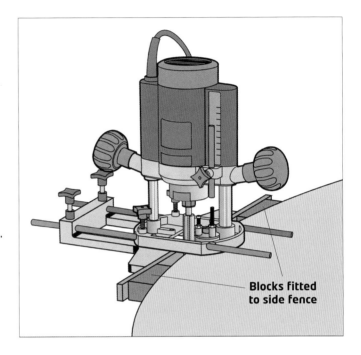

Blocks fitted to side fence

204 Small circle jig

This jig is a little time-consuming to make, but will be invaluable if ever you need to drill an exact-diameter hole. Fit the jig to your router using its base fixing holes and some pan-head machine screws. Plunge the cutter through and adjust the distance between the cutter and the centre pin; a vernier gauge is useful to set this distance. Always rout a test cut to check the exact diameter before using it on your real workpiece.

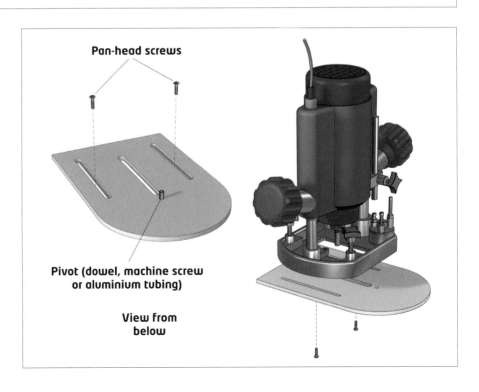

Pan-head screws

Pivot (dowel, machine screw or aluminium tubing)

View from below

205 Circle cutting

The pivot point supplied with some routers, fitting onto one of the rods, is not very effective: it is difficult to hold in place, and the rods supplied are rarely long enough for cutting large circles.

For a simple alternative, get hold of some steel bar to fit your router's baseplate, and cut it into two lengths of about 20in (500mm). Cut – or get someone else to cut – a short thread on one end of each piece. Make a steel plate with holes the same distance apart as those on the router's baseplate, and one in the centre.

Bolt the rods firmly into the outer holes. Into the centre hole attach an eyebolt, using a wing nut and locking nut. The eye pivots on a peg made from dowel trimmed to size, fixed into a mounting block that can be attached to the workpiece; double-sided carpet tape holds well enough.

It is almost impossible to make a mistake, as the pivot is held firmly while you concentrate on the router and where it is cutting.

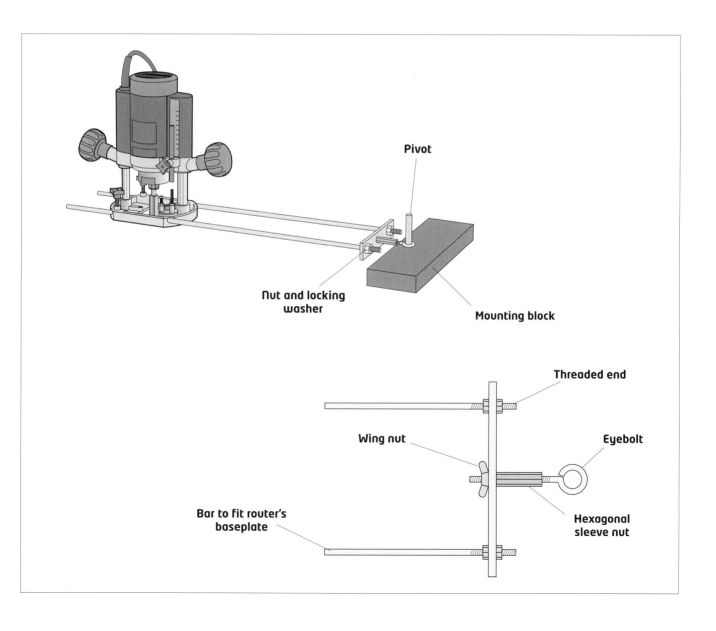

Pivot

Nut and locking washer

Mounting block

Threaded end

Wing nut

Eyebolt

Bar to fit router's baseplate

Hexagonal sleeve nut

Routing tips

206 Routing very small circles

A trammel bar cannot be used to cut recesses or holes
that are smaller in diameter than the router's base, but
a simple circle jig can be made from an offcut of MDF
in a couple of minutes.

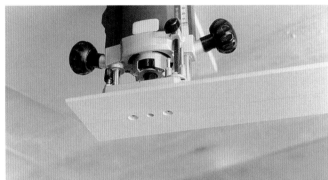

1 Start with an offcut measuring the width of your
router's base by about 18in (460mm). First, drill and
countersink two holes to fix the offcut to the router
using the guide-bush holes and screws.

Fit the cutter that you plan to use for circle cutting,
then plunge through the offcut – put a piece of scrap
under it first – leaving a neat, cutter-sized hole.

2 Measure from the edge of the newly cut hole and
mark the radius of the circle that you plan to cut.

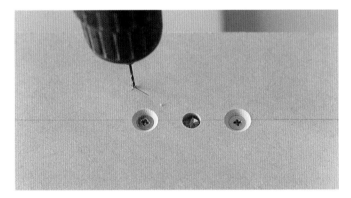

3 With a drill bit the same size as a panel pin, drill a
hole at your marked centre point.

4 Now snip the head off a panel pin and insert what's
left into the centre hole. You're now ready to rout a
circle – and for different-sized circles you can just move
the panel pin to a new hole.

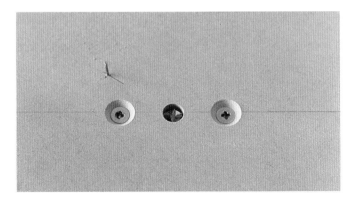

207 | Extended fence bar for circle cutting

Some manufacturers provide a pivot point to lock on the end of one fence bar. This allows cutting with a radius up to the length of one bar, but a router has two bars – if they can be joined, the possible radius is doubled.

A block of close-grained hardwood (beech or sycamore) joins the bars end to end. The block shown is 4in (100mm) long and 1in (25mm) square, drilled through to suit the bars. Four screws lock the bars in place. The ends of the screws are cut off and filed flat to provide a good bearing against the bars. Use fairly stout screws (no. 8) and drill pilot holes first, before driving the screws to cut a thread in the wood and then withdrawing them to cut off the points.

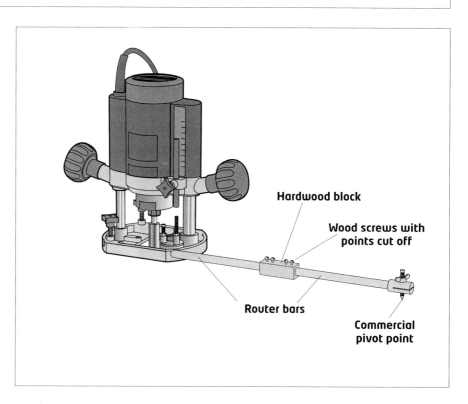

Hardwood block

Wood screws with points cut off

Router bars

Commercial pivot point

208 | Large circle jig

This trammel really couldn't be simpler. All you need are some recessed router fixing holes, a cutter aperture and a pivot hole drilled at the distance you require. To locate this centre, use the same drill bit to bore right through the jig and into the workpiece.

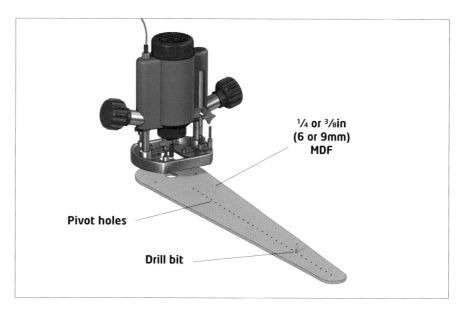

¹⁄₄ or ³⁄₈in (6 or 9mm) MDF

Pivot holes

Drill bit

Routing tips

209 | Routing a concave edge

The task here is to apply ⁵⁄₆₄in (1mm) thick solid timber edging strip to ¼in (6mm) ash-faced ply. The edging has to fit into a concave arc having a radius of 11in (280mm).

It can be difficult to cut the ply to the required arc and end up with cut faces that are spelch-free and at a true 90° to the top and bottom faces, so as to accept the edging which is to be glued on. Neither bandsawing nor jigsawing, even with narrow, fine-tooth blades, produces a really satisfactory finish, and in any case either of these methods would need the cut edge sanding to final size. Trying to sand a curve in ¼in ply while keeping the edges at 90° over its full width and length is not impossible, but extremely difficult. Regular two-flute straight cutters can be used, but here again the edge invariably needs sanding.

The solution is to rout the edge to final shape and size using a ¼in (6mm) spiral down-cut cutter and guide bush running around the edge of an MDF template.

The edging is cut and prepared to thickness but left overwidth (about ³⁄₈in or 9mm) and about twice the required length. The curvature is achieved by soaking it in warm water for a few hours and restraining it to the required radius while drying overnight.

The ply edges are left as cut by the router, and the edging strip glued into place with polyurethane adhesive and cramped in position with multiple strips of masking tape. The clean-up is quick, using a sharp, finely set plane.

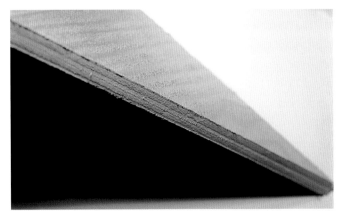

Top: **The edging strip attached**
Centre: **The clean-cut plywood edge**
Bottom: ¹⁹⁄₃₂**in (15mm) guide bush and down-cut spiral cutter**

210 | Large-scale trammel

This trusty trammel, with plywood arms and a single pivot block, can be made in whatever size you need. If the arm is 60in (1500mm) long, it will cut a diameter down to 20in (500mm); if you need to go bigger, make it the full 8ft (2440mm) length of a board. Leaving a rough edge on both the pivot block and the ply aperture helps to make the jig accurate and solid.

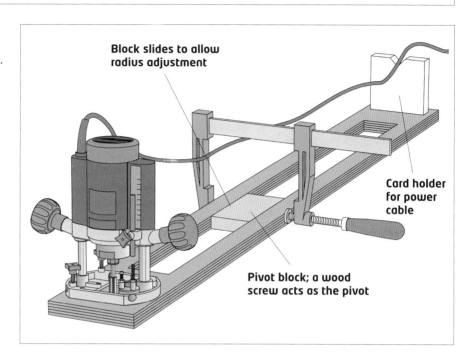

Block slides to allow radius adjustment

Card holder for power cable

Pivot block; a wood screw acts as the pivot

211 | Cutting an open-ended curve

If a router cut has to be made parallel to a curved edge, the usual way of guiding it is to attach temporary blocks to the fence, so their outer ends can bear against the edge (A; see also Tip 203). This works fine on a continuous edge, such as a table top. For a curve with an open end, the two-block guide system is unsatisfactory because there is a short distance at the start of the cut with no guidance.

But the router need not be used with its fence square to the cut. Instead, you can make a single block (B) which has its high point near the gap in the fence and is high enough to tilt the router, when it and the corner of the fence are bearing against the edge, so the cutter is in the correct starting position. The cut can be made successfully all the way from there.

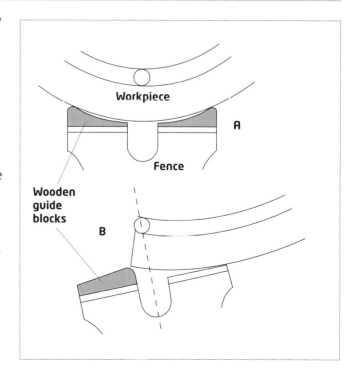

Workpiece

A

Fence

Wooden guide blocks

B

212 Stopped cuts

When cutting a stopped chamfer or moulding on a router table, it isn't easy to stop the cut exactly where you want it. To ensure complete accuracy, mark the guides with masking tape to show where the end of the wood will be once the cut has reached the intended limit. The tape can then be peeled off without leaving any marks.

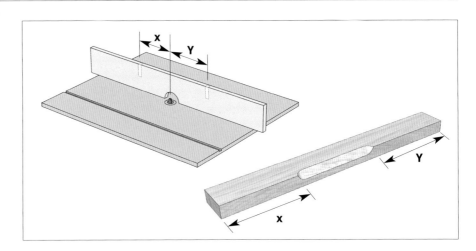

213 Quick repeats

When making a complex moulding, such as linenfold, always keep an offcut of your moulding. You can then quickly set fence and cutter height next time you want to make the same profile.

214 Crisper mouldings

When using a router cutter to mould across the grain, some woods tend to leave fibres of wood grain clinging to the surface edge. These have to be sanded off, and the result is always less sharp than edges cut along the grain.

This can be prevented by first cutting across to sever the fibres, using a cutting gauge. Cut a short length of moulding on scrap wood and set the gauge to that; it will then follow exactly the same edge as the bearing on the cutter.

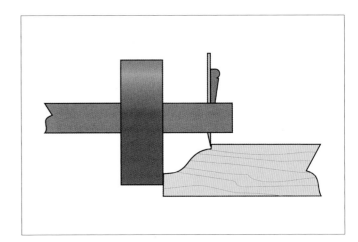

215 | Making narrow mouldings

It is impossible to make picture-frame mouldings from narrow strips with a hand-held router, and difficult and risky to do it with the router inverted in a table.

Instead, do the router work – hand-held or on a table – on the edges of a wide board, then cut off the moulding afterwards. If the board is as long as two sides of the frame, all the moulding you need can be made on the two edges.

Start by cutting the rabbets (rebates) on both edges, then move on to the chamfers and mouldings, leaving enough of the square edge between rabbet and chamfer for the bearing to travel on. The strips can then be cut off on the circular saw.

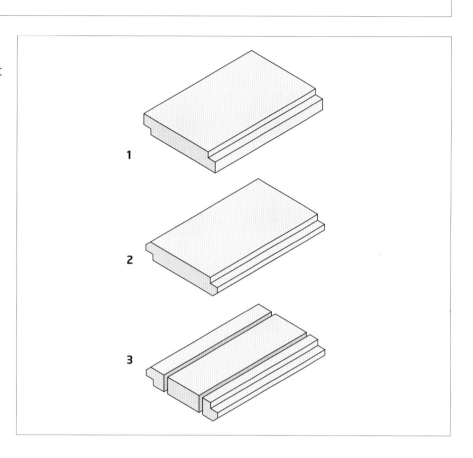

216 | Moulding samples

When designing something for yourself or a paying customer, it is extremely useful to make up a sample, either to help you in the process or to give the customer an idea of how the finished product should look. Make a sample piece that incorporates the most important section of a job, such as the top corner of a bookcase and maybe a short piece of plinth as well. Just a corner of a door panel plus the cornice moulding will suffice to display a proper finish, whether dyed, French-polished or varnished.

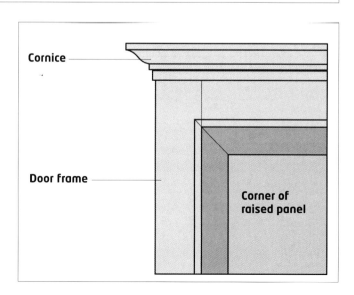

Cornice

Door frame

Corner of raised panel

Routing tips

217 Stopped mouldings in pre-jointed frames

A router and guided cutters permit the machining of rebates and mouldings around the inside edges of frames, after glue-up. Difficulties arise when stopped mouldings are required, for instance around the stiles and rails of a panelled door.

The following method allows edge treatment, to a precise distance, from each inside corner. It is important to machine these mouldings after cleaning up, and before you cut any rebates on the other side of the frame.

For small, rectangular frames:

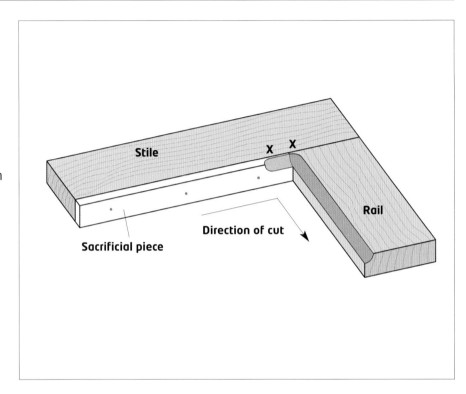

1 Prepare two sacrificial pieces, the same thickness as the frame members. The width must be equal to the distance required between the corner and the stop end of the moulding, X–X on the drawing. For absolute precision, cutter radius must be taken into account.

2 Cut these pieces to a snug fit along the longest sides, and butt them squarely to the short sides.

3 Temporarily pin them to the inside edges of the stiles, so that the pinholes will be machined out with the subsequent rebate on the other side. Otherwise, use G-clamps (C-clamps) or strong double-sided tape to secure the scrap.

4 The short sides (the rails) are now machined, treating the sacrificial pieces as part of the job. Rout straight into the scrap, for a couple of inches, turn the corner, and rout along the rail, turning the opposite corner and into the other scrap piece. Repeat at the other end of the frame.

5 Having machined the short sides first, you can now cut the same scrap pieces to fit the shorter sides. Remove the machining at the ends, so the scrap piece is square and will butt neatly.

Because the rail has already been moulded, there is less material to fix against, so make sure the scrap is secured well. Machine the stiles as you did the rails. Result: neat, stopped mouldings at a precise and predetermined distance from the corners of the frame.

Don't try to save on offcuts by using short pieces for each corner – they are inclined to slip, and will also have to be repositioned four times, creating more chances for error.

218 | Avoiding break-out

When cutting a large moulding in softwood, there is always a risk of splitting or breaking out, and the danger spots are not always apparent. This is particularly so if a large section of waste has to be removed (A). You might cut the moulding in stages, and still suffer from a bad spot. It helps to remove some of the waste first, with a chamfer (B) or a rabbet (C). Besides reducing the amount to be removed with the moulding cutter, it will usually show rough spots or potential tear-outs, so you can carefully ease past them with the final cut to produce a perfect moulding (D).

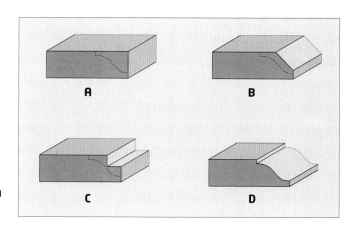

219 | Stopped mouldings

When running a moulding between two points on an edge with a router – for example, a stopped chamfer on a table leg – the most difficult part is obtaining a clean entry and exit at the same point on each edge.

To overcome this, square off a piece of scrap and then cut a 45° angle on it. Clamp this to your work, and a bearing-guided cutter will now run smoothly down the angle onto the work and just as smoothly off it at the other end, with no burning either.

220 | Clean corners

When moulding an edge all round a piece of wood, such as a table top, there is a risk of grain breaking out at the end of a cut across the grain. To prevent this – whether using the router hand-held or inverted in a table – cut across the grain first, but stop within a very short distance of the far side. Then machine the remaining section the 'wrong way', slowly. Any slight roughness this leaves will be removed by the cuts along the grain.

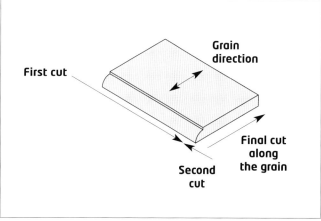

Grain direction

First cut

Final cut along the grain

Second cut

Routing tips

221 Trimming edges (1)

When the router table is used for squaring edges, the cutter is left slightly proud of the fence, removing maybe $1/32$–$5/64$in (1–2mm) in a pass. The problem with this method – especially with longer boards – is the tendency of the cut section to move in towards the fence. This can cause the uncut section to move away from the fence, causing a wavy edge.

The solution is to glue a length of worktop edging to the outfeed fence – use a sacrificial fence for this. Set your router cutter in line with the outfeed fence. Now, when you pass the workpiece through it will always remain in contact with the entire fence, ensuring a square cut.

222 Trimming edges (2)

When trimming or moulding all four edges of a natural timber panel, care must be taken to avoid excessive break-out at the end of the cross-grain cuts, so always cut across the short grain first. Any chipping or break-out at the end of the cut will then be removed when the side (long-grain) cuts are made.

Scoring the cutting line across the face of the workpiece with a cutting gauge or knife before routing removes any risk of tearing the surface grain.

When trimming or moulding only across the grain (leaving the long-grain edges square), spelch battens can be clamped at the ends of the panel to prevent break-out.

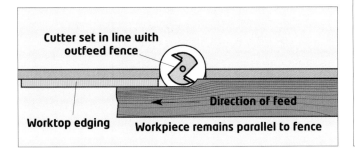

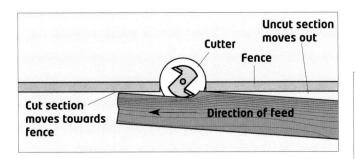

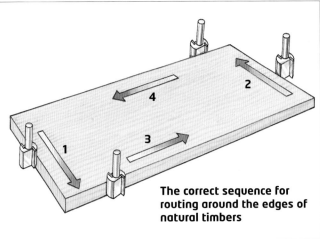

The correct sequence for routing around the edges of natural timbers

223 | Affordable housing

Here is a quick and simple method of making a housing (dado) joint, which can be a tight, snug or sliding fit. For this example we will use a ¾in (19mm) thick shelf in a ½in (12.5mm) deep housing. You will require a stepped trim guide to suit your router, a ½in (12.5mm) cutter, and an offcut from your shelf.

First clamp your trim guide on the end of the shelf offcut, and cut a rebate so you are left with a bare-faced tenon ½in (12.5mm) long and just under ½in (12.5mm) thick.

Next clamp the trim guide to the carcass side to align with the top edge of the intended housing (there is no need to mark out the bottom edge). Rout to the full depth, from left to right in stages, with a fine cut to finish. Remove any 'feathering' from the lower edge with fine abrasive paper.

Remove the trim guide and insert your shelf tenon into the ½in (12.5mm) housing with the bare face against the top edge.

Place your trim guide on the carcass and butt it up against the underside of the shelf. If you want to tighten the joint, push the trim guide hard up against the shelf and clamp it. If you require a loose sliding fit, place the trim guide gently against the shelf, sliding it from side to side to check the fit, and then clamp it.

Remove the shelf and rout from right to left to the full depth in stages, with a fine cut to finish. Your housing should now be complete, with nice crisp edges.

Fit the shelf. If everything has gone according to plan you should be able to tap it or slide it in. No maths is needed, marking out is minimal and any cutter can be used, so long as it's between half and three quarters of the shelf thickness.

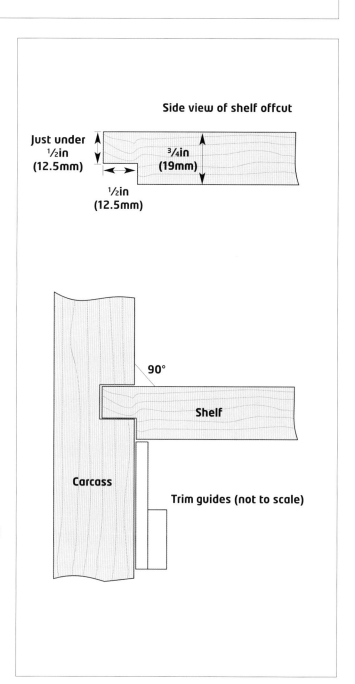

Side view of shelf offcut

Just under ½in (12.5mm)

¾in (19mm)

½in (12.5mm)

90°

Shelf

Carcass

Trim guides (not to scale)

Routing tips

224 Stopped grooves

Here is a set-up for routing stopped grooves along the edges of a workpiece.

A steel rule is used first, to set the work flush with the Workmate top. The rule is then used to measure and set the straightedge parallel to the workpiece

This method is safer and more accurate than lowering the work onto the cutter, with the router inverted in a table.

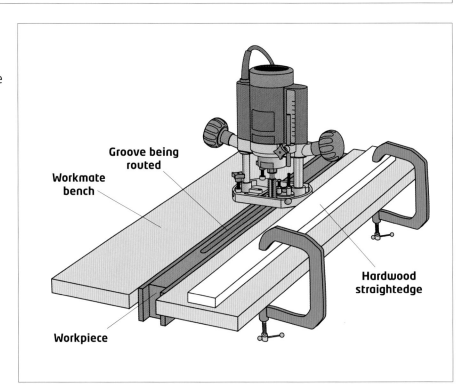

Groove being routed

Workmate bench

Hardwood straightedge

Workpiece

225 Clean grooves

A straight cutter in a router leaves the best edge when the direction the tool is moving opposes the direction of the cutter's rotation. If a full-width cutter is used to make a groove or housing joint, one edge will be rougher than the other, because the cut on that side will be in reverse.

Where the best edges are required, it is better to cut a groove in two passes with a smaller-diameter cutter, cutting the near edge first from left to right. The guide strip is then altered, or a packing strip used, so the far edge can be cut cleanly from right to left.

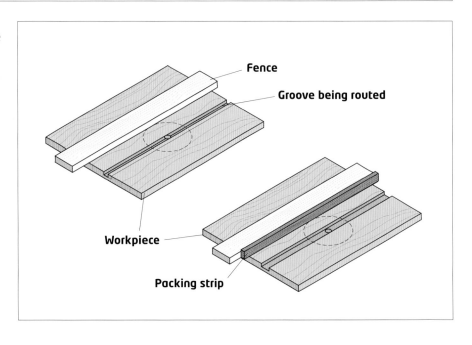

Fence

Groove being routed

Workpiece

Packing strip

226 Routing stopped chamfers

The easiest way to rout stopped chamfers is on a table. Stick a ¼in or ½in (6 or 12mm) fascia onto the fence and add stop blocks using double-sided tape.

Angle the workpiece against the right-hand stop before pivoting it onto the cutter and simultaneously moving it (in the correct direction against the cutter) up to the left-hand stop block.

227 Routing parallel grooves

If you want to make a succession of parallel slots or grooves, machine the first groove with a cutter of appropriate diameter, then fit a thin MDF sub-base to the router, with a machined strip of wood glued to it at the intended spacing from the cutter. Make sure it extends either side of the router base. Now sit the end of the strip in the first groove and proceed to cut the new groove. Repeat this procedure as many times as you want. The result is a set of parallel, equally spaced grooves, ideal for making CD racks and other such projects.

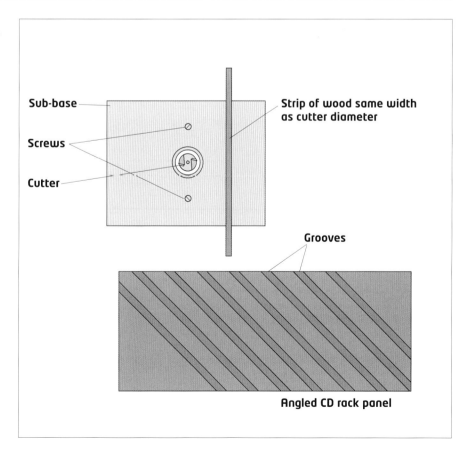

Sub-base

Screws

Cutter

Strip of wood same width as cutter diameter

Grooves

Angled CD rack panel

Routing tips

228   Routed door handles

This pair of pull handles can be made with the router and two cutters, working on the side of a board long enough for the two handles. The board should be wide enough to provide a smooth surface for the router base.

First, chamfer what will be the fronts of the handles (1). This is followed by deep cove cuts each side (2). Then the handles can be cut off on the circular saw (3). After trimming them to length, continue the chamfers around the ends with a small block plane (4).

Thin backing pieces are made from a contrasting wood, with chamfers all round (5). Finally, the handles are mounted with screws through the doors (6).

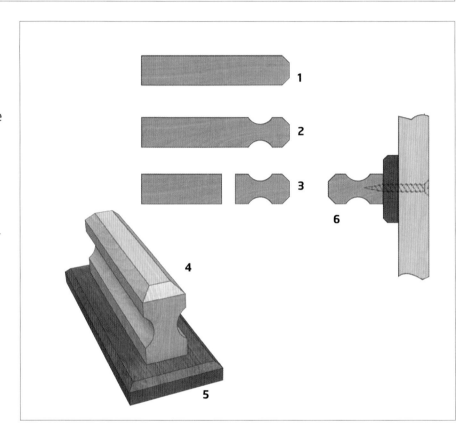

229   Removing glue squeeze-out

When gluing boards together edge to edge, there is always a certain amount squeezed out when cramping the joint tight. The usual thing is to scrape off the excess bead of glue with an old chisel, but this method is time-consuming and can often lead to surface damage on the timber.

Here is a simple method of using a router for this job. Attach a strip of ³⁄₈in (9mm) MDF either side of the joint, using double-sided sticky tape. Then, with a straight cutter in the router, and the router resting on the MDF runners, set the depth so that the cut just skims the surface of the timber. Just run the cutter along the joint, and the unwanted bead of glue will effortlessly disappear.

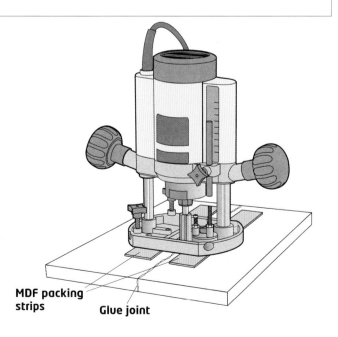

MDF packing strips

Glue joint

230 Routing large dowels

A 4in (100mm) diameter dowel rod for a table base is not an easy thing to find. If you don't have a lathe to turn one yourself, use your router instead.

First glue up a bottomless and topless plywood box the length of the dowel needed, then make a new plywood base for the router, clamping wood strips to the sides of the base so that it can slide back and forth along the sides of the box.

Next cut a 4 x 4in (100 x 100mm) blank and drill ³⁄₈in (10mm) holes at the centre of each end, into which you can drive ³⁄₈in (10mm) threaded rods to serve as a pivot. For ease of use, make a handle for one end. With a ³⁄₈in (10mm) straight cutter in the router, push it slowly away from you as you turn the handle. The device works best if you saw the corners off the blank first, and take light cuts with the router.

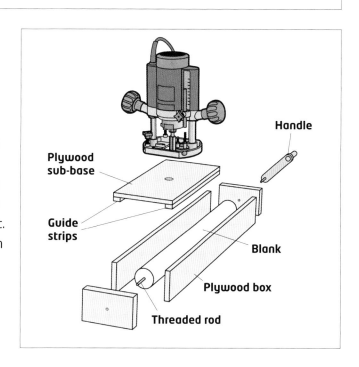

Handle
Plywood
sub-base
Guide
strips
Blank
Plywood box
Threaded rod

231 Routing long holes

Deep drilling from the tailstock of a lathe, as when boring a hole for the electric cable through a lamp standard, is always risky. The point of the drill may wander, and if you drill from opposite ends of the wood, the holes may not meet.

You can use your router to provide an accurate hole in wood of any length within the capacity of your lathe. Either cut the wood down the middle or use two matching pieces. With a straight cutter, groove down the middle of each piece, so they meet to make a square hole. A ³⁄₈in (10mm) cutter taken ³⁄₁₆in (5mm) into each piece suits most jobs. The grooves are stopped a short distance from each end to leave something solid for the lathe centres. The parts are glued and turned, then the ends drilled out. Of course, the same idea could be used for square-section lamp pedestals and other non-turned projects.

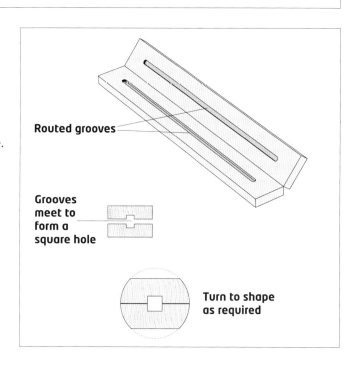

Routed grooves

Grooves
meet to
form a
square hole

Turn to shape
as required

232 | Secret shelf support

For a hidden shelf support without brackets, make a pair of bearers narrower than the thickness of the shelf and ½in (13mm) shorter than the depth of the shelf. Rout slots in the ends of the shelf to match these supports, stopping ½in (13mm) short of the front edge. The bearers are then screwed to the walls, and the shelf simply slotted over them.

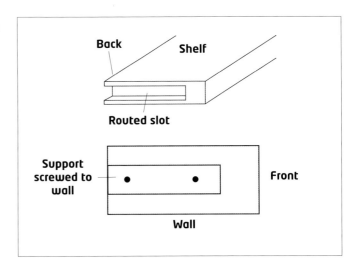

233 | Plug trimming

If you have to cut and clean off a lot of plugs, consider using a router. The alternative of sawing them carefully by hand while avoiding damage to the workpiece can be time-consuming.

Use an appropriately sized cutter with a bottom cut – most straight-fluted cutters are so designed. Set the depth stop so that the cutter is ever so slightly above the surface of the workpiece, and place the router over the plug.

Take light cuts until the stop is reached and the remains of the plug are just proud of the surface. Finish off by sanding the plug flush.

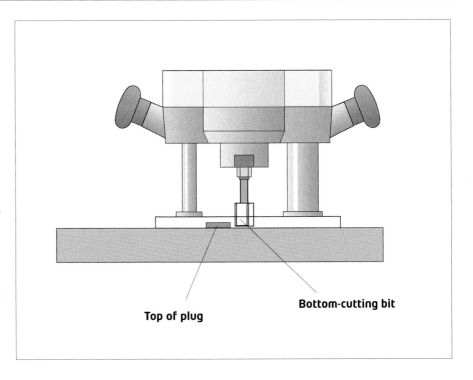

234 Secret fixing holes

Pocket holes with screws are a great way of secretly fixing two pieces of wood together without joints. To create them with a router, all you need to do is make up a ramp jig from some pieces of inexpensive sheet material.

Make up and attach two 6° ramps either side of a baseboard. In the near one fit a pair of T-nuts and bolts which will become the jig's clamping system.

On the baseboard, attach a stop for the workpiece, which also serves as a stop for the sub-base that you will need to make for the router.

The sub-base consists of a small sheet of perspex attached to the baseplate of the router, and a pair of guide runners fixed either side.

When the jig is complete, simply clamp the workpiece in it. Fit a ³⁄₈in (10mm) cove cutter into the router, plunge it to depth, then run the cut. It will take a few trial cuts to set the depth of cut and the end stop.

The last thing to do is drill a hole for the screw, using an overlength bit so as not to foul the chuck. Now all that remains is to screw the project together.

235 Precision drilling

One of the router's most underused features is its ability to drill absolutely perpendicular to the work surface, as well as to a precise depth. Ordinary power drills struggle to do this with precision, unless fitted in a drill stand. The router, of course, has its stand, although capacity is much more limited.

To optimize your router for this operation, stick a piece of clear polycarbonate to the base using double-sided tape. Plunge a small straight cutter through it, then use a knife to score 'crosshairs' on the underside. Now stick some fine abrasive under the solid part of the base to prevent 'wander'. Your router will now do all manner of drillings for shelf studs, hinges, etc.

Alternatively, you can go the guide-bush route and make up a jig for specific jobs using a set cutter/guide-bush combination.

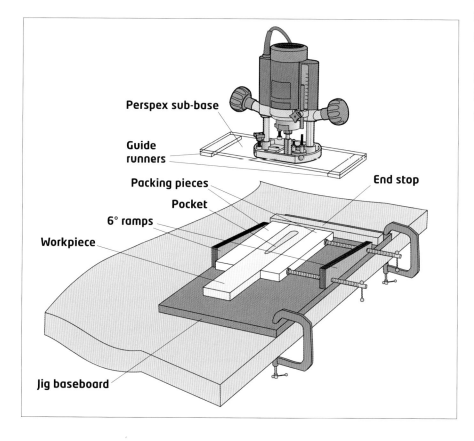

Perspex sub-base
Guide runners
Packing pieces
Pocket
6° ramps
Workpiece
Jig baseboard
End stop

Fences, guides and jigs

236 Easy fence setting

The cut-out in a router-table fence makes it difficult to measure the setting of the fence with a narrow rule.

Get hold of a piece of ½in (12mm) plywood approximately 3 x 6in (75 x 150mm) in size, and cut a 45° bevel on one end. Glue or pin a length of tape measure along the edge, with zero on the side that is placed on the router's fence.

With the gauge held against the fence and the scale lined up with the cutting edge of the cutter, any adjustments to the fence position are easily made. The gauge has a dual function, as it can be placed vertically on the bed while the cutter's height is positioned against the measure.

Cutter setting in the router table

Plywood offcut

Piece of tape measure

237 Improved fence for router table

This car-jack fence adjuster was originally designed for a tablesaw but works just as well on the router table. Two G-cramps (C-clamps) suffice to fix the fence in position, but no doubt some more sophisticated arrangement could be devised.

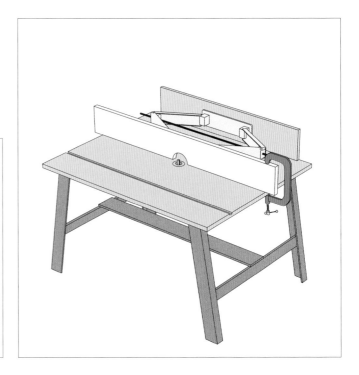

238 Continuous fence for mitre cutters

Using lock-mitre cutters in the router table is made much simpler by the addition of a continuous fence. Part of the cutter's profile is exposed, but only by the necessary amount for the job in hand.

239 Budget router fence

If a quick and easy fence for routing housings (dadoes) is required, a pair of sash-cramp heads joined with a wooden bar will perform the same function as some of the whizzo new guide rails, at a fraction of the cost. This should appeal to those who already have a pair of cramp heads, or to canny woodworkers who just won't part with their money.

The method involves nothing more than cramping a sash cramp sideways onto a workpiece to create an instant fence that will not need holding with lots of G-cramps (C-clamps). Ensure that the timber used for the bar of the cramp is straight and knot-free; a plain hardwood such as beech is ideal.

To make sure the router cannot wander, you could simply clamp another to the workpiece on the other side of the baseplate.

An added bonus of this method is that the bar can be made any length to suit a particular project.

240 Continuous side fence

Of all the accessories available for hand routers, the humble side fence is probably the most useful. As supplied, they have two cheeks fitted to leave a gap; this is fine for most work, but there are some situations where the gap is a nuisance.

The first of these is when routing along the edge of, say, a table top; for an inch or so at each end the router is guided by only one cheek and can pivot slightly, leaving a notch.

The second is when rebating or edge-moulding in solid wood; here the timber being cut can tear out where it is not backed up by the fence.

Both these problems can be solved by fitting a simple closed fence made of wood. Mount the existing fence on your router, with the cheeks removed. Offer up a suitably sized piece of wood to the fence, resting it on the router's base, and mark through the mounting holes. Drill and countersink holes for the screws, and fix to the fence. Before use, set the fence and then gently plunge the rotating cutter into it until the required depth is reached. It is a good idea to do this with router and fence on a piece of scrap. Now you have a fence which gives total support for both the router and the wood being cut.

Routing tips

241   T-square guide (1)

The T-square type of guide for the base of the router, used when cutting grooves across a board, can be improved by routing a central groove to clear a ¼in (M6) coach bolt, and attaching a block to bear against the far side of the board. This steadies the guide and holds it firm while it is clamped in position.

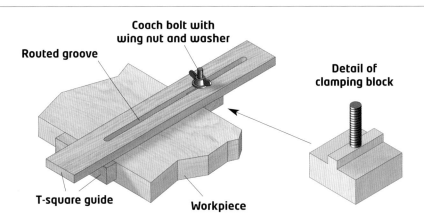

Coach bolt with wing nut and washer

Routed groove

Detail of clamping block

T-square guide

Workpiece

242   T-square guide (2)

To cut housing (dado) joints and similar grooves across boards, most of us clamp a guide for the router base to run against. If you find you are doing this frequently for the same size cutter – say ³⁄₄in (18mm) – you can reduce the amount of measuring needed each time by making this T-square guide strip. The parts are glued and screwed squarely. With the cutter mounted and the guide placed against scrap wood, cut through the stock piece on both sides of the blade deeper than you expect to need. Now all you have to do is locate a groove opposite the marked lines on the job and clamp the blade, knowing that the groove will be exactly right, without any further marking out.

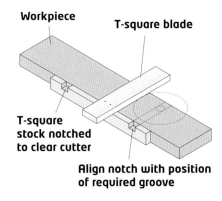

Workpiece   T-square blade

T-square stock notched to clear cutter

Align notch with position of required groove

243   Batten lines

A straight batten clamped to the workpiece is a good guide for routing trenches or trimming edges. However, the batten has to be offset from the line being worked to. Rather than measuring and marking the offset or using a loose (and invariably misplaced) spacer, make a batten with an integral spacer. This is prepared by screwing, gluing or nailing some ⁵⁄₆₄in (2mm) MDF to a straight batten, so that it projects slightly further out than the required offset. The router is then run along the batten to trim off the excess.

In use, the MDF lip is aligned with the cutting line and the batten clamped down. The router will then cut precisely along the line – no measuring required.

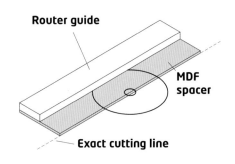

Router guide

MDF spacer

Exact cutting line

Fences, guides and jigs

244 Routing tricky housings

Here's a tip for when you're routing housings (dadoes) in a cabinet frame, maybe as an afterthought when something like a shelf or drawer is added.

To produce a consistent housing height on all parts, simply make a plywood fence the exact height that is needed. The size is calculated by measuring the distance from the bottom stretcher to the lower dimension of the housing, then subtracting the distance from the edge of the router's baseplate to the edge of the cutter. Cut the fence to size, then make a cutaway on either side to allow for clamping. Clamp the guide to the leg of the cabinet, and an accurately positioned housing is easily routed on all sides of the leg.

Make a set of fences in commonly used sizes.

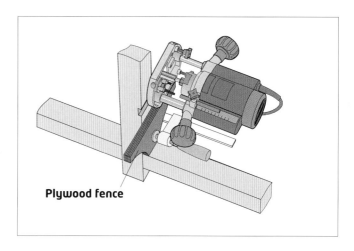

Plywood fence

245 Sash-cramp fence

Instead of using a batten and two G-cramps (C-clamps) as a fence when routing stopped housings, try using a sash cramp. It takes quite a bit of trial and error to get it right. If you just try to run the router along the cramp, the blocks get in the way and the edges will not be quite straight, so fix a strip of timber along it, secured through the peg holes. This works very well.

246 Grooving gauge

When grooving across wood, it is usual to have a guide strip cramped on for the router base to move against. If the cutter is the same size as the intended groove width, you have to locate the guide strip to match the distance from the centre of the cutter to the edge of the base.

The gauge shown here is a better alternative to using a rule each time. Even if several passes have to be taken, the gauge can be used for each setting. If you have more than one router you could make a double-ended gauge, marked accordingly.

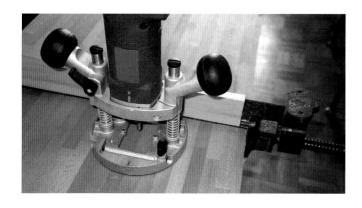

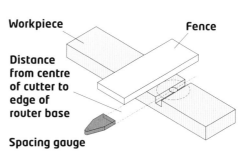

Workpiece   **Fence**

Distance from centre of cutter to edge of router base

Spacing gauge

Double-ended gauge

Routing tips

247 Long straightedge

Routing sheet material can be difficult, especially along the long edge, as not many people will have a straightedge long enough for the job. A long, straight piece of wood will do, if you can find one, but the natural tendency for timber to bend and warp means that your straightedge one day may be like a propeller the next.

A simple solution is to use a metal extension ladder, which most people have tucked away in their garage. Clamp it securely at either end of the workpiece, which is easily done with a bar clamp and a short length of wood, then run the router's baseplate along the outside edge of the ladder. This method can also be used with a circular saw or a jigsaw.

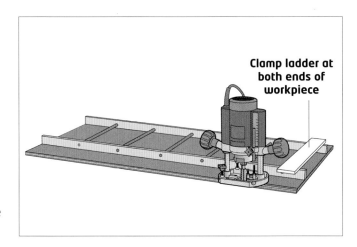

Clamp ladder at both ends of workpiece

248 Router guide channel

This simple device improves the versatility of a commercially available guide, and makes sure your router can't wander when routing housings (dadoes).

You will need a piece of aluminium channel to fit the groove that runs down the side of the guide. Machine a piece of wood to act as an infill for the channel; this will enable you to fix through the channel and the piece of perspex which is used as a base for the router. With countersunk machine-bolts, attach the base through the infill and the channel. You will now have a wander-proof housing system.

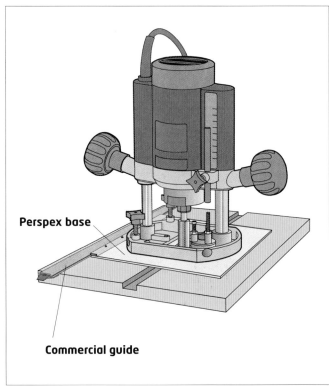

Perspex base

Commercial guide

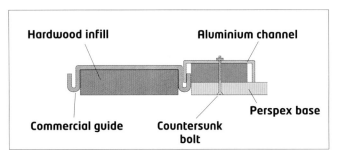

Hardwood infill

Aluminium channel

Commercial guide

Countersunk bolt

Perspex base

249 Bevelled rebates

Long bevelled rebates are difficult to make on a small tablesaw, so here is a way of routing them.

The problem is to tilt the router so as to get the correct angle using a straight cutter, as the rebate cutter available will not cut deep enough.

The problem is solved by making an adjustable hardwood fence to fit on the 'inboard' ends of the router fence rods, on the opposite side to the side fence. It is in two parts: the fixed part, secured with parallel, coarse-threaded woodscrews which act as grub screws clamping onto the rods, and the sliding part, which has slotted holes, and clamps at the desired height with two coach bolts and wing nuts.

The tilt can be further adjusted by altering the fence-to-router distance.

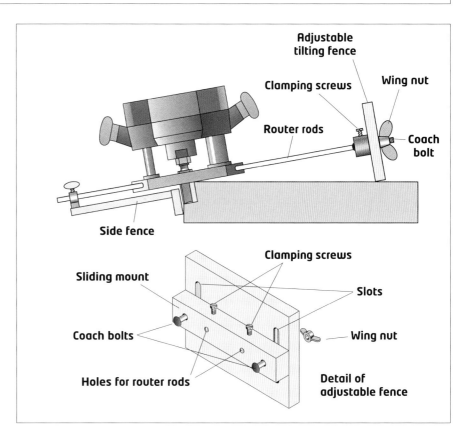

250 Repeat angles

This simple guide ensures accuracy and speeds up production of a rack for CDs which features a large number of narrow slots cut at an angle across the supporting sides.

The blade is made of ½in (12mm) plywood, cut to the same angle both sides. The stock or fence is cut so its ends come level with the line marking the nearside of the slot, when the router base is against the guide blade and the straight cutter is in position to make the slot. There is no need to mark the position of the guide each time – it can simply be cramped on with the certainty of getting the cuts at the correct angle and with the correct spacing on each side.

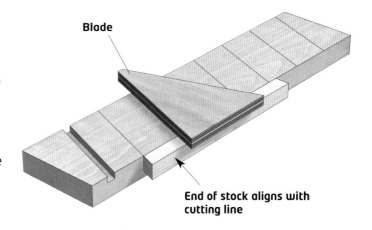

251 Improving router stability (1)

By their very nature, routers are top-heavy, and this makes them difficult to control, particularly when routing the edges of small workpieces. A simple solution is to use a scrap of wood the same thickness as your workpiece, positioned on the opposite side of the baseplate. It can even be fixed to the baseplate using a length of double-sided tape. This will stop the router from tipping, and help to make your routing that bit safer.

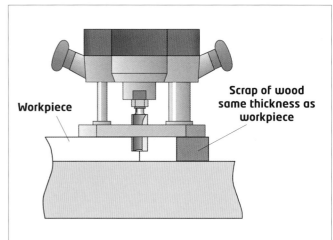

Workpiece

Scrap of wood same thickness as workpiece

252 Improving router stability (2)

When routing on an edge, rather than a flat surface – such as when doing hinge recessing – the router is unstable. Because of this, the base can drop into the machined slot. A solution is to make up an L-piece the same length as the edge to be machined. Make sure it is a true 90° and flat along its length. Cramp this in place, flush to the edge of the components. This provides a surface that in routing terms is 'big enough to dance on', and you can either use the router fence from the workpiece side, or work from the side of the L-piece, as convenient.

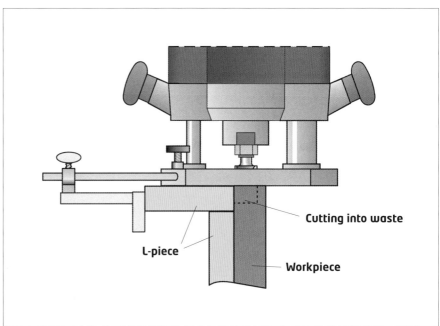

Cutting into waste

L-piece

Workpiece

253 Improving router stability (3)

Used freehand with the straight fence, the router can be unstable and dip in the workpiece at the start or finish of the cut. Usually it's possible to remove the existing fence facings and screw on a longer wooden through facing instead. If it is high enough, the cutter can cut a pocket in the fence and it will still remain intact – so why not do it? At the same time, clamp a longish board along the unfenced side of the workpiece. This will prevent the router tipping down. Now you have proper support in two planes.

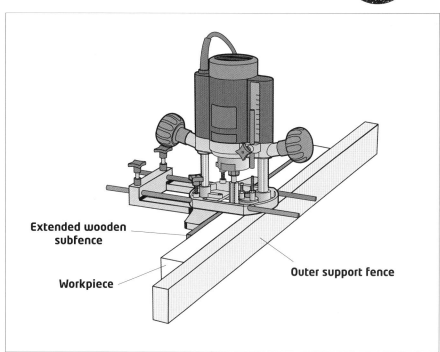

Extended wooden subfence

Workpiece

Outer support fence

254 Improving router stability (4)

Cutting a rabbet (rebate) for the back of a cabinet or bottom of a box after assembly should ensure an even depth all round and a level fit, providing you do not let the router wobble. If this does occur, the rabbet will be uneven. Cramp a thick strip of scrap wood with a true edge to each side in turn as cuts are made, to provide a wider surface to support the router base.

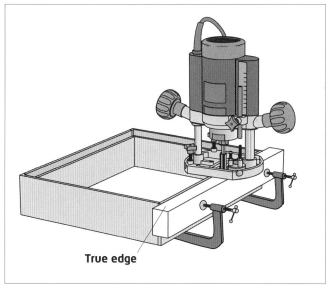

True edge

Routing tips

255 | Improving router stability (5)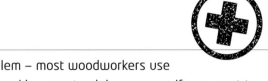

Most routers have a large base aperture, provided to help with dust extraction at source. The disadvantage of this is the lack of stability when moulding edges, especially when a hand-held router with a small-diameter cutter has to be taken around an external corner. The router easily tips – at worst, dangerous, at best, ruinous to expensive timber.

A simple solution for occasional workers is to fit a standard guide bush of suitable bore diameter, but inside out to the router. The projection of the guide-bush fence will lose you a little depth of cut, but this isn't a real problem with most cutters. If you own a full set of guide bushes you are bound to have one with a bore diameter to suit virtually any diameter of cutter. It will mean countersinking the holes on the reverse side of the bush, but this shouldn't be

a problem – most woodworkers use metalworking countersinks anyway. If you want to use dust extraction, it should be easy enough to replace the guide-bush idea with shop-made discs of polycarbonate, of suitable thickness to bring them flush with the Tufnol baseplate. Drill the discs to match the guide-bush locating holes, and bore centrally with various diameters to suit your cutters. To enable the dust extraction to work, bore a concentric ring of small 'breather' holes around the central one. This technique does not affect the depth of cut.

An alternative approach is to make full-size baseplates of $^5/_{32}$in (4mm) plywood or plastic, and fit these to the baseplate of the router itself. The depth of cut will be less with this method, but you can still use the breather holes.

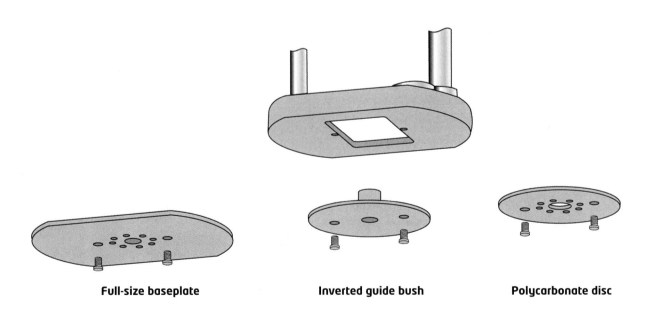

Full-size baseplate   **Inverted guide bush**   **Polycarbonate disc**

Fences, guides and jigs

256 Truing edges

When profiling a board in such a way as to slightly reduce its width, you will need to build out the lead-off fence to compensate for the difference in width between the two ends of the board. Some manufactured tables have an adjustable guide for this purpose, but some do not, and it is unusual for a shop-made table to have this facility.

If there is no such outfeed support, a simple alternative is to use a piece of card of suitable thickness, held to the fence above the working edge by masking tape, as shown.

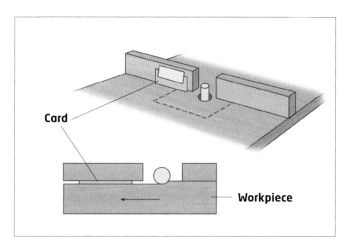

Card

Workpiece

257 Packing pieces

When work is held in the vice, packing pieces are often needed to give a broad surface for the router base to run on. Loose pieces are awkward to handle, so use a pair of guide strips located with dowels. To prevent assembling the wrong way, the dowels are placed irregularly. They are long enough to suit the thickness of the work being done, and one is made longer than the other so they can be engaged one at a time.

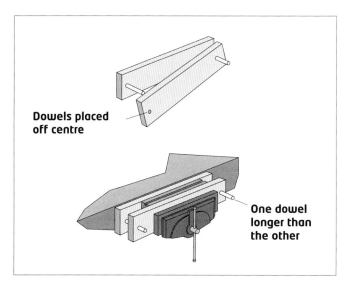

Dowels placed off centre

One dowel longer than the other

258 Non-stick strip

A strip of plastic laminate left over from a kitchen worktop can be used to provide a minimum-friction guide surface for when you are routing the edge of a board.

Just joint two 2 x 1in (50 x 25mm) strips of wood, about 24in (610mm) long, into an L-section, and glue the plastic laminate to the top surface. Grip the guide in a vice, level with the edge to be routed, to give a wide, non friction surface on which the router base can lie flat.

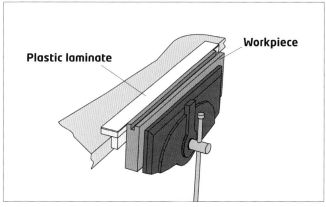

Plastic laminate

Workpiece

259 Multiple-pass routing channel ✚

When using a router table to make a complex profile, such as a dado rail or picture frame, where several passes are required, successive cuts can destroy the initial flat surface which registered with the router-table top, making subsequent cuts inaccurate. This device solves the problem, and also acts as a safety guard.

It is simply an accurately made channel consisting of two straight pieces of timber glued to a ³/₈in (9mm) plywood strip, into which the work is wedged.

The two narrow wedges are 6in (150mm) long, ¼in (6mm) thick tapering to zero, and ⁵/₈in (15mm) wide. With one placed at each end, they hold the workpiece surprisingly securely. A spacer can be added at the side of the work if necessary, and, when cutting small pieces, additional spacers can be put above the work to bring it down to the level of the cutter.

In use, the channel is inverted and moved along the router-table fence so that the workpiece, securely held within the channel, passes over the cutter. The position of the cutter in relation to the work can be checked before cutting, simply by looking through the open ends of the channel.

The sizes given are versatile enough for general work, but can be changed to suit your requirements.

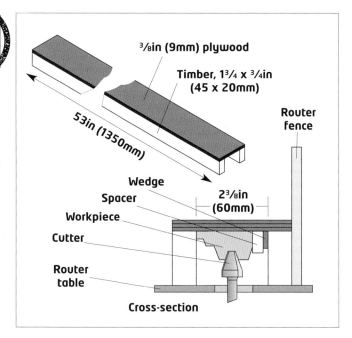

³/₈in (9mm) plywood

Timber, 1³/₄ x ³/₄in (45 x 20mm)

53in (1350mm)

Router fence

Wedge

Spacer

2³/₈in (60mm)

Workpiece

Cutter

Router table

Cross-section

260 The final pass

When machining, always make sure the work support and the fence setting are as good as they can be. If the cut width or depth is *almost* right, try repassing the router (or the workpiece, if using a table) at exactly the same settings. More than likely a further tiny amount will be removed, and this can be enough to make the difference with a critical fit.

Another trick when making a tight joint is to set up the router table and fence with a sheet of standard typing paper pressed against the fence, between it and the workpiece. If the fit is tight, on the final pass you can remove the paper and run the cut again; hopefully the slight extra cut depth will be enough to get a snug fit. This is particularly useful for dovetail housings and tongue-and-groove box joints.

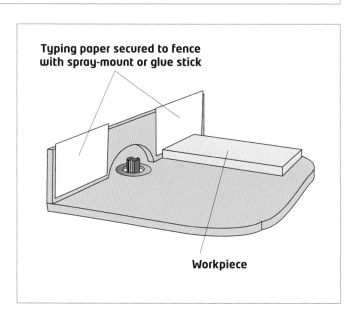

Typing paper secured to fence with spray-mount or glue stick

Workpiece

261 Jigs from laminate flooring

Laminate flooring is the ideal material for making jigs and templates for the router. This is the cheapo type, made from high-density fibreboard and with the pattern photo-printed onto the surface. It cuts accurately, has two smooth surfaces which the router just glides over, and wears better than MDF. It isn't expensive, either.

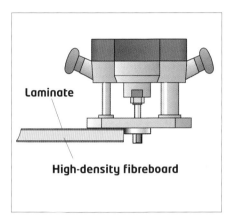

Laminate

High-density fibreboard

262 Dovetail aid

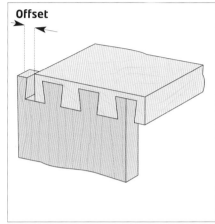

Offset

On some dovetail jigs the horizontal and vertical board stops are independent. Resetting these can be made easier by aligning to a guide consisting of two short boards joined at right angles, but displaced by the required offset.

The great thing is that you can use the dovetail jig to make this, without even having to take any measurements. Simply mount the boards as if making a normal dovetail joint, routing the tails and pins together, with zero offset. After routing, the members of the assembled joint will be displaced by half the dovetail pitch, which is exactly the offset required.

263 Flush-trimming jig

Instead of trimming timber lipping badly with a block plane, use this excellent little jig to produce perfect results in half the time. All that is required afterwards is a couple of passes with a block and sandpaper. Plunge a ½-1in (12-25mm) cutter onto a piece of paper while you set the depth adjuster. When you trim the lipping, the cutter will leave it proud by the thickness of the paper.

The same jig is also good for trimming the protruding ends of dovetails and through tenons.

Cutting list
Sub-base	MDF, 8 x 6¼ x ¼in (200 x 160 x 6mm)
Base	MDF, 10¼ x 8 x ¼in (260 x 200 x 6mm)

Screw to router base

Handle

Jig base

Sub-base or fence

Routing tips

264 Cleaning up dovetail sockets

Having cut dovetail sockets in the conventional way, with dovetail saw and coping saw, a quick way of cleaning them up is to use the router in conjunction with a simple but accurate L-shaped jig, instead of paring down to the shoulder line by hand. The jig can be constructed out of MDF or ply, using butt joints, and either screwed or mitred, using biscuits. Make it as long as the carcass you are dovetailing, or longer for future use. Clamp it in the vice, and set it dead level with the top of the pins. The jig acts as a platform for the router and a sacrificial fence to prevent spelching – although your carefully marked cutting-gauge lines should prevent this anyway.

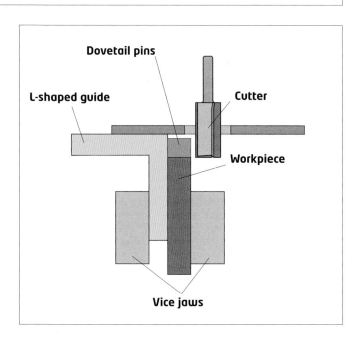

265 Far side jig

When making a router cut on the far side of the edge or end of a piece of wood held in the vice, something has to be done to provide extra surface for the router base to slide on.

The top of this simple jig is a strip of wood wide enough to give a good bearing, and deeper than the router fence. It is attached to a piece of plywood to go in the vice against the workpiece. The jig should be made a little longer than any piece of wood you expect to hold. For cutting the end of a workpiece that will not go in the vice, attach the jig to it with cramps.

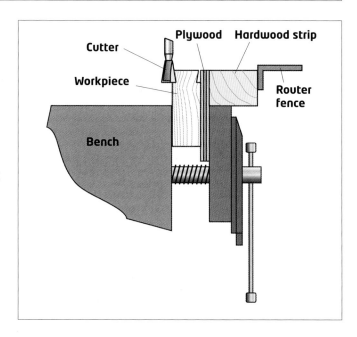

266 | Routing angled grooves

This jig is designed for grooving timber at any angle,
and is adjustable to any degree. The router slides along
a trackway made from offcuts of aluminium channel.
The workpiece rests in a cradle hinged to the wooden
supports, and is secured with small clamps.

Extra-long steel rods

**Fence jaws
replaced with
plywood 'skis'**

Nuts brazed on

**Machine
screws adjust
to alter angle**

Alloy extrusion   **Support strips**   **Brass hinges**

Routing tips

267 Variable slotting jig

This jig for cutting slots of various lengths consists of two identical interlocking parts cut from ⅜in (10mm) plywood. A block glued to each U-shaped component aligns them as they slide snugly together. To use the jig, slide the halves to your desired slot length, secure the assembly with two screws and clamp it to the workpiece. Use a flush-trimming plunge cutter with a top bearing. This has the advantage over a guide bush that you don't have to widen the slot in the jig to compensate for the offset between the guide and the cutter.

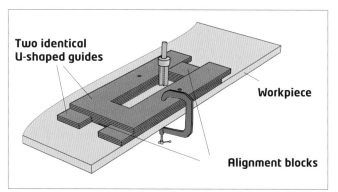

Two identical U-shaped guides

Workpiece

Alignment blocks

268 Dado jig

Although not foolproof to use, this housing (dado) jig has the added feature of a length stop. Once the first housing has been cut, this hardwood strip can be used for indexing repeated, equidistant cuts.

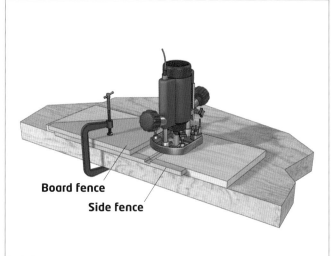

Board fence

Side fence

269 Jig for repeat housings

This set-up ensures an accurate and repeatable cut, and eliminates much tedious measuring. Lay a couple of battens, the same thickness as the workpiece, along the jaws of a Workmate or similar, so they are a snug fit on the width of the workpiece. Place a straightedge across these, with a card shim to raise it slightly above the battens, then clamp the whole lot tightly. Next, clamp another batten across the Workmate's jaws as a stop, so the housing will be formed in the correct place.

Now all you have to do is slide the workpieces under the 'bridge', clamp them so as not to foul the path of the router, and machine housings accurately in as many pieces as you like. The side battens not only contain the workpiece, but also support the router's baseplate at both ends of the cut.

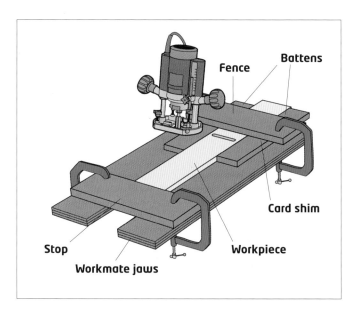

Fence

Battens

Card shim

Workpiece

Stop

Workmate jaws

270 Jig for bookcase housings

This jig was first made in the 1980s, but is still useful today. It was intended to help rout out slots in a set of bookcases. One end fits into the bench vice, and the other end goes under a batten on the workshop wall at the back of the bench. When you press the end into the vice and secure it, the workpiece is secured to the bench. The length is determined by the distance between vice and wall, while the distance between the guides is the width of your router. All the parts are made from offcuts of oak or hardwood, and secured with no. 12 screws.

A batten screwed to the bench forms a stop to help maintain the 90° angle, allowing the workpiece to slide into place for each slot. You can tap the block in the vice for fine adjustment, especially when the cutter is not the full diameter of the slot required. Release the vice to move the workpiece to the next slot. Occasionally you may need to use a G-cramp (C-clamp) to secure the workpiece to the bench.

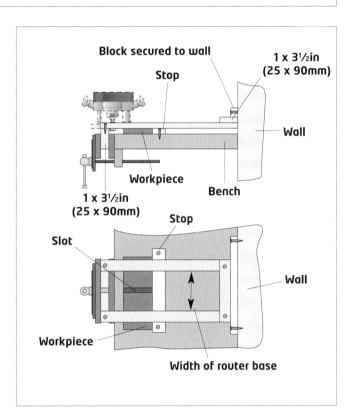

271 Modified housing jig

This variation on the previous jig has been used successfully to encourage craftsmanship and creativity among students, and to increase their confidence in the router. The movable back stop offers great flexibility. You could make several of these jigs, with the precut housing in various widths to suit the cutter being used. This makes it easy to line up the housings marked out on the workpiece with the precut housing on the jig. The long crossbar clamps into the vice, while the shorter, movable bar rests on the bench top. This device speeds up the production process because it is no longer necessary to clamp on a straightedge to guide the router.

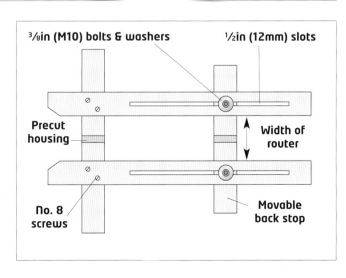

Routing tips

272 End-trimming jig for hand-held router

This simple jig can be used every time you want to trim the end grain of a workpiece cleanly. The results are so good that the face often does not need sanding. Remember always to rout in the correct direction, towards the workpiece fence.

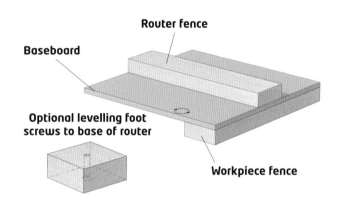

Baseboard

Router fence

Optional levelling foot screws to base of router

Workpiece fence

Cutting list:
Baseboard	MDF, 8 x 8 x ¼in (200 x 200 x 6mm)
Workpiece fence	Pine, 8 x 1¾ x ⅝in (200 x 45 x 17mm)
Router fence	Pine, 8 x 1¾ x ⅝in (200 x 45 x 17mm)
Levelling foot	Pine, 2 x 2in (50 x 50mm) x thickness of workpiece

273 End-trimming jig for router table

This jig for squaring up the ends of boards makes use of the mitre-guide slot on the router table. The diagram shows a thin board with a backing piece to support the work. The strip underneath is a good fit in the mitre slot. Hold the work against the backing piece and push the whole assembly past the cutter to trim the end. Any tendency of the cutter to pull the workpiece into it can be counteracted by clamping the work to the backing piece.

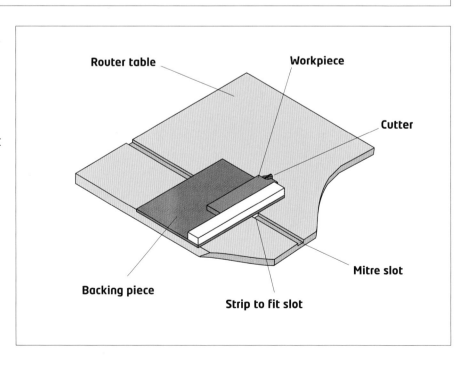

Router table

Workpiece

Cutter

Mitre slot

Backing piece

Strip to fit slot

Fences, guides and jigs

274 | Surfacing jig

In a small workshop, surfacing large pieces of wood can be time-consuming and difficult if you don't have a planer. If you have a router, here is a jig that could solve the problem. Built from ³⁄₄in (19mm) plywood, it consists of a track for the router to slide along, supported by a pair of runners fixed to the workbench.

Cut the runners 3in (75mm) high, and long enough to span the work. Fix them to the bench using angle brackets, allowing enough space between them to take the widest pieces you will want to surface.

The components for the sliding track should also be 3in (75mm) high, and long enough to overhang the runners by 2in (50mm) or so at each end. Screw the pieces together to make a pair of L-section runners. The crosspieces that run against the runners are now attached to them. Make the whole assembly about ³⁄₄in (19mm) wider than your router baseplate.

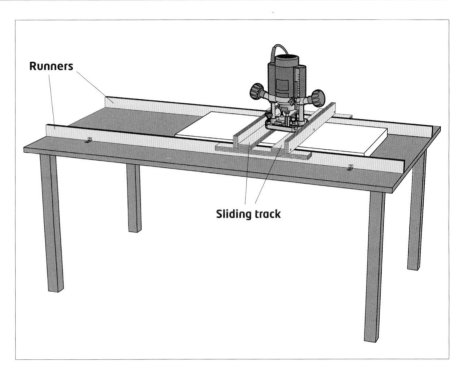

Runners

Sliding track

To use the jig, secure the workpiece to the bench between the runners with cleats. Using a ³⁄₄in (20mm) straight flute cutter, place the router on the sliding track. Set the cutter depth at the lowest point on the surface of the wood, and, starting at one end with the router against one side of one of the runners, make a pass across the work. Then bring it back in the opposite direction, against the other side. This will give a cut 1½in (38mm) wide. Move the track along to the next section and repeat. Continue the process at different depths along the whole length until you have a board that is uniform in thickness.

Routing tips

275 Round-tenon jig (1)

A close-fitting mortise-and-tenon joint is to be made between the sections of a pole which is 2in (51mm) in diameter. The plug or tenon A is turned first to a diameter of 1¼in (32mm). Mine proved to be a slightly slack fit in a test hole made with a 1¼in (32mm) Forstner bit.

In order to rout the socket part of the joint, the clamp C is made from an offcut of MDF with a 2in (51mm) hole, split across the middle. Two countersunk screws clamp the two halves onto pole B, which is held in the bench vice with the clamp C sitting astride the vice jaws. The template D is then fixed with two countersunk screws to the top of the clamp C. To overcome the slight slackness in the fit of the plug, it was necessary to reduce the size of the template. This was done by sticking two thicknesses of masking tape to the circumference of the template. Diagram E shows the base of the router and the guide bush with the cutter in position for routing the socket.

To copy the precise set-up shown here, you will need to use a 1½in (38mm) guide bush and a ½in (12mm) plunge bit.

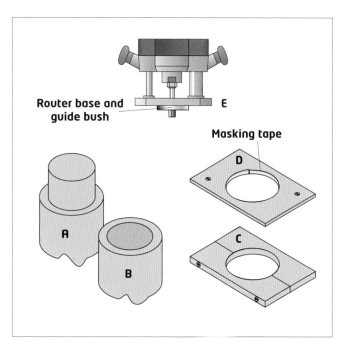

Router base and guide bush

E

Masking tape

D

A

B

C

276 Round-tenon jig (2)

This router jig is for stepping ½in (12mm) dowels to create a round tenon, as may be used on a plate rack, for example. This method is quicker than using a lathe.

When creating the stepped end of the dowel, ensure that you rotate the dowel in the opposite direction to the rotation of the cutter.

You can adapt the jig to suit any size of dowel by making alternative top plates.

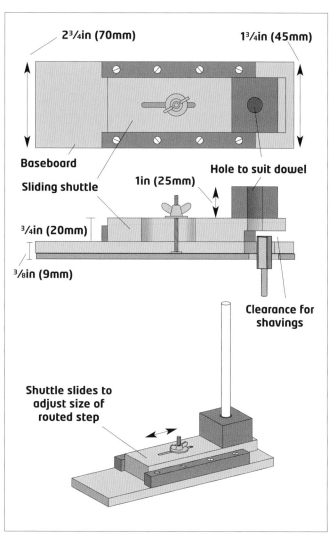

2¾in (70mm)   1¾in (45mm)

Baseboard

Sliding shuttle

Hole to suit dowel

1in (25mm)

¾in (20mm)

⅜in (9mm)

Clearance for shavings

Shuttle slides to adjust size of routed step

277 Mortising box

This is probably one of the most low-tech ways to rout mortises. You will need an extra fence for your router, either a standard-issue or a home-made version.

The workpiece is supported by packing and held in place by cramps. The whole assembly is screwed to the workbench.

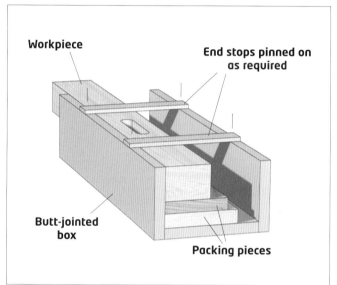

Workpiece

End stops pinned on as required

Butt-jointed box

Packing pieces

278 Adjustable mortising jig

This jig can cope with timber which is too long to handle on the router table. It is made from birch plywood, and sized to suit the router you have. A groove is routed in the main bed to accept a standard mitre fence, and a curved slot is routed into the swivelling router mounting bracket so that the cutter can be positioned for mortises in timber of different thicknesses. The jig can be mounted in the workbench vice, to handle boards of almost any size.

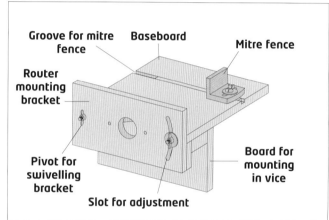

Groove for mitre fence   Baseboard   Mitre fence

Router mounting bracket

Pivot for swivelling bracket

Board for mounting in vice

Slot for adjustment

279 Easy scarfing

Scarf-jointing is a neat way of creating longer pieces of wood. It can be difficult to do accurately, but this router jig does the job quickly and precisely. The joint is traditionally made with straight cuts, but a curved surface either end is easier to make and gives a larger gluing area.

Only two pieces of wood are needed, and the guide bush and cutter do the rest of the work. The radius at either end of the joint is the same as the diameter of the cutter, and the guide bush is twice its diameter. Simply place a piece of wood in the jig, rout the shape on the end, then do the same with another piece of wood. Flip one piece over, and they will fit perfectly.

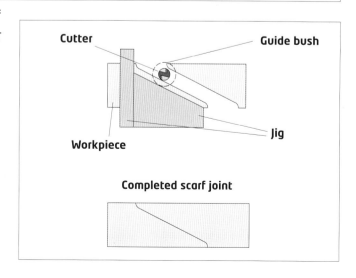

Cutter   Guide bush

Workpiece   Jig

Completed scarf joint

Router cutters

280 Bearings make cutters more versatile

Bearing-guided cutters are easily set up (only the height needs adjusting), but you can increase their versatility by using different-sized bearings.

A straight cutter with a same-size bearing is ideal for laminate trimming and pattern work, where the template is the same size as the workpiece. Pop on an oversize bearing, and the same cutter becomes an overlap trimmer, leaving an overhang for jointing purposes.

The popular rebate cutter's range of cuts is likewise extended with different-sized bearings.

Slotting cutters, useful for biscuit jointing, have the capacity to make slots for the three standard biscuit sizes, nos. 0, 10 and 20, just by changing the bearing to adjust the depth of cut.

Profile cutters can have their range of profiles greatly extended by swapping bearings and adjusting the height so that either all or part of the cutter is used.

So investing in a set of bearings is an excellent way to extend the uses of the cutters you already have, without spending a lot of cash. They are quite cheap, and most routing accessory suppliers will have them; but do check with your supplier to make sure that the bearings and cutters you want to combine are compatible.

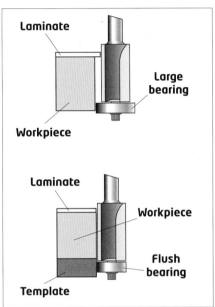

Above: **Straight cutter**

Below left: **Moulding cutter**

Below: **Slotting cutter**

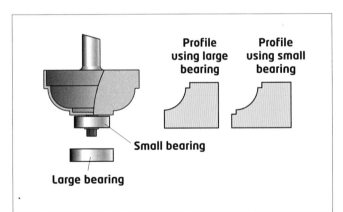

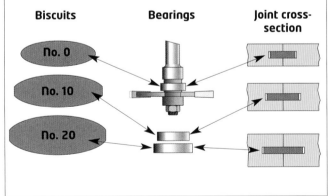

281 Rabbet cutting

Rabbet (rebate) cutters will cut cleanly along the grain, but in many woods they tend to tear out when used across the grain. It is better in this case to use a straight cutter guided by the fence. With open-grained wood, do not cut the full width in one pass, but leave a little waste which can be taken off in a final pass along the line; this usually leaves a clean edge which needs no further attention.

282 Trimming haunches and dovetails with a laminate trimmer

This particular design of laminate trimmer is also excellent at flush-trimming dovetails, finger joints and dowels. It's not worth buying one just for this, but if you're considering buying a trimmer then this model's extra talents might help you make up your mind.

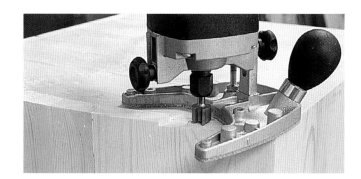

283 Down-shear cutters

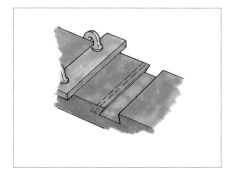

When cutting veneered or laminated sheets, a down-shear cutter is highly recommended, since it completely eradicates break-out. They are particularly good for kitchen worktop joints that require nothing short of perfection.

284 In praise of straight cutters

Most people assume that fancy profiles are essential in a good cutter selection. Actually, a wide variety of straight cutters is more useful for general work. They come in a huge number of types and sizes, from $5/64$in (1mm) up to massive 2in (50mm) cutters that challenge a spindle moulder. However, a series of the more usual sizes, including shortish $1/4$in-shanked versions and long $1/2$in-shanked versions, makes many operations possible. All kinds of joint making – tongue and groove, housings (dadoes), half-lap and biscuits – are possible. Even decorative detail can be added, such as the stages on a cornice, or a dentil moulding. If you have just a couple of straights in your box, buy some more and have fun!

285 Dovetail cutters

When making dovetailed housings (dadoes) for shelf ends, the dovetail profile, unlike a straight housing, must be cut in one pass. Always cut the housing before the dovetail tongue, and adjust the tongue width to suit. For ease and safety while cutting the tongues, consider using the router mounted in a table.

If a router below 750W is to be used for this kind of work, it is worth routing a relief cut with a straight cutter first, in the centre of the housing. This lessens the amount of material that has to be removed by the dovetail cutter, and consequently reduces the load on the router motor.

286 | Coping with collets

Many routers have a three-piece collet system, consisting of a tapered collet 'thimble', a collet nut, and a machining taper in the motor shaft.

With collets of this type it's absolutely essential that the collet thimble is snapped firmly into the collet nut. If it is not, the cutter can still be inserted after a fashion, but will remain stuck in the motor shaft when you try to remove it. Failing to snap the thimble into the nut is the cause of more queries and problems than any other routing topic.

This design of collet also needs two bites of the spanner (wrench) to release the cutter. The first bite releases the initial friction of the nut, after which you can take several turns of the nut with your fingers before it tightens up again. You then need to apply the spanner for a second time to undo the nut and pull the collet up out of the tapered motor shaft. This is the second most common cause of confusion for newcomers to routing.

The situation is complicated slightly by the fact that some routers with the three-piece collet system have

Above: **It's essential that the collet thimble is snapped firmly into the collet nut**

the thimble embedded into the collet nut by the maker; with these collets the thimble cannot be removed for cleaning or changing collets, and the problem of stuck cutters should not apply.

287 | Uneven wear

Particleboards such as MDF are especially harsh on router cutters, and even the edges of tungsten tips will suffer. If a routing operation is carried out frequently in one position on the side of a cutter - for example, when using a straight cutter for profile work - it will tend to wear a step in the cutter. To reduce this problem it is advisable, when setting up, to position the cutter at a slightly different depth each time; this will spread the wear along its cutting edge.

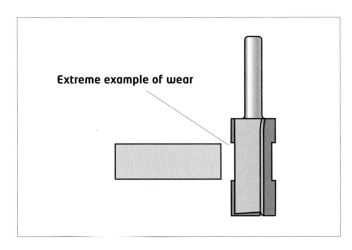

Extreme example of wear

288 Shank length

Always insert as much of the shank as possible into the collet – at least three quarters of the shank length, as a minimum – to decrease the risk of cutter deflection under load. This in turn will prevent damage to the collet, reduce wear and stress on the router's bearings, and minimize the likelihood of shank breakage. Do not allow the end of the cutter to touch the inside end of the armature recess; a gap of $^{1}/_{32}$ to $^{5}/_{64}$in (1 to 2mm) is needed (A) to avoid inducing a hammer action, causing the cutter to creep from the collet.

Ensure that the collet does not engage on the webbed flange of the cutter – that is, the curve between cutter body and shank (B). Never

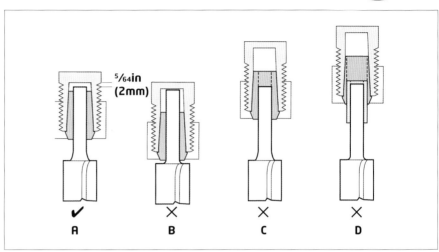

clamp a short portion of the shank in the collet, so as to 'dangle' the cutter, to get extra length (C); and never use collet reducers to extend the length of the shank (D).

289 Collet inserts

Any seasoned router user will know that a good-quality collet is vital for safe and reliable routing. The practice of manufacturers supplying collet inserts as alternatives to different collet sizes is, quite frankly, deplorable. An insert isn't a very safe or effective means of holding a shank when it already has the collet around it, adding to the number of installed shank-holding devices. An insert is simply a sleeve with a slit, and does not compare with a collet when it comes to precise holding power. When you buy a new router, ensure that alternative collet sizes are available. If you already own a router, then try the specialist firms who supply collets for a variety of machines; they may stock the size(s) you require.

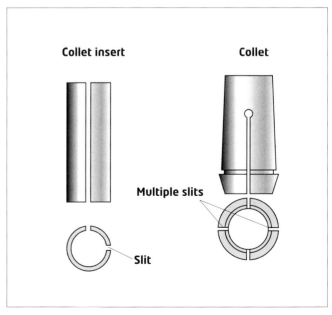

Routing tips

290 Easy cutter removal

Router bits do not always come away freely when you slacken the collet nut and pull them. It helps if you do not push the cutter fully in when you fit it. Leave a gap of $1/32$ to $5/64$in (1 to 2mm) before you tighten the nut. Then, if release is difficult, you can lever in the gap. Use a tapered piece of wood in preference to a screwdriver, to avoid causing damage.

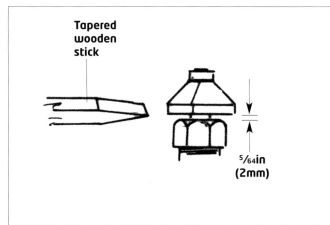

Tapered wooden stick

$5/64$in (2mm)

291 Easier cutter installation

One of the main problems when changing cutters in a router inverted in a table is the cutter falling out of the collet. A solution is to place an O-ring over the cutter shank. This allows you to put the cutter in the collet in exactly the place you want. It also leaves both hands free to tighten the collet, making the cutters very easy to fit. Use $1/4$in (6mm) O-rings for $1/4$in shanks and $1/2$in (12mm) O-rings for $1/2$in shanks.

O-ring

$1/4$in (6mm) O-ring for $1/4$in shank

$1/2$in (12mm) O-ring for $1/2$in shank

292 Cleaning collets

If they are to remain undamaged, it is important that a router collet and the shank of the cutter which goes in it are clean. It is easy to wipe the shank of a cutter, but not so easy to clean inside a collet. Use a spray lubricant, then rub and twist a piece of dowel of the right size ($1/4$, $5/16$ or $1/2$in; 6, 8 or 12mm) inside the collet.

293 Rust-free collets

Store your collets away in old film canisters with either silica gel (the little packets of moisture-absorbing stuff from packaging) or... rice! A few grains of this staple will do the trick, and on a larger scale it can save all sorts of kit from an attack of rust.

294 Beware the loose washer

When using a bearing-guided cutter with the router mounted in a table, you may be tempted to change the bearing with the cutter still fitted in the inverted router. This seems a logical thing to do, as you can utilize the router's spindle lock to stop the cutter from rotating.

Some cutters have bearing retaining screws with captive washers, but others unfortunately have a loose washer, and if you are not careful this can fall straight into the guts of the inverted router! In my case, careful examination showed that it was resting on the blades of the cooling fan, and with great care it was retrieved with a blob of thick grease on the end of a thin screwdriver. I was lucky: it could have dropped further into the router, which would have involved an expensive strip-down.

So be warned: remove cutters from routers before changing bearings.

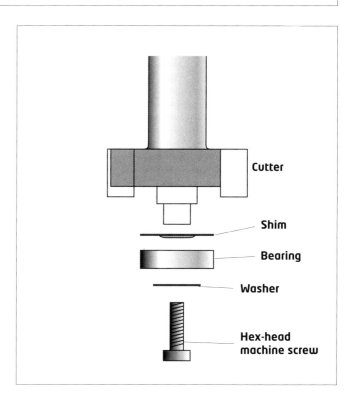

Cutter

Shim

Bearing

Washer

Hex-head machine screw

295 Changing cutters

Buy a box spanner (tube wrench) to fit your collet nut and use it to install and remove narrow cutters when your router is inverted in a table. It will make life easier when using narrow straight cutters and flush trimmers.

Routing tips

296 Sharpening with diamond

A small, folding diamond whetstone is great for sharpening saw blades, but it is difficult to sharpen router cutters accurately with the cutter in one hand and the stone in the other. To avoid the expense of buying a large diamond bench stone, use a glue gun to attach a small wood offcut to the back of the small stone and hold it in a vice. Both hands can then be used to control the cutter, with vastly improved results. The offcut is easily removed when finished.

297 Looking after bearings

The bearings of bearing-guided cutters are worth looking after. Now and again, take them off to remove wood waste or dried glue and muck trapped between bearing and cutter. While you're at it, give the cutter a good clean and possibly a diamond honing. Resist the temptation to spray on a cleaning or anti-rust agent, which will thin the grease in the bearing and shorten its working life. Instead, just wipe it with a small amount of lubricant on a cloth or tissue. Keep all spare bearings in a dust-free container so they don't get caked in dust. It's also worth getting one or two different-sized bearings when buying a cutter, as this makes them more versatile.

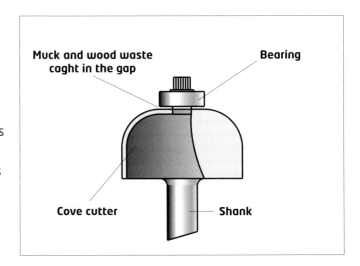

Muck and wood waste caght in the gap

Bearing

Cove cutter

Shank

298 Clean cutters

The best way to remove dust and resin build-up from cutters is to wipe them carefully with a cloth dipped in contact-adhesive remover.

299 Holding cutters securely

If a router cutter has to be sharpened, cleaned, or have its guide bearing removed, it has to be held in some way by its shank, usually in a vice. Gripping the shank directly may damage it.

To make these simple clamps, drill a hole to suit the cutter shank centrally in the end grain of a block of hardwood, then cut across the hole. The waste removed by sawing allows the clamp to close tightly on the shank when squeezed in the vice.

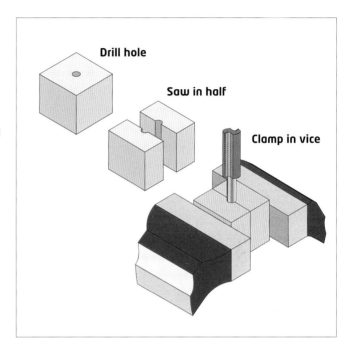

Drill hole

Saw in half

Clamp in vice

300 Improved cleaning brush

The little brass brushes used for cleaning router collets are worth having, although their twisted wire handles are not very long, which makes them fiddly to use, especially when the collet is still in the router.

You can improve it by mounting two sizes at opposite ends of a piece of dowel. Cut off the loop ends and epoxy the twisted wire into drilled holes. Of course, if you have a lathe you could create a better-looking handle instead of the dowel.

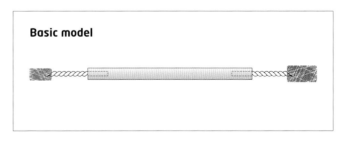

Basic model

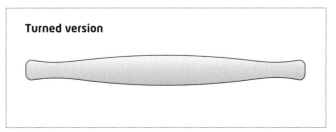

Turned version

301 Rustproof storage

As you accumulate router cutters there is a temptation to make storage racks by drilling holes in strips of wood. This may not matter for temporary storage, but in the long term there is a risk of rusting. Even well-seasoned wood can have 10% water in it, which can cause irreparable damage to the steel cutter spindles. Instead, make cabinet shelves from perspex drilled to take the cutters, and mount them on wood with oversize holes so the wood will not touch the steel. Another advantage of using perspex is that, unlike wood, it doesn't suffer from expansion or contraction, so it is always easy to lift the cutters in and out.

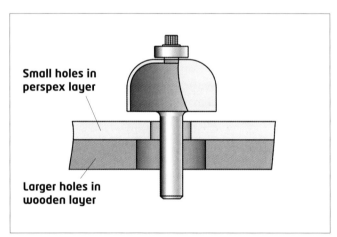

Small holes in perspex layer

Larger holes in wooden layer

302 Storing collets

A good way to protect collets is to put them in an old plastic 35mm film container. With a piece of foam at the bottom and another on top, the collets are held snugly, and if the foam is sprayed with penetrating oil or PTFE this should keep rust at bay too.

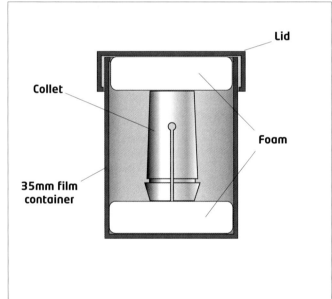

Lid

Collet

Foam

35mm film container

303 Toolboxes

We all know cutters need safe storage. So too do all the accessory bits and pieces, including collets, nuts, bolts and washers. You may be surprised by the solutions on offer at your local DIY superstore. Gone are the all-steel cantilever toolboxes – now there are umpteen varieties of ingenious plastic toolboxes with natty compartments, lids, etc. You should find several that will suit your particular needs.

Plastic is kind to cutters, won't rust, and therefore won't transfer rust to the contents. The neat little compartments are ideal for proper segregated parts storage, and larger items like dust spouts, fence rods and spanners (wrenches) can be easily accommodated in the bottom. This is one recent development that can be welcomed – look after your kit and it will always be ready for action!

304 | Protecting cutters

We all know how important it is to protect router cutters from getting chipped. Nowadays some makes come in neat little cases, but many just have a plastic pouch that falls apart at the slightest touch. Instead, cut an old, soft piece of leather into suitably sized squares, apply contact adhesive to three edges, then fold and press to form a soft pouch. A refinement is to apply a sticky label to each pouch showing the cutter type, size and shank. Now place all the pouches into a suitable tin so they lie cosily together.

305 | Dangers of foam

Cutters which are kept in tight-fitting foam case inserts can become stuck in the foam. The reactive nature of foam and condensation can stick the shanks fast, and there may also be a small risk of rusting. Squirt a generous dose of spray lubricant into the boxes to free the cutters from the foam.

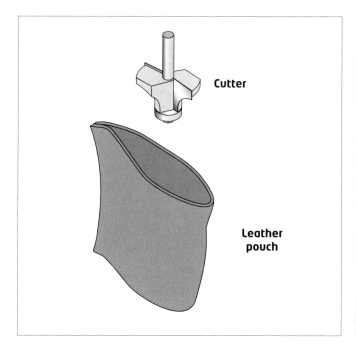

Cutter

Leather pouch

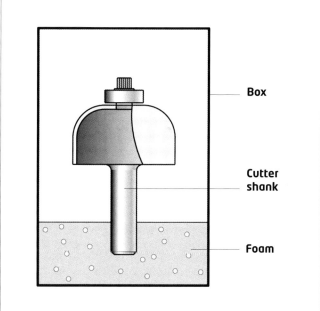

Box

Cutter shank

Foam

Measuring and setting up

306 Setting depth of cut (1)

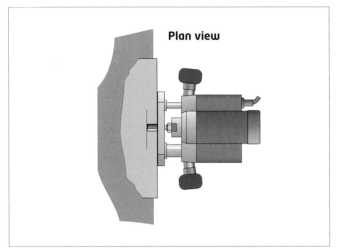

Plan view

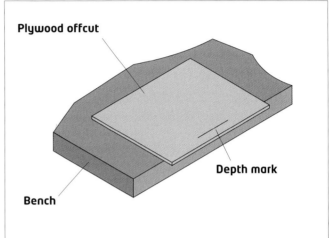

Plywood offcut

Bench

Depth mark

When setting the amount of extension of a router cutter it is habitual to think in the up-and-down mode, because that is the way the tool will normally be used. However, it is often easier to set the depth of cut with the router horizontal.

Mark the depth of cut as a distance from the straight edge of a scrap of plywood, then fix this on the edge of the bench so you can push the base of the router against it, while holding the router horizontal, and adjust the cutter to the line.

307 Setting depth of cut (2)

When you need to adjust the plunge depth of your router, take advantage of the ready availability of your bench vice. Simply open the jaws of the vice to provide clearance for the cutter, then make the adjustment. The vice is more than sturdy enough to provide a sound support, and it is always – or nearly always – there ready to use.

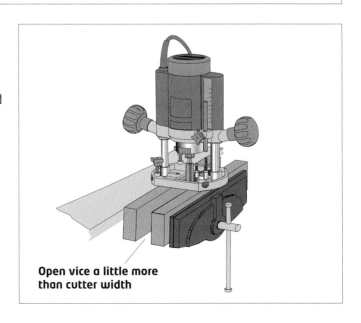

Open vice a little more than cutter width

308 Gauge block to set cutter depth

Setting the height of your router cutter can be time-consuming and fiddly, but the job can be done quickly with gauge blocks made from a 3in (75mm) length of 2 x 4in (50 x 100mm) with rebates cut around the underside to correspond to the settings you most frequently use. It is quite convenient to make a number of blocks, each giving all the settings for a specific job. These gauge blocks serve just as well for setting the fence to the blade on a tablesaw.

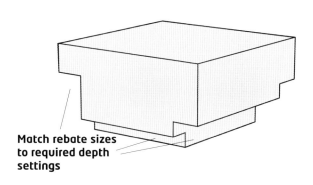

Match rebate sizes to required depth settings

309 Using drill bits to set plunge depth

For a quick and reliable way of setting a router's plunge depth, simply plunge a motionless cutter onto your workpiece, then use of drill bit of the appropriate diameter to set the depth of cut.

310 Home-made feeler gauge

The three-stage depth-setting turret on the average router seldom gives the intermediate plunge stages that you need. The result can be passes that are too deep or too shallow. A way around this is to have a small pack of pieces of ply or MDF about ½in (13mm) wide, all in different thicknesses, that you can slip in turn under the depth stop and thus get any plunge setting you want. A refinement is to drill them and use a piece of bath-plug chain or string to tie them together so they can't get lost.

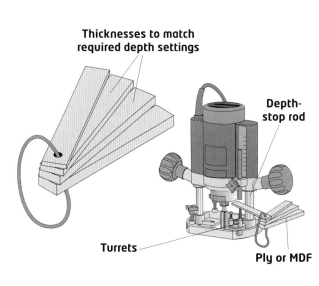

Thicknesses to match required depth settings

Depth-stop rod

Turrets

Ply or MDF

311 Router positioning on jigs and table inserts

When fixing a router on a jig, or beneath a router table, it is quite hard to mark the position of the screw holes accurately. The collet is in the way, and there really isn't enough space to get a bradawl or a small pencil in the space – besides which there is no way of marking them from the other side.

A simple solution is to buy a couple of 1½in (40mm) machine screws and, having sharpened them to a point, insert them into the threaded base holes. Carefully pressed down, they will leave a mark in exactly the required place. In the same way, a sharpened, unthreaded piece of bolt can be used as a centre point for the collet.

The job of sharpening the bolts with a true centre is best accomplished on a metalworking lathe, but a woodturning lathe should work, providing it is a variable-speed version used on a slow setting.

With the edge of the file, take off the head of the bolt, leaving a sharpened point. Alternatively, use a drill press, again set at a slow speed, and apply a file in the same way as before.

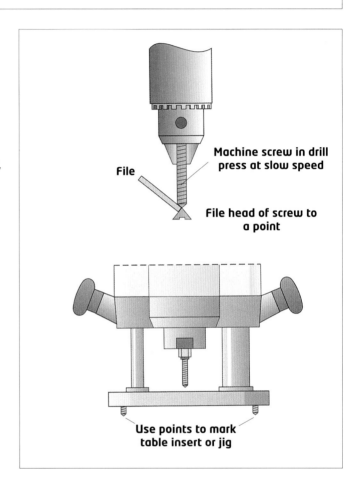

File

Machine screw in drill press at slow speed

File head of screw to a point

Use points to mark table insert or jig

312 Measuring from cutter to fence

When measuring the distance from the cutter to the fence – either the router's side fence or one on a router table – a common beginner's mistake is to measure from the body of the cutter and not from the cutting edge, thus giving a false measurement. To make sure of a correct reading, rotate the cutter so that its cutting edge is at the closest point it can get to the fence, then measure from the tip.

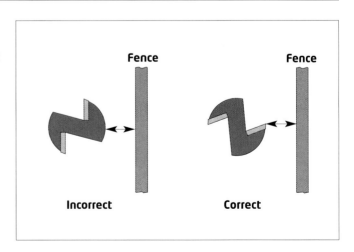

Fence   Fence

Incorrect   Correct

313 Simple set-up guide

When making a housing (dado), rebate or similar joint, you will need to set a straightedge to the correct distance between any particular diameter of cutter and the edge of the router baseplate. Here is a way to achieve this consistently without the use of a ruler.

Take a piece of board – scrap material will do – and attach a fence or straightedge along one edge. Then place on the board a reasonably sized offcut of ¼in (6mm) ply or MDF and, keeping the router baseplate firmly against the straightedge, cut off a series of strips using different sizes of cutter. Mark each strip with the cutter size used, so each one shows the exact distance between the router base and the outside cutting edge of that particular cutter.

When setting up a fence for routing a housing, for example, mark the joint's position on the board with a line. Select the cutter to be used, then place the matching strip for that cutter against the line. Butt the end of a straightedge against the guide strip and clamp it tight, repeating for the other end. If you make two strips in each size, both ends of the straightedge can be set at the same time.

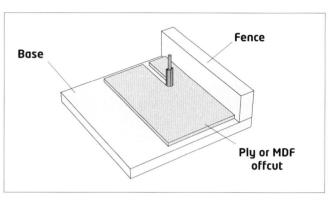

Above: **Make a simple jig to rout strips exactly as wide as the distance from the cutter to the edge of the baseplate**

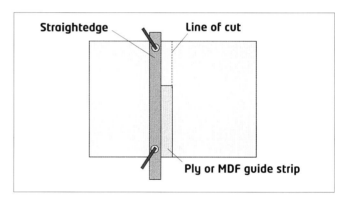

Above: **The routed strip is placed on the line of cut and a straightedge butted up to it**

314 Setting out grooves

When removing the waste from grooves with a straight cutter, using a cramped-on guide strip, you can avoid frequently measuring for the strip's position by making template strips of the correct width for locating the line of the first side. Mark the size of the cutter on both sides of each piece. Round one end of the template and drill it so it can be hung up. You should still measure for the cut on the other side of the groove, as this could vary to suit the actual thickness of the other piece of wood used in a housing joint.

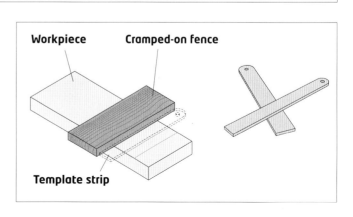

Routing tips

315 Finding the centre

Here is an easy way to run a cutter down the centre of a board, no matter what its width – within reason.

Make up a thin base and attach it to the baseplate of the router. Fix a couple of pins into this plate, as wide apart as is comfortable – the distance isn't critical, but make sure that each is the same distance from the cutter, and that the line between them passes through the centre of the cutter. If a couple of rollers are fitted onto the pins it will make the jig run more smoothly .

It is then a simple matter of placing the router onto the workpiece then twisting it until the pins make contact with the outside edges of the board; the cutter will automatically be centred.

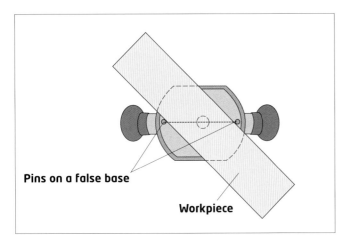

Pins on a false base

Workpiece

316 Using ski supports

When the router is to be mounted or held in 'ski'-type supports, the position of the guide rods can easily be marked on the skis by inserting lip-and-spur drills in place of the rods.

A piece of wood is then pressed sideways onto the drill points, giving the exact centres for drilling. The wood can be used on its own, reinforced with plates, or clamped to the metal skis to act as a template.

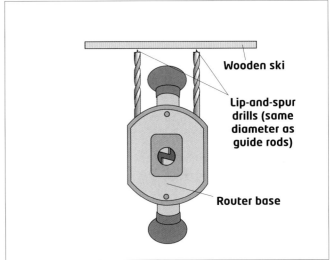

Wooden ski

Lip-and-spur drills (same diameter as guide rods)

Router base

317 Stopped chamfers

When cutting stopped chamfers that have to be a uniform distance from a joint or other point, it is best to mark where the edge of the router base has to come, rather than trying to look through the router base to see when the cutter is there. Make a trial cut on the edge of a piece of scrap to obtain the precise distance.

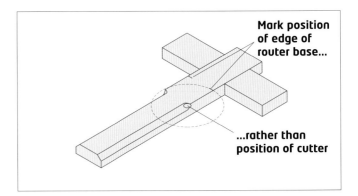

Mark position of edge of router base…

…rather than position of cutter

318 Washer offset

The best way to repeat complex shapes consistently is to make a template and use the router freehand, with a bearing-guided straight cutter and a guide bush. Calculating the offset between cutter and bush is simple enough, but transferring it to the template can be difficult.

The solution is extremely simple: find a washer with the same inside-to-outside diameter as the required offset between cutter and guide bush. Rest it against the shape that needs to be reproduced, and insert a pencil through the hole.

While applying pressure towards the shape, roll the washer around to place a pencil mark at the correct offset. The template is made by cutting around this line, then cleaning up the edge. If a suitable washer cannot be found, ask a friend with a lathe to make one.

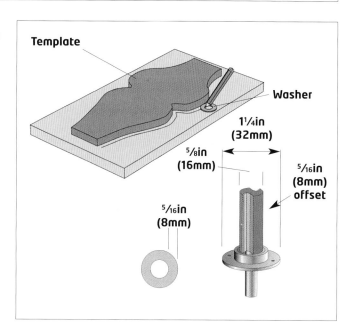

319 Curve calculation

A formula from schooldays will take away the guesswork involved in finding the radius of a curve.

$$A^2/C + C = \text{diameter of the circle}$$

where A = half the length of the chord, and C = the rise of the curve (see lower diagram).

For example, if you want a curve 20in long and 5in deep, then A = 10in and C = 5in. By the formula:

$$10^2/5 + 5\text{in} = 20 + 5\text{in} = 25\text{in}$$

This gives 25in as the diameter of the circle, so 12½in is the required radius. For the same example in metric units: $254^2/127 + 127\text{mm} = 508 + 127\text{mm} = 635\text{mm}$ diameter, 317.5mm radius.

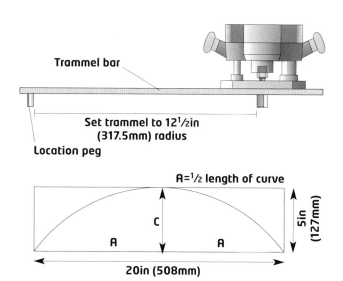

Workholding

320 Versatile holdfast

One of the major problems in routing is to hold the workpiece securely. The method shown here is extremely useful and versatile, and has the advantage of not being expensive. The are only three parts to the clamp, and it is easy to make.

The first part is a bench screw, which you may already have; if not, buy one, as they have many uses. Fit the bench screw into the bench.

The jaw is straight-grained oak or similar hardwood, 2in (50mm) square by about 20in (500mm) long, with a hole drilled in it, a loose fit on the bench screw, about 7in (180mm) from the back.

Lastly, there is the stepped block which is made from a short length of 4in (100mm) square hardwood. Into this, cut a series of five steps at convenient heights to suit the

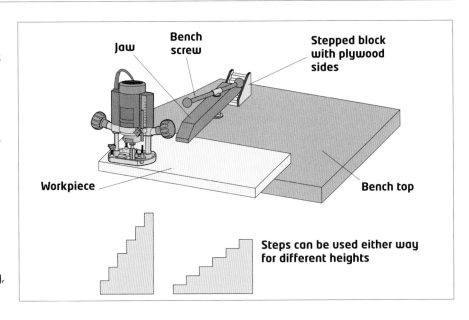

thicknesses of commonly used material. Make them longer one way than the other, so that the block provides another five settings when flipped round. It is worth pinning some thin pieces of plywood to the

block's sides to contain the jaw and stop it spinning.

You will soon find that this simple hold-down is useful not only for routing but also for sanding, planing and jigsawing.

321 Sash-cramp support

For some router work a useful holding arrangement is a sash cramp mounted in the vice. It holds the wood by both ends, leaving the top surface clear of obstructions.

It can be a nuisance having to arrange packing pieces to hold the bar of the cramp in the right place in the vice, unless you make the combined packing and holder shown. This hooks over the bench top, has a packing thick enough to keep the cramp heads clear of the bench side, and provides a narrow supporting lip for the bar, which is held reliably in the correct position as the vice is tightened.

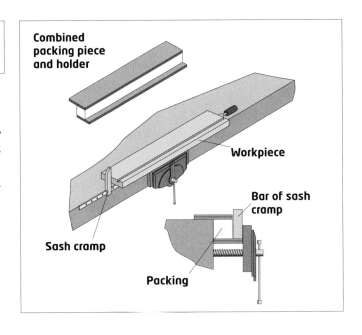

322 Routing small items (1)

Small items can be difficult to hold safely when routing rebates or mouldings. Machining the profile on a larger piece of stock first, then ripping it to size afterwards, is not always possible, especially in the case of glazing bars with rebates and mouldings on both sides.

A simple method is to have a small push stick, about 2 x 1in (50 x 25mm) and as long as you need, with the sides bevelled to get right into the corner of the fence. Cut a long bird's-mouth on the underside, then attach a small piece of plywood to the end to act as a stop. When machining with this, the length will allow you to apply pressure much more evenly along a greater amount of the stock.

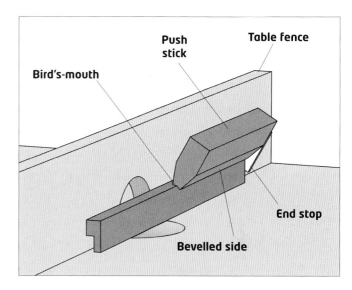

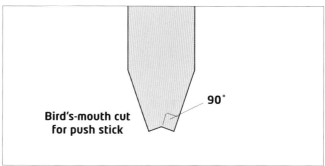

323 Routing small items (2)

When machining small components, do as much of your routing as possible before the finished piece is finally cut to shape. If you're routing on a table, it's always safest to employ a lead-in pin or point to hold the work against; this will stop it from snatching on the first contact.

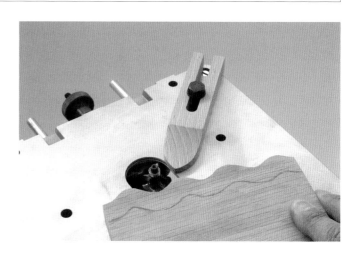

324 Hot-melt glue

Cramps and router mats qre excellent for holding parts down, as are cam clamps and vacuum tables, but when all else fails, use the woodworker's friend: hot-melt glue. It is an underrated fixing device, but makes irregular or small workpieces quick and easy to fix.

Don't forget that small pieces can be machined by fitting an oversized sub-base to the router (with hot-melt glue) and allowing it to slide on battens either side of the workpiece. This is an ideal solution for freehand router carving, for example.

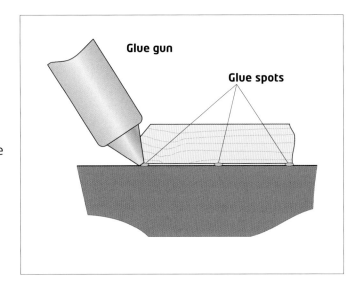

Glue gun

Glue spots

325 Home-made toggle clamp

Here's a very simple tip to save buying a toggle clamp. The wood to be routed is placed next to the fence or shoulder, and the wing nut tightened down. If a router mat isn't available, a piece of inner tube or sandpaper could be used for grip.

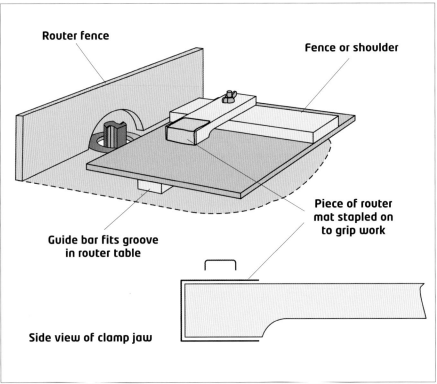

Router fence

Fence or shoulder

Guide bar fits groove in router table

Piece of router mat stapled on to grip work

Side view of clamp jaw

326 Horizontal table

This design is based on a suggestion by router expert Ron Fox. It uses a cheap router of the kind found in many DIY superstores. The wobbly turret is gutted of all its fittings and tightened down hard with a plain replacement screw. The depth stop is discarded and replaced with 6in (150mm) of $^5/_{16}$in (8mm) steel tubing. A 10in (250mm) length of $^3/_{16}$in (M5) studding (threaded rod) is fitted through the tube and locked into one of the turret holes. Running on the studding is an MDF disc fitted with an M5 T-nut. By holding back the weight of the plunge string manually, the disc will spin freely for rapid adjustment. One full turn of the disc moves the rod $^1/_{32}$in (0.8mm), so four equally spaced marks on the rim of the disc give fine adjustment in increments of

$^1/_{128}$in (0.2mm). The switch was replaced with an insulated connector block, and the router is connected via a no-volt-release switch.

The horizontal table can be made more versatile by fitting simple legs which allow it to be used the normal way up when required.

327 Sliding carriage

If you are making your own table and are including a sliding carriage (which can be much more useful than a mitre fence), try this design that runs along the edge of the table as well as in the groove. If made really accurately, with wax applied to the meeting surfaces, it provides a very rigid 90° fence.

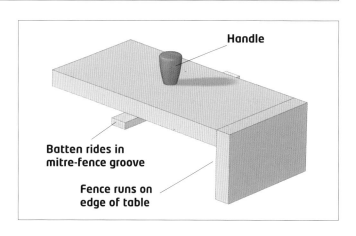

Handle

Batten rides in mitre-fence groove

Fence runs on edge of table

Routing tips

328 Back-door table

Here is a makeshift solution for those temporarily without a workshop. The bench is attached to the door, and can be dropped down to become a router table.

329 Cheap mounting plate

Although it is possible to make your own router table both easily and cheaply using offcuts of MDF or other such material, the router mounting plates are very expensive. One possibility is to use the now redundant plain steel circular saw blades.

The router is bolted to the blade, which is then fitted into a rebate in the table top. The arbor hole in the blade is enlarged with a metal-cutting jigsaw to accept the largest cutter you are likely to use. This large hole is then reduced for better support of material by fastening a piece of perspex, or the like, to the plate with self-tapping screws, or possibly double-sided tape. The perspex must be the same diameter as the blade, and can have centre holes to suit the cutter in use. The same idea can be used with an inverted jigsaw or circular saw.

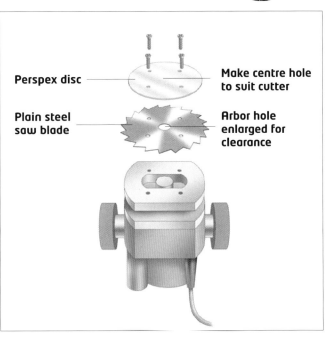

Perspex disc — Make centre hole to suit cutter

Plain steel saw blade — Arbor hole enlarged for clearance

330 Rapid fence adjustment

When using a router fence of the separate-face type, it can be useful to have fore and aft adjustment, particularly on the outfeed side for planing or shaping the edge of a workpiece. It is also useful not to have to unclamp the fence each time, only to find that it needs resetting to its original position a few minutes later.

Two sets of plastic laminate shims provide the necessary adjustment. The thickness isn't important, provided it is uniform throughout the sheet of laminate – a typical thickness is ³⁄₆₄in (1mm). Cut ten rectangles of the same length as each of the fence's split faces, but slightly taller to allow for the removal tabs. Using contact adhesive, glue four pairs of the rectangles together so that you end up with two rectangles of single

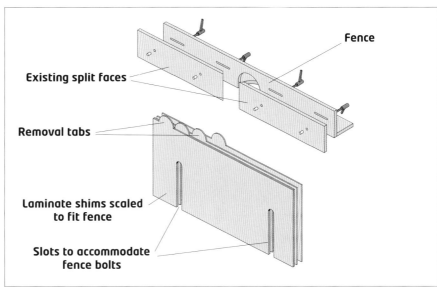

Fence

Existing split faces

Removal tabs

Laminate shims scaled to fit fence

Slots to accommodate fence bolts

thickness and four of double thickness. Slots must be cut to allow the shims to be inserted over the fence bolts. For edge-planing operations, the single-thickness shim on the outfeed side should be

sufficient. The other shims are useful when you want to back the fence away from the cutter in small increments.

331 Quick clamp

For a quick, easy and cheap method of clamping your router to the underside of a home-made table, simply use the rods that hold the fence. Make two blocks big enough to span the distance between the rods. Using a core-box cutter, rout some semicircular grooves in the blocks to take the rods. Drill each block for two bolts. Attach the bolts to the underside of the table, either with epoxy or by counterboring from the top. Slide the fence rods so they are equidistant, then, using wing nuts, bolt your router to the underside of the table.

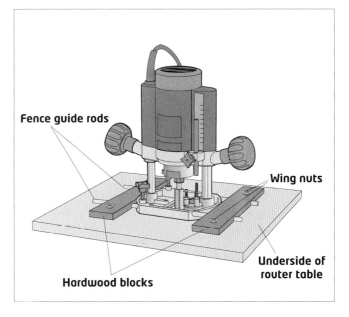

Fence guide rods

Wing nuts

Underside of router table

Hardwood blocks

Routing tips

332 Loose fittings

Before fitting a router into a table, remove all unnecessary fittings, such as clamp screws, depth-adjuster rods, etc. These can vibrate loose and fall off while you are machining, getting lost in a pile of shavings. Worse stilll, they could be drawn into the cutter by the extractor and by uplift from the motor.

On some large machines the weight of the tube-type depth adjuster causes it to shake loose and drop off when used for long periods, even with the locknut well tightened. You can use just a nut in place of the adjuster, using a long box spanner (tube wrench) for fine adjustment and to nip the nut up against the locknut. This also makes cutter changing quicker, as the nut is quickly spun down the thread before the router is lowered.

The problem of things coming loose seems to be worse on the better-quality, more rigid router tables.

333 Quick cutter changing

When using the router inverted in a table, push a tight-fitting O-ring onto the shank of the cutter at the position where you want the shank to rest in the collet. When the cutter is put into the collet, the O-ring rests on the nut, so it does not need to be held in position while the nut is tightened. The O-ring is also useful in preventing dust and chippings getting into the collet or nut, and allows rapid repositioning if the cutter needs changing between cuts.

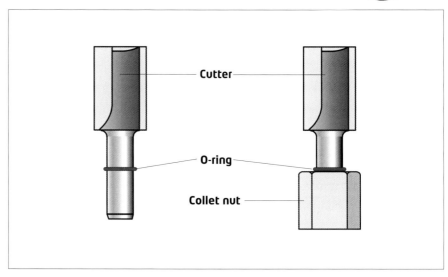

Cutter

O-ring

Collet nut

334   Router jack

If you have difficulty in pushing the router up into position in its table, it is possible to buy a device consisting of a long thread, with a wheel on it, to attach to the router. A much cheaper option is to buy a scissor jack from a scrapyard, and bolt this to a length of timber laid across the stretcher bars on the table. You can now adjust the height of the router, and, if you wish, use it as a fine adjuster.

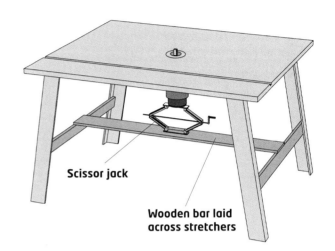

Scissor jack

Wooden bar laid across stretchers

335   Cheap threaded inserts

Threaded inserts for use in router tables and jigs are quite expensive and can be hard to get hold of. A cheap and simple way of making them is to file the corners off a plain hexagon nut and glue it in a pre-drilled hole. An alternative method is to file them to a wedge shape so they will grip the hole without gluing. To make them 'shake-proof', you can use locknuts with a nylon insert. To speed up the filing job, carefully insert them in a drill chuck and hold a file against the revolving nut.

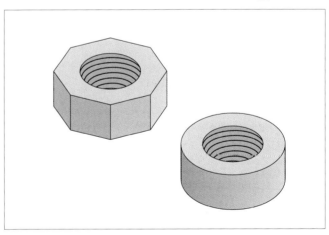

Routing tips

336 | Router lifter (1)

This device for lifting an inverted router into its table is designed to fit a 5in (127mm) gap between the base of the router and the shelf of the cabinet; the measurements could be adjusted if necessary to accommodate a smaller gap.

WARNING

Before making or using any lifting device for the router, please refer to the safety tip, no. 354 (page 177).

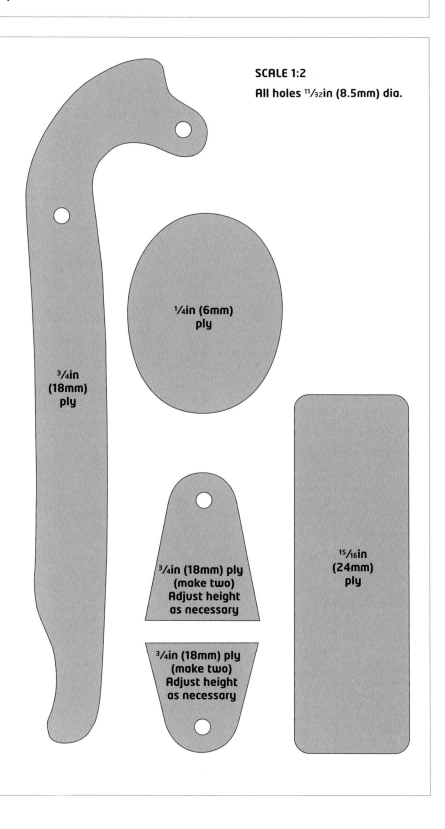

SCALE 1:2
All holes ¹¹⁄₃₂in (8.5mm) dia.

¹⁄₄in (6mm) ply

³⁄₄in (18mm) ply

³⁄₄in (18mm) ply (make two) Adjust height as necessary

³⁄₄in (18mm) ply (make two) Adjust height as necessary

¹⁵⁄₁₆in (24mm) ply

337 Router lifter (2)

This system allows the router height to be adjusted quickly and without effort. All you need is a couple of roofing bolts and some ¾in (18mm) ply. Using the depth gauge with the turret stop, you can get the full range of adjustment in seconds, and if you raise the router before removing it from the table the adjusting arm does not have to be removed.

338 Home-made height adjuster

Here is a simple and cheap way to make a fine height adjuster for a router table. You'll need a long ⅜in (M10) bolt and two nuts to fit it. Take a block of scrap wood and drill a ½in (13mm) hole in it, then cut a recess for one of the nuts, which is fixed in with superglue. The second nut acts as a locking nut; thread it onto the bolt, then thread the bolt into the block of wood. Now mount a shelf under the router, and insert a protective pad with ventilation holes between the bolt's head and the router. Now you can easily make fine adjustments by threading the bolt up and down.

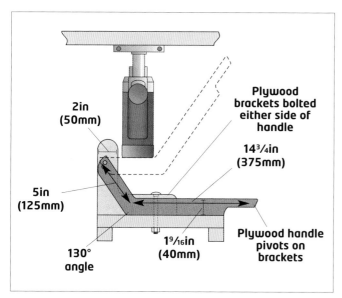

2in (50mm)

Plywood brackets bolted either side of handle

14¾in (375mm)

5in (125mm)

130° angle

1⁹⁄₁₆in (40mm)

Plywood handle pivots on brackets

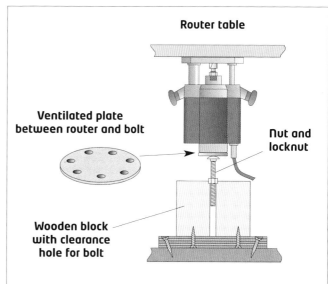

Router table

Ventilated plate between router and bolt

Nut and locknut

Wooden block with clearance hole for bolt

339 Router lifter (3)

This hardwood lever and roller provides a means of adjusting the cutter height without resorting to three hands. The cutter height can be set by using a piece of wood marked at the required height and placed across the hole in the table.

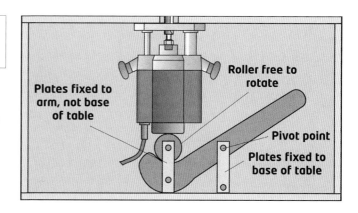

Roller free to rotate

Plates fixed to arm, not base of table

Pivot point

Plates fixed to base of table

340 Router lifter (4)

Here is another solution to fine adjustment of cutting depth.

1 Fit a length of roofing batten as a crossbar across the front legs of the table. Bolts and slotted holes allow it to be removed easily.

2 Make up a simple rectangular frame to support the router, again using roofing battens.

3 Use the frame as a lever to adjust the router height before locking it in place. Very fine height adjustment is possible in this way.

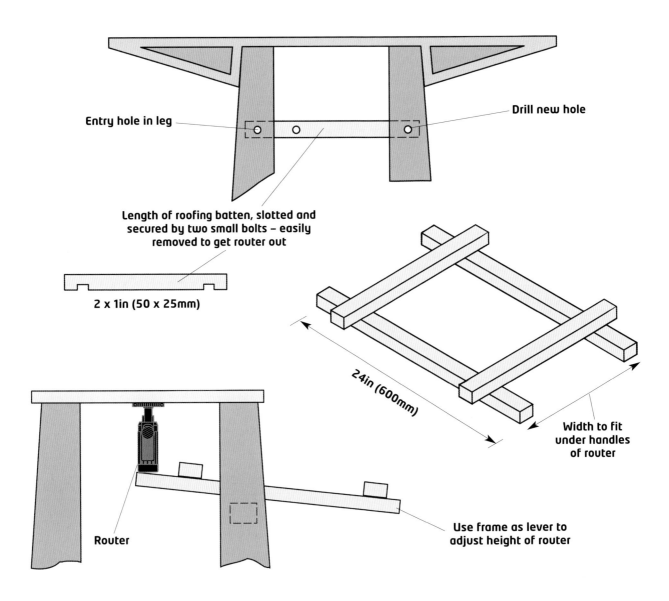

Entry hole in leg

Drill new hole

Length of roofing batten, slotted and secured by two small bolts – easily removed to get router out

2 x 1in (50 x 25mm)

24in (600mm)

Width to fit under handles of router

Router

Use frame as lever to adjust height of router

341 Angled push stick

If your router table has a transparent protecting cover over the cutter, the usual push stick (similar to those used with a circular saw) will stop short when it hits the cover, leaving the last section of the workpiece to be moved on by lifting the cover, so it no longer provides protection.

This design lifts the edge of the cover sufficiently, without any break in the thrust. It is made from 2 x 1in (50 x 25mm) wood, with the base measuring 6in (150mm) long. The 12in (300mm) handle is screwed and glued to it at about 45°. The end, curved almost to a sharp edge, overlaps the notch by about 1⅝in (40mm). If you make the notch a few degrees less than a right angle, it grips better. When the end gets worn it can be recut more than once before a new push stick is needed.

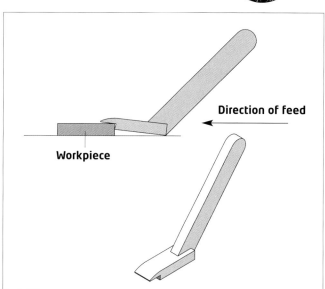

Direction of feed

Workpiece

342 Improved push stick

When feeding a piece of wood over a router table, it is necessary to press the work against the fence as well as pushing it forward. You may have to use both hands on some jobs, but it helps if the push stick also provides some sideways pressure. This can be done by arranging the handle, whatever its type, diagonally to the push stick. This one is at about 30° to the line of thrust.

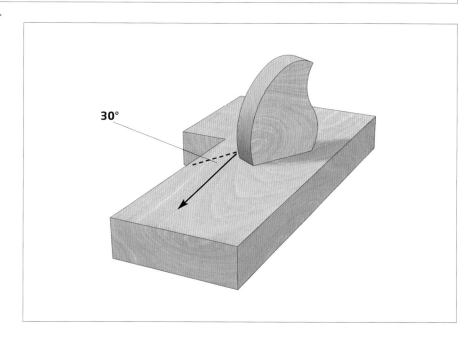

30°

Router accessories

343 | Fine height adjusters

Here are two fine height adjusters to suit different makes of router. Both work well and were made at little cost.

Mark I

This router has a threaded bar which fits into its base. Replace this with a piece of threaded rod long enough to come above the top of the router body when it is at maximum height. A piece of pipe about 3/8in (10mm) in diameter fits snugly over the rod.

The two knobs are made from offcuts drilled through, with 5/16in (8mm) nuts glued in place with epoxy. They are designed to lock against each other. A washer is placed on top of the cap, and another on the adjusting knob above. Infinitely fine adjustment is now possible by using the flat knob. The second knob is then tightened against the first to stop it vibrating loose. This works well, even upside down in a table, provided the depth lock is always used.

Mark II

This adaptation is intended for the smaller type of demountable router with the motor held in a clamp. The motor clamp is held on the spring-loaded pillars of the base by a set screw and large washer on one side only. The diagram (*below right*) shows this version.

Remove the screw and replace it with a piece of threaded rod, locked in place with a nut. A piece of 9/16in (15mm) copper pipe slids easily over the pillar, so by soldering a cap on a piece of suitable length and drilling a 1/4in (6mm) hole in the cap, pressure can be applied to the motor clamp and the depth adjusted. The knobs are formed in the same way as before.

It should be possible to adapt at least one of these two adjusters, or devise some variation on them, to fit a wide range of machines.

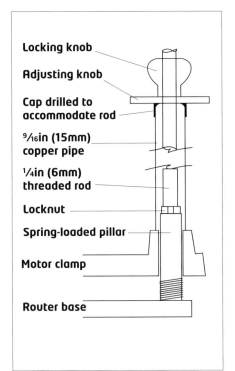

Locking knob

Adjusting knob

Cap drilled to accommodate rod

9/16in (15mm) copper pipe

1/4in (6mm) threaded rod

Locknut

Spring-loaded pillar

Motor clamp

Router base

344 Safe height adjustment

Being disabled poses particular difficulties when routing, not least of which is safe control of the router. If you are unable to stand, you will not be able to provide much downward pressure or exercise firm control of the router, unless you have a height adjuster to safely lower the cut into the workpiece in consistent increments. These can be expensive to buy, but you can make your own.

Measure the threads of the three-way turret, and buy a length of screwed rod of the same pitch and diameter; you will only need about 6in (150mm) of it. The new rod replaces one of the screws in the turret.

Next, take a wing nut of the same size, and file it down until it can be jam-fitted to a piece of metal tubing large enough to slip over the threaded rod. Fix the nut to the rod with epoxy. Make up a winding handle and fit this to the other end of the tube.

The final result is excellent to use, as it gives very precise control – each complete turn of the handle advances the cutter by $\frac{1}{32}$in (0.75mm) – and you can cut any shape safely.

With just a little ingenuity it should be possible to adapt this technique to suit many different makes of router.

345 Height adjuster

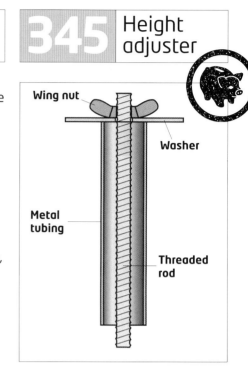

This fine height adjuster fits a number of popular models. It consists of a 5½in (140mm) length of tubing, about 6in (150mm) of $\frac{3}{16}$in (M5) threaded rod, and a washer and wing nut to fit.

Screw the rod into the shortest of the depth turrets, placing the tube over it, with the washer and wing nut on top. The plunge spring of the router keeps everything taut.

This will save the often difficult job of releasing the plunge lock, pushing the router up to the correct position, then resetting the plunge lock. To adjust the height of the router accurately, simply turn the wing nut.

Proprietary versions can be bought, but if you are on a tight budget this simple device can be easily made without the need for any complicated tools.

346 Flexible depth gauge

This design can be made quickly from leftover softwood, and suits any size, metric or imperial, router or saw. A hardwood version would make a really nice tool.

Make it wide enough so it will not fall over. Sometimes you need two hands to adjust your router or saw, and it helps if the depth gauge stays where you put it. Make it any size to suit the work you have to do.

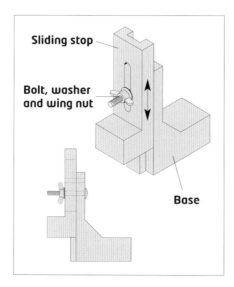

347 Improved roller follower

This device addresses the problem of the router
pivoting on the roller follower and spoiling the job.

It utilizes the original follower bracket supplied with
the router, but the single wheel bracket and the wheel
itself are taken off. A new two-wheeled version is
made, using a couple of pieces of small angle welded
together and then welded to the single wheel bracket.
Drill a couple of holes for the axles of the new wheels;
their positions will depend on the size of the wheels
chosen. Sturdy buttons make adequate wheels.
The axles are made from thick steel wire, riveted over
at each end.

The device can be adapted to suit the materials to
hand, but the principle of having two wheels on the
follower, rather than one, will automatically keep the
cutter at 90° to the edge of the work, and prevent any
more pivoting problems.

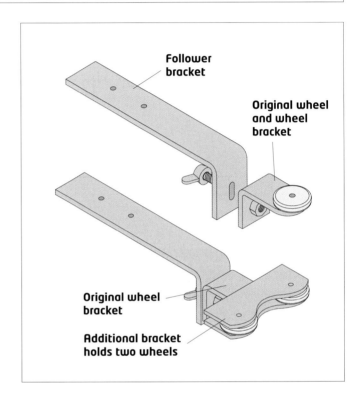

Follower
bracket

Original wheel
and wheel
bracket

Original wheel
bracket

Additional bracket
holds two wheels

348 Tool caddy

When you are about to tackle a routing project, both a
spanner (wrench) and the cutter you are going to use
need to be ready to hand. The stand shown here keeps
them together and accessible. The spanner hangs on
two small cup hooks on one side, and there are holes
for cutters on the other side. A dowel through the top
serves as a handle.

The timber is ¾in (18mm) thick and the base is 4in
(100mm) square; the height is decided by the length of
the spanner. You could make two in different sizes, for
¼in and ½in cutters and their respective spanners.
Paint them a conspicuous colour to ensure there is no
difficulty in finding them amongst the shavings and
general clutter on the bench.

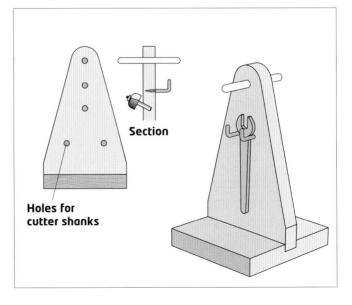

Section

Holes for
cutter shanks

349 Temporary support

Supporting the weight of an inverted router with one hand, whilst trying to bolt it to the underside of a table with the other, can be a little tricky. This simple temporary clamp is constructed using two pieces of wood, each 6 x 1¾ x ⅜in (152 x 45 x 10mm), one ⁵⁄₁₆in (M8) coach bolt, a penny washer and a wing nut. A clearance hole is drilled through the centre of both pieces of wood, and the square of the bolt is pressed into one of them.

To fix the router to the table, the half of the clamp with the bolt fitted is passed through the gap between the columns, so that the bolt protrudes through the bottom of the baseplate. The clamp and router are then offered up to the underside of the router table and held in place with one hand. The other half of the clamp is then passed over the protruding bolt and secured with the penny washer and wing nut. The nut is left loose to permit the router to be centred with respect to the hole in the insert plate.

You can now use both hands to fit two of the three securing bolts. The clamp is then removed, the third bolt fitted, and all three tightened.

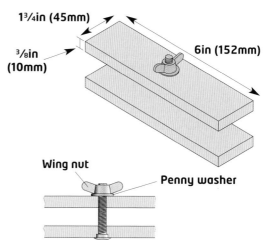

1¾in (45mm)

⅜in (10mm)

6in (152mm)

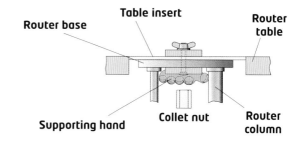

Wing nut

Penny washer

Table insert

Router base

Router table

Supporting hand

Collet nut

Router column

350 Safer inversion

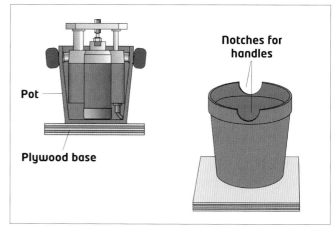

There are times – such as when changing a cutter – when it is convenient to have the router inverted on a bench, but even if the top of the router is flat, it is not a very big area for stability.

Simply drill and screw a plastic flowerpot to a piece of plywood, and you have a reliable support. If you require notches for the handles, cut them with a fretsaw or a junior hacksaw.

Notches for handles

Pot

Plywood base

Router safety

351 Safe routing procedure

1 Secure the cutter in the collet.

2 Set the depth of cut.

3 Set up whatever guides you plan to use.

4 Check that the workpiece is secure and there are no obstacles in the way.

5 Make sure the router is not switched on and the cutter is free to rotate. Only then connect to the mains and switch on.

6 Allow time for the motor to reach full running speed.

7 Perform the routing operation.

8 Retract the router cutter by releasing the plunge mechanism.

9 Switch off and let the cutter come to a complete stop

10 Put the machine down and isolate from the mains.

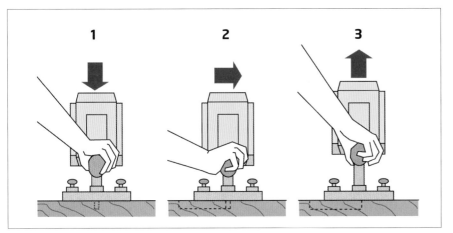

Plunge-routing sequence

Step 1: **Plunge down and lock the motor carriage**

Step 2: **Carry out the routing operation**

Step 3: **Release plunge lock; motor carriage returns to normal position**

352 Router cutter safety

Never use damaged or worn-down cutters – a damaged or worn cutter may disintegrate with disastrous consequences; a worn cutter will produce an inferior finished cut.

Always work at the proper feed speed; forcing the cutter through the wood at too fast a speed will exert unnatural forces and increase the risk of breaking the cutter.

Pay particular attention when making the initial cut. Clear any clutter away from the path of the router to avoid accidents. Also double-check measurements, as a wrongly positioned cut will be costly.

Do not cut deeper than the diameter of the cutter in one pass – a ½in (13mm) cutter can be used to cut ½in (13mm) deep at each pass.

When working with small-diameter cutters, set your maximum cutting depth to only half the cutter diameter – a ⅛in (3mm) cutter should be set to cut a maximum of ¹⁄₁₆in (1.5mm) deep at each pass.

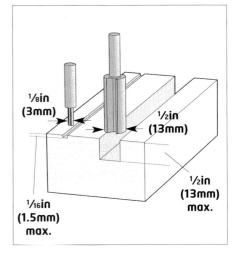

⅛in (3mm)

½in (13mm)

½in (13mm) max.

¹⁄₁₆in (1.5mm) max.

353 Handling cutters

Boxed sets of cutters are often packaged in very tight-fitting plastic holders, and it is all too easy to cut your fingers, especially when removing straight cutters. To avoid this, wear an old gardening glove, or wrap a piece of rag around the cutter when first removing it from its housing.

The same technique can be used when removing the Allen bolt holding the bearing on bearing-guided cutters. They are often tightened excessively, and without protection they can easily take lumps out of your fingertips.

Above right: **Gardening gloves protect hands when removing cutters from their box for the first time**

Right: **Undoing a tight Allen bolt on a bearing-guided cutter can cut unprotected fingers**

354 Using a router lifter

There is a potential problem awaiting those who employ a lifting system for their table router. When using any kind of block or platform to support your router, there is a danger that the main air intake for the motor can be covered, to the extent that the router may overheat if used for any length of time. Careful positioning of the block, or the provision of grooves or holes within it for ventilation, should solve the problem.

Routing tips

355 Power-cord safety (1)

Power-tool and extension cables, and even air hoses, can be a danger if allowed to trail on the workshop floor. The mechanism from an old loose-leaf binder will help you contain the mess safely and tidily.

Simply fasten one more of these mechanisms to walls, machines or benches at the appropriate height, click them open and insert your cord between the jaws of the device. This cord is kept off the floor but is free to move as the tool is used.

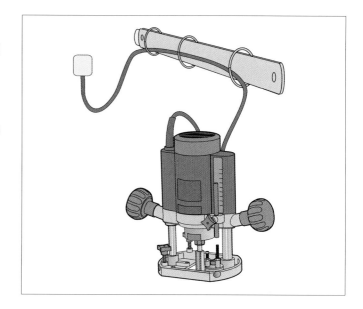

356 Power-cord safety (2)

The dangling power cord is a persistent and potentially dangerous nuisance. Slide a 16in (400mm) length of ½in (12mm) clear plastic hose onto the power cable and push or tape it onto the cable strainer. This stiffens the cord so that it stays well clear of the cutter.

This technique could be used on any power tool with a wayward cable.

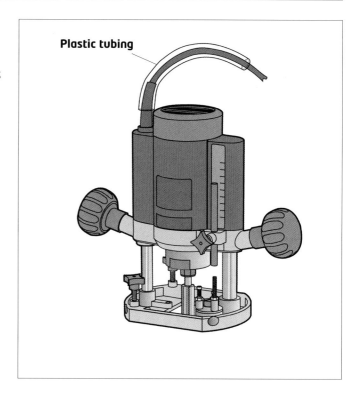

Plastic tubing

357 Power-cord safety (3)

Put hooks in the workshop ceiling to support your router cable and extractor hose. Position them above where you normally work, and suspend the cables from them with a length of shock cord for maximum flexibility in use.

Alternatively, use the flex holder from an ironing board to hold your router cable clear of the work.

A hook in the ceiling and a bungee cord help to keep wires out of the way

The flex holder from an ironing board does the same

358 Finger tip

Anyone who has spent some time routing will have picked up the odd scrape on their hands. Changing bits on two-wrench routers can be a particular problem, until you realize that by using only one hand you can prevent your fingers getting caught between the handles of the two wrenches.

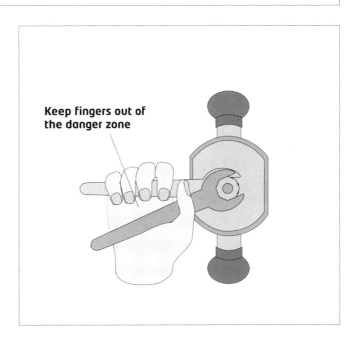

Keep fingers out of the danger zone

359 Dust control (1)

In order to remove coarse chippings and ultrafine dust particles, such as those produced by the router, it is necessary to use an efficient vacuum system. Commercial ones tend to be somewhat expensive, but you can build your own.

You need a wet-and-dry vacuum cleaner with a 1000W motor, a large water butt and a tumble-dryer venting-hose connector.

The drum of the vacuum cleaner is fixed into the hard rubber lid of the water butt by simply cutting the correct-sized hole in the lid and pushing the drum into it so that approximately half the drum is above the surface of the lid. This produces a good tight fit, but an additional fixing can be made by applying a fillet of adhesive above and below. A large hole is then cut in the bottom of the vacuum-cleaner drum and the lid replaced on the butt. In order to get a good seal, fix some soft rubber draught excluder to the top of the butt where it is in contact with the edge of the lid.

Cut a 4in (100mm) diameter hole in the water butt, near the top, and attach the venting-hose connector with self-tapping screws and a suitable sealant.

Finally, the inlet hole in the vacuum-cleaner drum is sealed using a patch cut from the scrap hard rubber removed from the water-butt lid. Again, this is fixed with sealant and screws. The extractor is connected to the various machines using plastic soil pipe and flexible tubing, both 4in (100mm) in diameter.

The extractor is very efficient, easily emptied, and access to the dust filter within the vacuum cleaner is simple. The cost of the components is very reasonable.

360 Dust control (2)

The problem of attaching a vacuum line to a router's dust spout is complicated by the differences in size between the smaller hose nozzles and the spout outlet. A simple solution is to stretch a section of bicycle inner tube over the spout, folding over the spare end and pushing it inside. This allows the spout to adapt to the smaller vacuum nozzle. The rubber can be kept in place by a couple of turns of duct tape. It can easily be turned out again when you need to clean the spout.

361 Extraction box

This 'extraction box' is easily connected to your dust extractor, and is intended to complement the extraction systems supplied by the power-tool manufacturers. Whether you use it for routing or sanding, it will help to keep the workshop dust levels down.

Make up a shallow box, about 3in or so (80mm) deep and 16in (400mm) square, from your preferred sheet material, plywood or MDF. Run a rebate around the inside edge of both the top and bottom of the box. Place a solid sheet in the bottom rebate, fixing it in place, and a drilled sheet in the top, leaving this loose for easy removal. Bore a hole in one of the box's side walls so it is a tight fit on a dust-extractor pipe, and you are nearly there. Rubber feet on the bottom will stop it sliding around, and a router mat laid on the top does the same for the workpiece, but still lets the dust through.

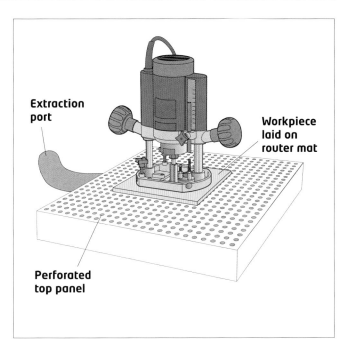

Extraction port

Workpiece laid on router mat

Perforated top panel

362 Dust collector

A plastic bucket fixed to the underside of a router table makes a good dust-extraction collector.

Take a bucket of suitable size, cut a hole in the bottom and then pop-rivet it to a flanged 4in (100mm) standard PVC soil-pipe fitting.

Before screwing the bucket to the underside of the router table, cut a hole in the side of the bucket to take the plug cable; this is because the switch on the router will be covered, so the flex must be taken to a separate switch. Cutting a few ventilation holes around the rim of the bucket helps the airflow over the router.

Attach flexible hose to the pipe fitting and link up to your dust extractor. Now screw a no-volt-release switch to the table and plug the router in.

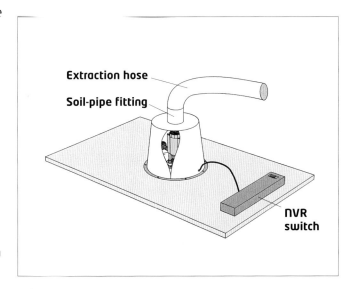

Extraction hose

Soil-pipe fitting

nVR switch

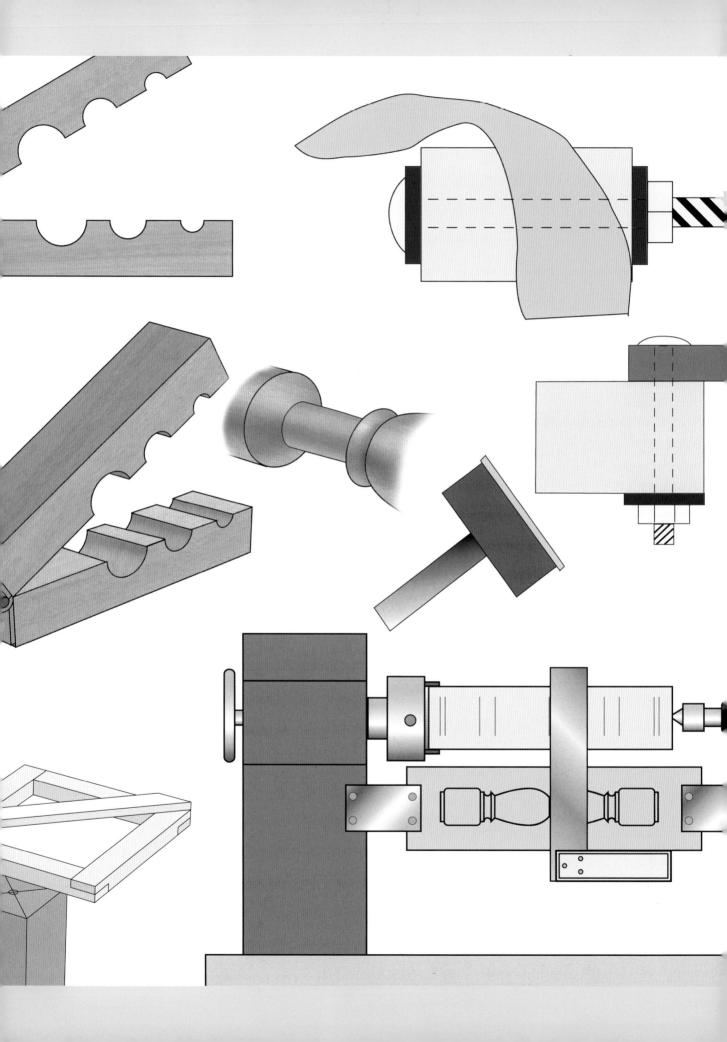

Woodturning tips

Lathes

363 Banjo support

When working with the banjo near its forward limit, even solid steel bed bars may show some vertical flexing during turning. This results in the toolrest bouncing as the bars flex, meaning that the turned surface is not perfectly smooth.

A cheap and effective answer is a free-standing support for the front of the banjo. This can be made from a length of hardwood 1⅛in (30mm) square cut ¹¹⁄₁₆in (17mm) longer than the distance from the floor to the underside of the banjo. On one end the sides are cut away to a depth of ⅜in (10mm), leaving a central tenon approximately ⅜in (10mm) square. To use, position this central pillar against the front edge of the banjo and then give the other end a kick towards the lathe bench, which wedges the wood in position, supporting the banjo.

This simple prop provides a rigid support to the banjo and eliminates the ripples which would otherwise occur on the turned surface.

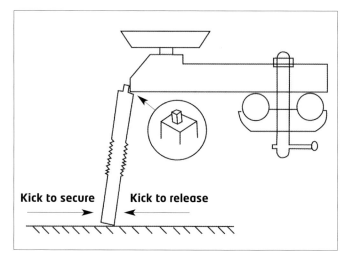

The support can be quickly removed by a good kick in the opposite direction, and the central tenon makes the support equally useful when turning large items with the end-turning arm fully extended.

364 Banjo adjustment

The means of securing the toolrest banjo to the bed bars on some lathes works adequately, but falls short of perfection.

In models where the slot and the housing above it are cast in, rather than machined, the hexagon nut which slides in the housing may tend to jam, so a bit of waggling about is needed to free it and move the banjo.

This can easily be remedied. Take a piece of steel bar 1 x ¾ x ⅜in (25 x 20 x 10mm) and drill it centrally, starting with small drills and finishing (for the model illustrated here) with 10.2mm. Tap this at M12 – if you lack the tap and tap wrench, a friendly garage might oblige. File off all the contacting corners at a quarter-circle, finishing off with emery cloth. This nut should now slide sweetly in the housing. A mere slackening of the clamping screw releases the whole banjo to slide freely in all directions.

Toolrest extension

Even if your bowl turning very rarely exceeds 10in (255mm) in diameter, the uncorrected blank will often be larger than this, and after swivelling the lathe head to clear the bed bars the standard banjo may not be long enough to position the toolrest outside the edge of the blank.

An economical solution is to use a mild steel bar 15in (380mm) long by 2in (50mm) wide and ½in (13mm) thick as an extension. The bar is the only addition, as all existing parts are used. The dimensions are not critical, provided that the bar is strong enough to prevent vibration.

Easier locking

On some lathes it can be difficult to exert enough finger pressure to lock the tailstock quill with the knob supplied. Here is a way to give yourself more purchase.

First tighten the knob in the locking position, using pliers. Next, with a felt-tip pen, mark the position to drill a ³⁄₁₆in (4.5mm) hole through the centre of the knob, and insert a ⁵⁄₃₂ x 3⅛in (4 x 80mm) steel bar. Turn two round knobs to secure the bar in place. It is now easy to lock the quill with just a light push on the tommy bar.

This tip can be used on any lathe with a similar locking device, and would be beneficial for those with arthritis or a weaker grip.

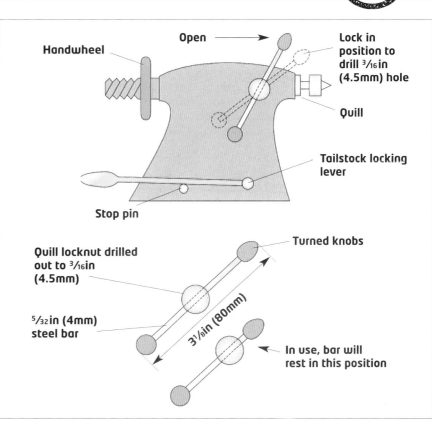

Handwheel

Open

Lock in position to drill ³⁄₁₆in (4.5mm) hole

Quill

Tailstock locking lever

Stop pin

Quill locknut drilled out to ³⁄₁₆in (4.5mm)

⁵⁄₃₂in (4mm) steel bar

Turned knobs

3⅛in (80mm)

In use, bar will rest in this position

Woodturning tips

367 Keeping the lathe clean

Keep your lathe's bed bars spotless. When using sealer, wax, oil, varnish or glue, cover the bars with an apron.

Plastic sheeting, sold for covering table tops and shelves, is ideal – provided it is not the adhesive type. Cut it to fit, and form a hem at either side, either by stitching or by using parcel tape. Slip a piece of metal strip into the hem to give enough weight to hold the apron in place across the bars.

An occasional spray of silicone or other lubricant makes sure that both banjo and tailstock slide easily and freely along the bed.

A hardboard splashboard propped behind the bed will also collect spray which otherwise would go on the wall and the tools hanging from it.

Note the build-up of deposits on the apron and splashboard, which would otherwise be on the lathe bars

368 Emergency stop

Ever wished that you had a third hand to stop your lathe when both hands were busy? Parting off is one such instance, when steadying the work with one hand and holding the parting tool with the other.

Let your leg do the work. The picture shows the controls - they don't have to be variable - mounted under the bench, so a separate stop button is all that would be required.

A strip of wood is hinged to the front of the bench so that it moves away from you, and the end of the wood is cut to fit over the stop button. It needs to be carefully positioned in front of the stop button so that it only just touches it. You can now stop the lathe whenever you need to by pushing anywhere on the wood with your leg; then all that is required to restart is to press the 'on' button.

A spring-loaded stop button is best, as it saves you having to reset after each operation.

Removing the tailstock centre

It doesn't do to keep the tailstock centre in place when not required. It is all too easy to stab an elbow on it during faceplate turning, so it should be removed.

Obtain a piece of steel 1¾in (45mm) long by 1⅜in (35mm) diameter, and drill it centrally to take a piece of ⁵⁄₁₆in (8mm) steel rod. Secure this either by drilling for an 'interference fit', by threading, by brazing, or with degreaser followed by superglue. Make the length to suit your lathe – 6in (150mm) in the example shown – then glue on a leather or rubber washer.

This 'lathe hammer' should be hung in a large screw eye near the lathe so that it is always to hand.

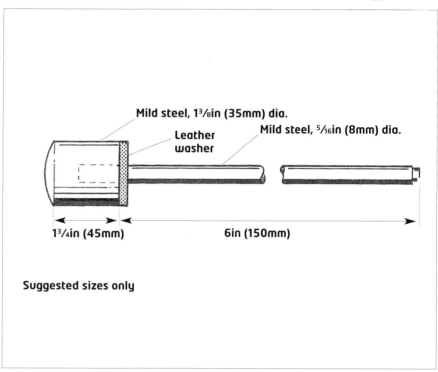

Mild steel, 1⅜in (35mm) dia.
Leather washer
Mild steel, ⁵⁄₁₆in (8mm) dia.
1¾in (45mm)   6in (150mm)

Suggested sizes only

Covering the tailstock centre

An alternative to removing the tailstock centre is to cover the sharp point. A small piece of spare wood and a quick turning job are all that is needed. Turn a cylinder about ½in (13mm) wider than the tailstock centre, then hollow it, initially with a Forstner bit and then with a parting tool, to create a tight fit. This turned piece can be placed directly over the point of the tailstock centre.

Turn a cylinder about ½in (13mm) wider than the tailstock centre

To ensure a tight fit, complete the hollowing with a parting tool

The offending point is now 'muzzled'

Workholding

371 | Make your own screw chuck

An old-fashioned carvers' screw can be converted into a screw chuck. The example shown fits a Multistar Duplex chuck with 'C' jaws.

The screw used was 3½in (90mm) long and ⅜in (9.35mm) in diameter, with two different-pitched threads, both 1¾in (45mm) long. For the body, a length of 2½in (62mm) iroko proved ideal.

Turn the wood down to this diameter and square it off at the tailstock end. Moving back ⁵⁄₃₂in (4mm) from this end, reduce it to 2in (50mm) diameter. Another ¼in (6mm) back – that is, ⅜in (10mm) from the squared-off face – reduce the diameter further to 1½in (38mm) for a length of 1⅝in (40mm). Slightly chamfer the smaller end, and part off at a total length of 2in (50mm).

Having checked that this turned-down piece fits your chuck, drill a ⅜in (10mm) hole right through the centre while it is turning, to ensure that the screw will fit centrally through the hole.

Countersink to a diameter and depth of ½in (13mm) to allow for the threaded grip, then turn a recess 1in (25mm) diameter by ⅛in (3mm) deep, so the grip can sit in the recess and remain flush with the squared-off face.

Finally, remove the piece from the chuck and then, using a pillar drill, make a recess 1in (25mm) diameter by ½in (13mm) deep at the other end, inserting a ⅜in (10mm) steel washer and ⅜in (10mm) hexagonal nut into the recess. There should be enough space around the nut to use a socket spanner (wrench). Then insert the screw from the other end and tighten the nut. As the screw is pulled deeper into the nut, the spikes on the grip will dig into the wood and pull it deeper into the recess, so as to ensure that nothing can move.

Make up a range of wooden washers in different thicknesses. These can be slipped over the screw to control the depth to which the screw enters the workpiece.

The turned hardwood block

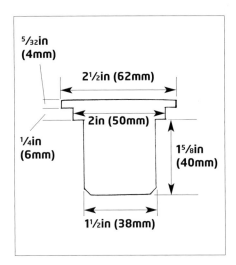

⁵⁄₃₂in (4mm)
2½in (62mm)
2in (50mm)
¼in (6mm)
1⅝in (40mm)
1½in (38mm)

The block drilled and countersunk

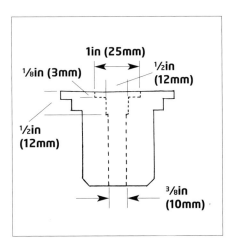

1in (25mm)
⅛in (3mm)
½in (12mm)
½in (12mm)
⅜in (10mm)

Getting the most from a chuck

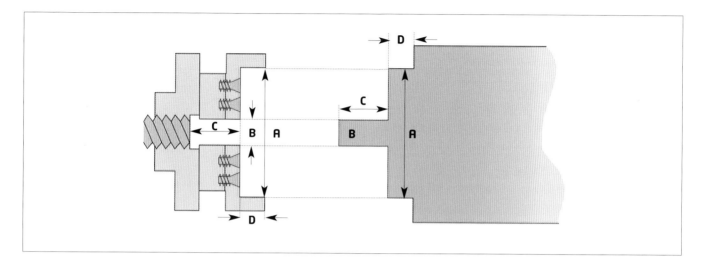

A four-jaw chuck with standard 2in (50mm) jaws is not really adequate for bowl work; this is not what they are designed for.

Rather than buying another set of jaws, you may find that there is gripping power in the chuck that isn't being used. With a little thought, the following advice will probably apply to any scroll chuck.

Set the jaws to roughly the middle of their travel, then measure lengths A, B, C and D as shown in the cross-section view, *top left*. Turn spigots in a piece of hardwood to match these

dimensions, as shown *top right*. If anything, make C slightly underlength so the wood doesn't bottom out on the headstock spindle, and make A slightly oversize so that, when mounted, the jaws make contact before the jaw carriers, and the main gripping power is where it should be. As the jaws compress the wood, so the small spigot B will be a snug fit.

Once you are happy with the dimensions, make up a hardwood template, *right*, with cut-outs for A and B, and marked lines for C and D.

This will enable future spigots to be turned quickly and accurately.

This method works very satisfactorily, without any loss of concentricity.

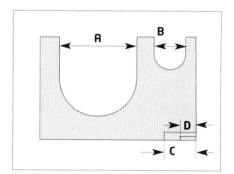

Prevent chucks jamming

To prevent chucks from jamming on the lathe spindle, it has become common practice to use a leather washer between the two. However, oil from the bearings soaks the leather, resulting in a black sludge which is quite difficult to avoid.

Instead of leather, use nylon washers, which can be bought from plumbers' merchants very cheaply.
Two can be used together if necessary. The washers are available to buy in ½in (13mm) or ¾in (19mm) bore to suit most lathes.

Woodturning tips

374 A smaller faceplate

Very small faceplates – smaller than the lathe spindle – are not commercially available. One solution is to attach a face ring to a 1in (25mm) thick hardwood disc. After truing the face, the centre space is available to drill holes in the required positions.

You don't actually need a face ring: you could turn suitable dovetails into your disc and drill close to the centre, as needed. However, repositioning with a face ring is easier and more accurate.

The arrangement shown in the photo could be improved on by using threaded inserts fitted into the wooden disc and countersunk Allen screws, so that the face ring can be removed or refitted easily.

375 Wine-bottle stopper jig

When making wine-bottle stoppers, a dowel is used to hold the stopper while turning, and is afterwards glued to the cork. You can hold the stopper with your hand while cutting off the stub of the dowel, but this is not a safe practice.

It is better to make a jig to hold the stopper while you cut off the stub. The jig consists of two pieces of 1 x 3in (25 x 75mm) wood glued at right angles. Turn a tapered hole, the size of the cork, in the vertical piece. Using this to hold the stopper while you push it through the bandsaw blade is a much safer method of cutting off the stub end of the dowel.

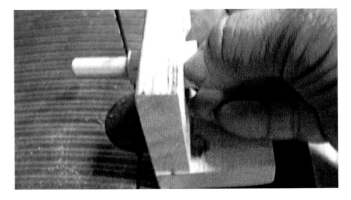

Tailstock support

It is quite often necessary to provide additional support with the tailstock when the separate parts of a piece of work, such as a box and lid, need to be held together on the lathe in order to size or finish the sides.

When using a revolving centre in the tailstock for such support, a thick pad has to be put over the point to avoid damage to the work.

A safer method is to use a car-bonnet stud; these are found in the bonnet (hood) area of a car, where they are used to stop the bonnet lid from vibrating.

These mushroom-shaped studs are made of plastic with a rubber pad on the cap end, and can be fitted between the revolving centre and the workpiece.

The stem of the stud can easily be drilled and trimmed to fit over the point of the revolving centre, while the cap end – being made of rubber – easily compresses onto a box top or over a finial without causing any damage.

The stud revolves with the workpiece and the centre when the tailstock is screwed up, thus keeping the lid securely in place. Bonnet studs are readily available from vehicle dismantlers and car-spares outlets.

Bonnet stud

The bonnet stud in action

Safe chuck

While the method of this wood chuck is not new, it is often shown with a jubilee clip to secure the workpiece. This can be dangerous because of the screw whirling round. Three or four heavy elastic bands, wrapped around the workpiece a few times, will hold it securely and no damage will be caused.

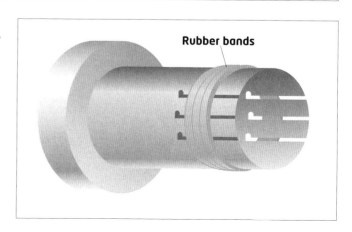

Rubber bands

Woodturning tips

378 Longer-lasting jigs

We often find ourselves shaping small rounds of wood for the purpose of making jigs and mounting fixtures for repetitive projects. The difficulty is that, after only a short while, the tenon used to mount the jig in the chuck gets deformed by the jaws, resulting in the jig running out of true. We are then forced either to reshape the jig or to reverse-mount it and reshape the tenon, which can be annoying.

A solution is to purchase a short length of 2in (50mm) PVC water pipe. When making a fixture which you intend to re-use multiple times, turn a round blank of hardwood and size the tenon on one end to fit snugly inside the pipe. Leave a wide shoulder – approximately ½in

(13mm) – on the round. Next, cut a short section of the PVC pipe about ⅝in (15mm) in length and, using epoxy-resin adhesive glue, secure it to the tenon.

Part off the excess length of the PVC, truing the end of the collar. Leave the outer surface of the collar flat if that suits your chuck, but if your chuck has tapered jaws, you can simply shape the PVC to match. Turn the shoulder behind the tenon to an appropriate width to seat on the face of the chuck jaws. You now have a tenon that can be remounted dozens of times and run true each time. The pipe will not mar easily, and the solid wood centre will prevent it from distorting. After many uses, the small amount of

marring that occurs can be turned away, enabling the device to be used many more times.

At times it is necessary to hold in the chuck jaw a round that we don't want marred by the jaws. There are smooth jaws available for some models, but it takes time to change them, and sizes are limited. Also, there are times when the piece you want to hold has a tenon just a little bit smaller than the chuck jaws will close on.

PVC water pipe can also be used in both of these situations. Simply mount a short section of PVC on the lathe and part off rings ⅜in (10mm) to ½in (13mm) in width, then halve them with a bandsaw and remove an extra ⅛in (3mm) or so from each piece. Depending on how much flexibility is needed to fit the tenon snugly, cut either a single wide notch or several small kerfs on the interior face.

Usually 1½in (38mm) or 2in (50mm) PVC will fit the bill, but any size of pipe can be used for the job in hand. You will now be able to convert to smooth jaws quickly when you need them, and easily mount undersize pieces in a snap. Save the pieces and re-use them whenever you need them.

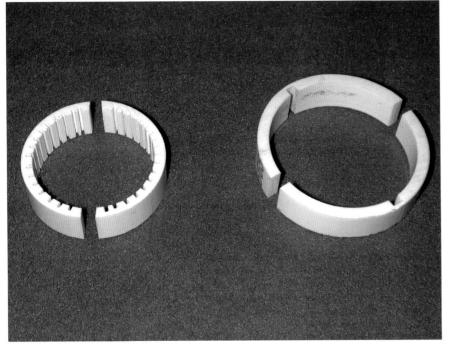

379 A long-turning steady

The long-turning steady shown here takes work of up to 4in (100mm) diameter. G-clamps hold the steady in place on the lathe bed. Adjustment is made by moving ballraces into contact with the workpiece and locking with nuts either side of the brackets. These are welded to the bottom of the frame and straddle the lathe bed.

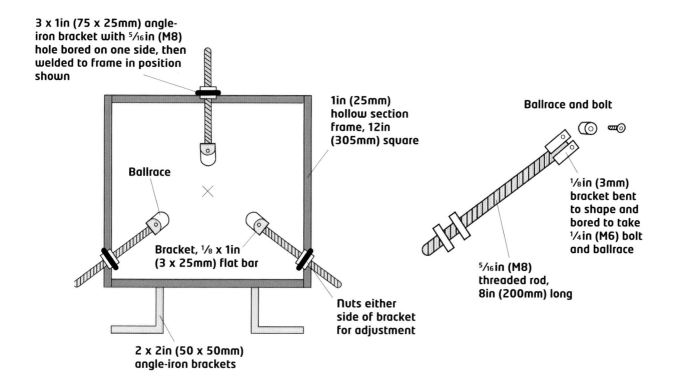

3 x 1in (75 x 25mm) angle-iron bracket with ⁵⁄₁₆in (M8) hole bored on one side, then welded to frame in position shown

1in (25mm) hollow section frame, 12in (305mm) square

Ballrace and bolt

Ballrace

⅛in (3mm) bracket bent to shape and bored to take ¼in (M6) bolt and ballrace

Bracket, ⅛ x 1in (3 x 25mm) flat bar

⁵⁄₁₆in (M8) threaded rod, 8in (200mm) long

Nuts either side of bracket for adjustment

2 x 2in (50 x 50mm) angle-iron brackets

380 Easier to handle

The spanners (wrenches) accompanying some chuck sets are inconveniently short. Drilling two holes in the spanner and screwing it to a turned hardwood handle gives much more leverage and makes it more comfortable to use. Drill pilot holes for the screws in the handle to prevent splitting.

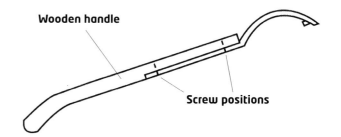

Wooden handle

Screw positions

Tools

Improving a long-hole borer

Here is a useful modification to the tail centre to facilitate long-hole turning.

On the model shown, it is necessary to locate the centre into the end of the section to be drilled, wind in the quill in the tailstock to engage the ring centre, then loosen the quill and ring centre in order to undo the Allen screw, so enabling the removal of the centre pin, only to have to bring up the tailstock and quill to relocate the ring centre.

The solution is to extend the centre pin with a rod which passes right through the tailstock, and is MIG-welded to the centre pin. Locate the centre and wind in the tailstock to locate the ring, slacken the Allen screw and withdraw the centre pin through the hollow quill of the tailstock.

This also saves spending 10 minutes going through a heap of shavings, having dropped the small centre point while removing it in the conventional manner.

The same method will probably work with other makes than the one shown here.

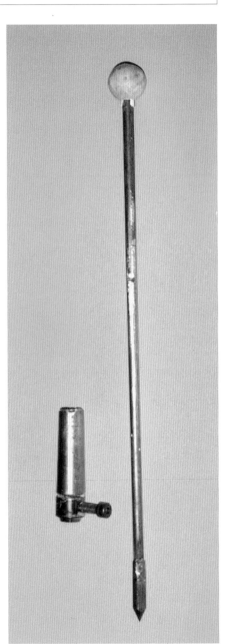

Modified long-hole boring set-up

A commercial long-hole boring kit

382 Spiralling system safety

With some commercial spiralling systems, the user's left hand has to be on top of the clamp, pushing forward towards the cutting wheel.

For a safer method, take the baseplate off and reduce the cutting-wheel end of it by 1⅝in (40mm). Then turn the clamp itself through 180°, so that the angle markings on it still match up with the centre line on the tool shaft. Reassemble it and move the clamp and baseplate forward by 1⅝in (40mm) from the original position, so the cutting wheel centre is now 1⅜in (35mm) from the clamp screw centre. This also allows the widest part of the baseplate to rest on the lathe toolrest when in use, giving greater stability.

The left hand now naturally holds the tool shaft behind the clamp, which is much more comfortable. Most importantly, the hand cannot slip forward onto the cutting wheel, as the clamp is now in the way.

383 Using scrapers

The old adage that turners do not use scrapers is untrue. On really dense woods you may find that you can achieve a better cut with a scraper than with a gouge. If this is the case, use the scraper for profiling if you want to.

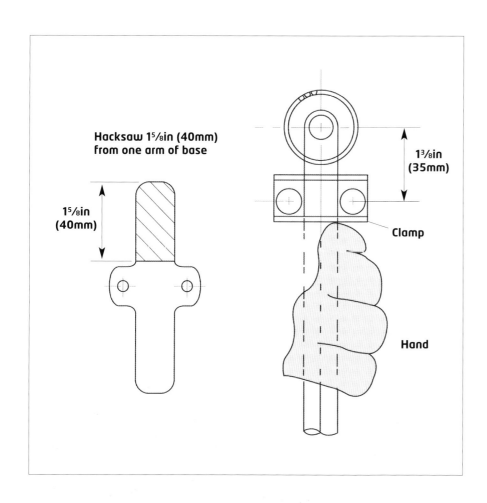

Hacksaw 1⅝in (40mm) from one arm of base

1⅝in (40mm)

1⅜in (35mm)

Clamp

Hand

Woodturning tips

384 Sharpening carbon-steel tools

Some mature turners may still have carbon-steel chisels and scrapers, so here is a tip for sharpening them without the frustration most of us have experienced. As the edge gets thinner, it becomes more susceptible to 'bluing', which must be avoided because it draws the hardness from the metal.

My grandfather was a cutler and a maker of pikes, so he probably knew plenty of things about sharpening. In his day, carbon steels were the norm, and when he was working on fine edges he quenched the work in a tub of water, to which he would add a small quantity of soap – you could try a drop of washing-up liquid. This was just enough to break the surface tension so that, when he returned to the grinding wheel, the surface of the work was wet.

As the grinding wheel generated heat while removing metal, it would make the damp surface dry and, when it was dry, you knew it was time to return to quench the work – or the chisel, in our case – keeping the edge cool.

Nowadays, carbon-steel tools are often available in club auctions at good prices. If you are just starting to turn, or have a limited budget, don't shy away from them on the grounds that they are old-fashioned, or not as good as the latest technology. This tip may be helpful to keep your edges keen and your *temper* under control.

385 Sharpening small tools

Here is a simple method for sharpening small cutters and scrapers which may not fit on a commercial sharpening jig such as the one shown here.

First turn a hardwood rod of 5/16in (8mm) diameter and drill holes in each end for the shafts of the cutters. The cutter shafts should rotate freely in the holes. The pictures below show how it works. Place the rod parallel to the existing universal support, which should be locked close to the grindstone. Allow the grindstone to rotate the cutter slightly as you work, and you will achieve a perfect grind. Use your thumb to control the rotation.

This method works in the same way as 'centreless' grinding, a technique which is also known in the metalworking industry.

Cutters 5/8in (15mm) and larger can be sharpened normally in the manufacturer's own jig.

Make a wooden rod with bored ends...

...fit the cutter into the rod...

... and place the rod parallel to the universal support, thus enabling an even grind

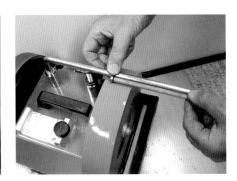

386 Lathe-bed tool rack

Setting up your lathe in the centre of the workshop gives you good access to all sides, but leaves you with no convenient place to rest your tools without walking across to the bench. You may be tempted to leave them on the bed bars, but you will certainly regret it: you will find yourself dancing backwards to protect your toes as the tool falls to the floor (because all tools land sharpest-end down), and then spending ten minutes resharpening. Try making this simple toolrest instead.

Find an offcut of board about 18 x 8in (460 x 200mm) and screw on a few pairs of tool clips to take your two or three most commonly used turning tools. On the back, mount a pair of larger clips to go over the bed bars; when not on the lathe, these fit onto two suitable lengths of plastic pipe mounted on the workshop wall. Cover the blades of the clips with insulation tape to protect the tool handles and bed bars and prevent any sounds of vibration. The end result is very effective.

387 Grinding aid

This tip is from an old professional turner. If you are finding it difficult to grind consistent bevels on your tools, use a marker pen to colour the bevel before grinding. If there is any ink left on the bevel after you have sharpened the tool, you know that it hasn't been ground consistently. The ink also shows you which part of the bevel you need to concentrate on in order to correct the shape.

388 Mobile tool rack

This wheeled rack has three shelves to hold chucks, toolrests, centres, etc. Use it to house the tools you use most often, and you can easily move them into position wherever they are needed.

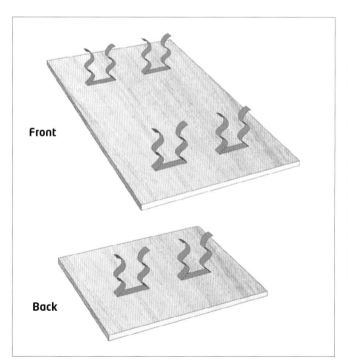

Front

Back

Marking and measuring

389 Improving dividers

Instead of sharpening your dividers to a point, grind the tips to a chisel edge. These can be used to mark out divisions on spindles, for example.

The chisel point will incise clear lines which are easier to see and more accurate than pencil marks. Always keep the toolrest close to the work and just below the centre line.

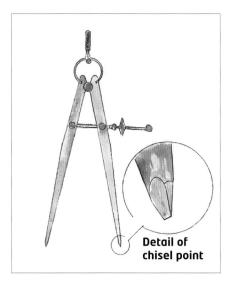

Detail of chisel point

390 Transferring measurements

A board mounted on the lathe to hold a paper pattern helps to speed up the transfer of measurements. Use a combination square on the back edge of the board to transfer the points from the pattern to the turning. The pattern's centre line, the far edge of the board and the line between lathe centres must all be parallel.

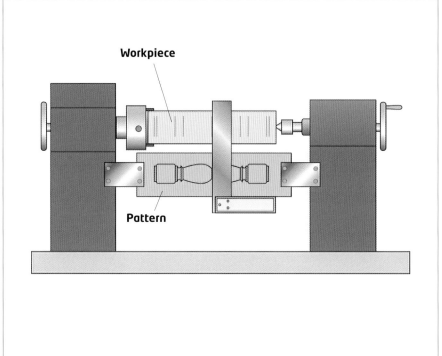

Workpiece

Pattern

391 Accurate repeats

If you regularly make repeat items of the same size – such as collets for chuck jaws – keep several pairs of callipers, set to your usual sizes. This saves having to set your callipers each time.

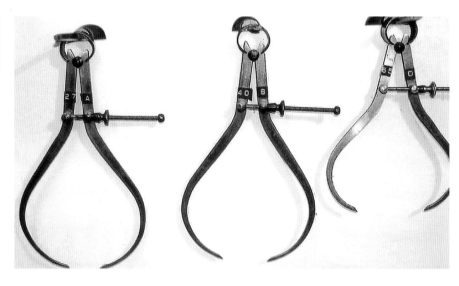

Marking and measuring

Better callipers

All commercially available callipers are produced with angular measuring tips. Though these may provide accurate measurements, they invariably mark the wood, and do not glide smoothly along the surface. If one side is already turned to a finish – as is often the case when making bowls or hollow forms – having to go back and smooth it again is very annoying.

The skin-measuring callipers used by doctors and veterinary surgeons are ideal for woodturning. The ends of both legs are bulbous, so as not to hurt the patient – so they will not hurt the wood either – and there is a scale providing an accurate measure of the gap in millimetres. Medical callipers are a little on the small side for most woodturning purposes, but it would not be too difficult to scale them up to suit most requirements; perhaps one of the tool manufacturers might be interested in taking up this suggestion.

Alternatively, attach a wooden, rubber or plastic ball to each end of your standard callipers.

Bulbous-ended skin callipers protect the wood...

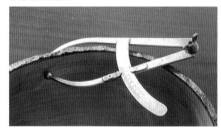

...and do not mark finished surfaces

Centre finder

This device ensures accurate and easy marking of the centre on the end of any square or round piece of wood. It is much less tedious than using a ruler to draw crossing lines. It can be made to suit any size of stock; a capacity of 3in (75mm) is particularly useful.

Make four identical pieces, say ½in (13mm) in section, with halving joints at the ends. Glue these together and check that the diagonals are equal. Add a ⅛in (3mm) strip on top, corner to corner. If you put the wood to be marked inside the corner and draw along the strip, move the wood through 90° and repeat, then the crossing of the two lines must be central.

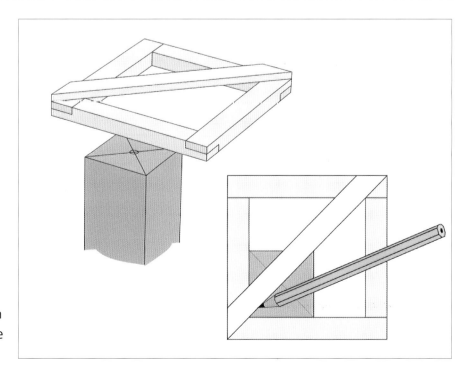

Woodturning tips

394 | Measuring base thickness

This device makes it much easier to measure the wall thickness at the base of a deep hollow form.

You will need:

- A piece of ¼in or ⅜in (6 or 10mm) ply, cut to shape as indicated
- A piece of ¼in (6mm) rod
- A piece of tube with a slightly bigger inside diameter than the rod – you could drill a suitable clearance hole in a piece of ½in (12mm) dowelling.

Method

Cut the plywood as shown. Hot-glue the tube to the top section of the cutout as indicated. Insert the measuring rod and let it rest on the bottom of the cutout.

Now mark the rod where it protrudes from the top part of the tube. From that mark, and working downwards, make further marks at, say, ¹⁄₁₆in or 1mm intervals, up to the maximum thickness you want to measure.

In use, the wood thickness is indicated accurately by the measurement that shows above the top of the tube. The device is versatile because you can make it to any size, and can insert and remove the rod when the gadget is in place.

You could refine the device by making it extendible, and by colour-coding the extension and measuring rod to correspond, but the example shown, which is 17¾in (450mm) long, has proved very satisfactory. Of course, you can still measure the smallest of hollow forms, as the top measure is always constant.

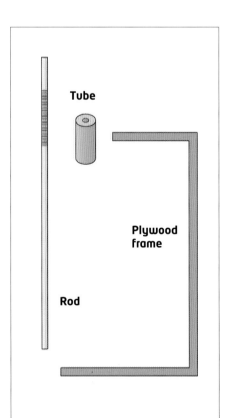

Tube

Plywood
frame

Rod

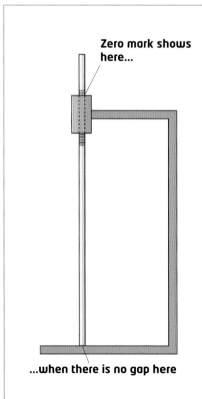

Zero mark shows
here...

...when there is no gap here

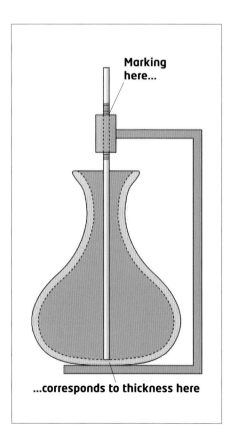

Marking
here...

...corresponds to thickness here

395 Measuring wall thickness

When making long-necked hollow vessels, it can be difficult to judge the wall thickness at the top, as double-ended callipers will not reach, and shining a light through the wood only works on certain woods.

One method is to bend a piece of strong wire as shown, and cut a piece of dowel to fit accurately between the ends of the wire. The amount by which the dowel overlaps the wire is the wall thickness.

396 Dowel gauge

When you turn dowels at the tailstock end, you can use a hole in the job, or drill one in scrap wood, to test the size. If the dowel part has to come at the headstock end, try this simple gauge, which has three commonly used hole sizes, divided between two hinged strips. It is made by cramping the pieces together and drilling through the meeting edges.

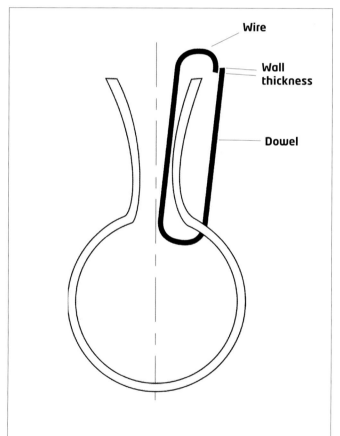

Wire

Wall thickness

Dowel

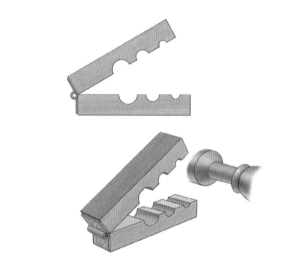

397 Tile recess gauge

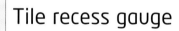

This time-saving gauge was designed to measure the recess for 6in (150mm) diameter ceramic tiles fitted in a circular frame. It ensures that the recess is level and of the required diameter. Make it an easy fit, to allow for any future shrinkage of the timber.

Stock preparation

398 Sawing round stock

Here is a method of holding round material safely
when cutting with a bandsaw.

Between-centres turnings can be difficult to cut
square or hold steady. Wooden blocks don't hold the
work securely, and you would need different sizes;
but this jig adjusts to cover a wide range of sizes.

Clamp together two 1in (25mm) pieces of angle iron
cut to 8in (203mm) long, and drill a hole ³⁄₈in (10mm)
in diameter near each end.

Braze or weld an extension piece about 1in (25mm)
wide on to the top of each piece of angle iron, and
drill two small holes in each of the extensions to take
woodscrews. Cut two pieces of wood to fit between the
metal jaws, with slots or notches cut in them to clear
the threaded rods. Cut two pieces of ³⁄₈in (10mm)
threaded rod 7½in (190mm) long.

Insert the two lengths of threaded rod into the holes
in one of the angle irons, and braze securely in place.
Then place the first wooden piece over the threaded
rod and securely screw to the metal side. Put on a pair
of nuts, followed by the washers. Securely screw the
second wooden piece to the second angle iron. Slide this
on the threaded rods, followed by another pair of
washers and nuts.

By adjusting the nuts, the blocks can be opened or
shut to suit the size of the workpiece and then locked
into place. The material just sits between the wooden
jaws, which do not need to be tightened onto it. Using
a small bandsaw, small to medium-sized branches or
dowels can be cut quite safely, without jamming.

A garage or small engineering workshop should be
able to make up the metal sides if you do not have the
facilities to do this yourself.

Above: **An ingenious method of holding round work**

Right and below:
**An end of an old
broomstick shows
how thin the cuts
can be. The dowel
is held in place by
hand pressure
only, and won't
jam the saw
while cutting**

Stock preparation

Saw slices in safety

Here's a safe method of cutting slices of branch wood or banksia nuts on the bandsaw to make coasters.

Cut a hard piece of wood, such as oak or beech, about 8in (200mm) long, and plane it so that it slides easily, without side play, in the mitre-fence groove of your bandsaw table. Fit it flush with the table surface or slightly below.

To this, fix a piece of thin plywood approximately 6 x 5in (150 x 125mm), so that it can slide just clear of the saw blade. Then nail two battens at right angles to the slide groove and exactly parallel to each other at approximately 3in (75mm) apart, to act as guides.

Cut pieces of thin scrap plywood about 12in (305mm) long so that they slide between the guides without any play. Your piece of branch wood or banksia is then fixed to this with the help of the hot-melt glue gun at several points along the plywood strip. Be sure to fix the tail end of a banksia nut, as illustrated, to stop it rocking on the final few cuts.

Make a truing cut across the end of your stock, then set the bandsaw fence; I set mine for ¼in (6mm) slices. Now you can cut all the slices to exactly the same thickness, with no risk of twisting, jamming or having to put your fingers anywhere near the blade.

Use hot-melt glue to fix the banksia nut to the plywood

Make sure the nut doesn't rock by gluing its tail end to a purpose-made end block

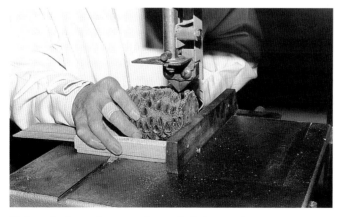
Make a truing cut across the end of the stock

All the slices have been cut in safety

Turning technique

400   Cutting large blanks accurately

When turning large pieces on a swivel-head lathe, the size of the work is not limited by the height over the bed, but by the physics of rotating objects.

Most bowl blanks seem to have been cut by eye and are not as round as they ought to be. You can turn them to a cylinder while putting up with a few seconds of vibration during the initial cuts – which is not advisable, as the noise is alarming and there is no telling what it is doing to the bearings of your lathe – or you can simply avoid using larger sizes because of the vibration problem.

The answer is very simple: a piece of board with a nail right through it and a channel to fit the bandsaw blade. Having decided which side is to be the top, drill a hole in the centre of the blank, just wide and deep enough to fit the nail. Clamp the jig to the bandsaw table, locating the nail at the desired distance from the blade, and start cutting at the part of the circumference which is closest to the centre. Then just turn the piece on its axis as you cut.

It is quite possible simply to nail a disc to the top of the blank and cut round it by eye, but the method described here is more sure, and will allow bigger pieces to be turned because the result is more even. The largest piece turned so far by this method was a sycamore offcut 15in (380mm) in diameter. There was hardly a wobble, and larger sizes would surely be possible.

There will of course be a limit to the size you can manage on any given lathe, and this will probably be determined by the natural variations in the tree around the circumference of the blank; but this method allows you to deal with larger sizes than would otherwise be advisable.

401   Hollowing

When hollowing through a restricted opening, make the hole through which you work at least ³⁄₁₆in (4mm) wider than the hollowing tool you are using. This will allow you just enough clearance to manipulate the tool – although, of course, working through a much larger hole is easier still.

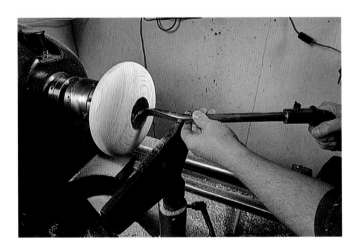

402 Balancing odd shapes

To find the centre of balance of an odd-shaped piece, use this simple centre finder. It is made from a block of wood 2in (50mm) thick, and a 10in (255mm) length of ½in (13mm) dowel. Drill a ½in (13mm) hole in the block, then glue in the dowel and cut it flush underneath.

Place the workpiece on top of the dowel, then move and adjust it until it is perfectly balanced. It is balanced when it sits atop the dowel without any other support. Then hold it steady while you mark around the dowel with a pencil.

Now you can drill or centre your faceplate over the pencil mark. Once on the lathe, even odd-shaped pieces turn smoothly.

At first it might sound time-consuming to find the balance point by trial and error, but with a little practice and a good eye you can do it in less than a minute.

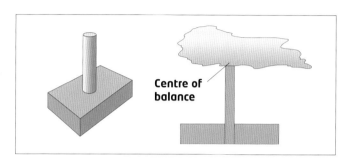

Centre of balance

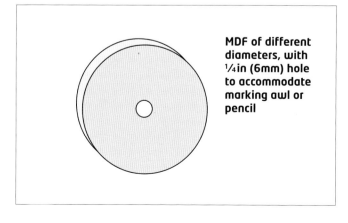

Right: **Finishing off a piece of burr that was centre-balanced**

403 Thin-walled turnings

On thin-walled work, use freshly sharpened tools and take gentle cuts. Pushing the tool hard against the wood will result in unnecessary flexing of the walls, and could ruin the work. Once the initial bulk has been removed inside, work down in stages, from the rim towards the base, in sections of about 1–2in (25–50mm). Turn each section to its finished thickness and sand, then move to the next section. This will mean that if there is movement, the area that is likely to move will already have been completed, so will cause no problem. Apply a finish when all the turning is complete.

404 Finding the centre

Stock for natural-edge work can sometimes be hard to centre. A selection of MDF discs will help. They range from 2 to 10in (50–255mm), each with a central hole. Choose one slightly smaller than the blank, and use this to get a rough centre. With practice, it's surprisingly quick and accurate.

MDF of different diameters, with ¼in (6mm) hole to accommodate marking awl or pencil

Woodturning tips

405 Finishing to thickness

When making a three-footed leaf-shaped bowl, involving several reverse mountings, the final task was to remove the dovetail mounting on the base and finish the bowl wall to thickness – from the outside, without access to callipers. Here is an easy and accurate method.

Finish and sand the interior of the bowl and the outer skirt down to the base, then proceed as follows:

1 With the piece off the lathe, make three evenly spaced pencil marks on the underside of the bowl section, one in the centre of the dovetail mounting and the other two along the curve of the bowl bottom.

2 Measure the thickness at these points with wide-mouth callipers, and write the measurements beside the pencil marks. Decide on the wall thickness you require, and subtract this amount from each of the measurements you have marked. The resulting figures give the thickness which needs to be removed. Drill small holes to the appropriate depth at each of the three points, using a depth stop or masking tape on the drill bit.

3 Remount the piece using Cole jaws or a jam-chuck, and carefully turn away the bowl base until the drill holes just disappear.

4 Take a thin final cut in a smooth curve across the entire bowl bottom and sand to a finish. The result will be a nice, even wall thickness.

Right: **A summary of the stages involved in turning the bowl**

Below: **Three holes are drilled to correct depth for wall thickness**

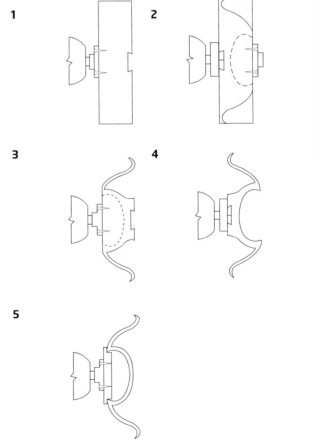

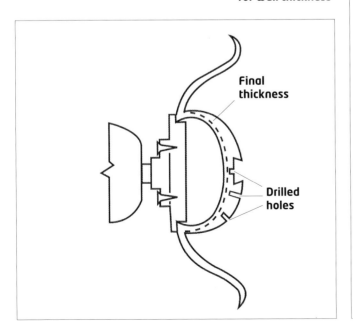

Final thickness

Drilled holes

Reducing waste

Woodturners are well known for converting 70% of a beautiful piece of wood into shavings on the floor; this method helps to reduce such waste.

Turn the wood to a cylinder, face off the ends and hold the piece in a three- or four-jaw self-centring chuck on the headstock. Remove the pilot drill from a holesaw and mount the holesaw and arbor in a Jacobs chuck in the tailstock.

Set the lathe to its lowest speed and slowly feed the holesaw into the blank, withdrawing frequently to clear the waste. Continue cutting to almost the full depth of the holesaw, then turn the blank around in the chuck and continue from the other end until the central core is freed. This can be redrilled with a smaller holesaw. Try a 1½in (38mm) holesaw on a 2in (50mm) cylinder, and a 2½in (64mm) saw on a 3in (75mm) cylinder. This provides an allowance for cleaning up the inside of the cylinder. There is a limitation on the length of the hollow cylinder, due to the length of the holesaw.

These hollow cylinders can be used to create boxes by adding a top and bottom, possibly from a different wood to provide a contrast. You could also cut rings from the cylinder and use these to ornament your work, or fix various-sized cylinders together to make a vase – it saves all that deep hollowing. The picture shows a set of three boxes made from a 3in (75mm) cube of wood. The technique can be used for other materials, such as polyester resin rod and possibly other plastics.

Next time you spend good money on a nice piece of timber, think twice before throwing most of it away.

Recycling offcuts

When turning a bowl, the outside bottom of the blank is often wasted. Try turning off one or two picture or mirror frames first.

Mark up an area about ⅞in (22mm) wide by ⅞in deep. Turn the inside waste wood away to give clearance for working. Then put in your rebate to take glass and backing.

Part off both marks and use the bowl blank as a holding chuck. Reverse the frame and finish as required.

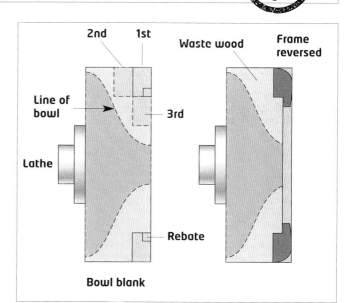

408 | Making wooden eggs

Nicely formed and finished eggs are very popular at craft fairs, and it is useful to be able to knock out a batch quickly and efficiently. One of the difficulties is to find a simple and reliable rechucking system; the usual wooden jam-chuck is not really satisfactory.

The solution lies in a plastic plumbing fitting: a 1⁹⁄₁₆in (40mm) expansion drainpipe connector, to be precise. This is fitted with a wooden plug turned to suit the jaws of your scroll chuck. With the device installed in the lathe, it is a simple operation to pop the tapered end of a part-finished egg into the rubber gasket to obtain a secure and damage-free hold.

After insertion, rotate the lathe by hand and adjust as necessary to centre, using thumb and forefinger. For finishing, use a ¹⁄₁₆in (1.5mm) parting tool to obtain the final shape, then sand and apply finish. The egg can then be popped out by hand, with the chucked part still in pristine condition.

It is, of course, important that the egg diameter is within the capacity of the fitting; for the fitting shown, an ideal size is 2⁵⁄₈in (67mm) long by 1³⁄₄in (44mm) diameter, although the diameter can go down to about 1²¹⁄₃₂in (42mm) with no problem.

Please note that the chuck shown here will only accept the tapered end of the egg, so this must always be finished first.

Turning procedure

Here is the general method for making eggs from yew branch wood. Start by cutting blanks to approximately 7in (175mm) long, which is enough to make two eggs. Then turn these between centres to a cylinder of 1³⁄₄in (45mm) diameter. Mount the cylinder in chuck jaws and bring up the tailstock centre. Turn the two eggs to shape after defining their length with a parting tool. Leave a ³⁄₈in (10mm) nib at the tailstock end to avoid any bruised wood, and leave a minimum ½in (12mm) spigot between the eggs. Always work with the tapered end of the egg toward the tailstock.

With shaping completed, withdraw the tailstock and carefully cut away the remaining nib using a freshly sharpened fine parting tool. Complete sanding and finishing before parting off at the rounded end, using the same tool. Finish the second egg in the same way. Both eggs are now ready to be rechucked as described.

Egg with expansion pipe fitting

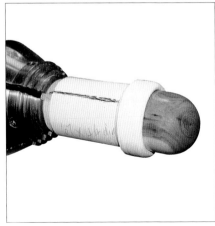

Home-made chuck in use

Egg inserted into expansion fitting; note the dovetailed wooden plug glued into the other end

Turning technique

409 Segmented turning for beginners

If you don't have a bandsaw, the easiest way to rough out bowl blanks from square pieces of wood is by cutting off the corners using a mitre saw. Don't throw away the triangular 'waste' pieces from the corners, because they can be glued together and turned to make a low pedestal. Make sure the grain in each piece runs as shown in the diagram, so that the tool is always cutting 'uphill' and will not dig in.

The best way to align the grain in each of the four segments

rotation

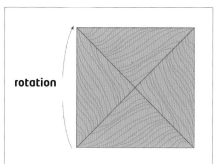

410 Chasing threads

Here are two tips that make it possible to chase threads in softer woods. The first tip concerns the grinding of the external chaser.

These tools are normally used with the handle angled up, while the teeth cut either at or just below lathe-centre height. The chaser seems to cut best when held this way. The disadvantage is that, when lifting the handle up, the teeth of the chaser are angled away from the wood. The result is less guidance of the chaser in the early stages of cutting the thread, meaning less grip from the teeth.

The solution is to grind off the top of the chaser to produce a negative rake angle. Ground this way, the chaser can be held horizontally to achieve the best cutting angle and at the same time enable more grip from the teeth.

The second tip is to use oil as a lubricant while cutting the thread. To prevent crests crumbling, some turners use wax or superglue, but far better results can be got from ordinary vegetable cooking oil – sunflower oil, to be precise. This penetrates deep into the wood, does not get sticky, dries fast and does not smell. During chasing, apply the oil regularly with a piece of kitchen towel. As a rule, the softer the wood, the more often the oil needs to be applied – sometimes as frequently as every two or three chases.

Good-quality pear is an excellent wood to start with, but good threads can also be achieved in lilac, apple, box elder, yew, birch, robinia and laburnum. The mushroom box in the photograph is made of yew, and the acorn boxes of holly, pear, cherry and spalted laburnum. The small acorn box shown open has a 30tpi thread made with home-made chasers.

Woodturning tips

411   Curtain-rail toolrest

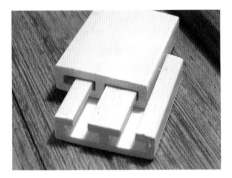

Note how the rails link nicely

The rails are incorporated into a jig

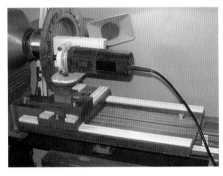

Ready to rout: the complete set-up

The common type of curtain rail shown here has a cross-section such that one piece will, when reversed, fit inside another to form a pretty good guide rail.

This can be used to make a sliding jig that enables a router to be mounted in a commercial drilling jig to carry out decorative faceplate and spindle work.

As the pictures show, the jig replaces the lathe toolrest, and features a crosshead like that of a metalworking lathe. For spindle turning it can be slid along the work with the crosshead locked, while for faceplate work it can be slid across with the longitudinal slide locked. Note in the right-hand picture that rotating the drilling jig in the

toolpost can also change the angle of attack. The router can, of course, be replaced with a power drill for basic hole-drilling jobs.

The device works well, but particular attention should be paid to the positioning and fixing of the guide rails, both to minimize any play and to give a good, parallel movement of the router or drill.

412   Coloured inlays

Here is a new suggestion for adding colouring to decorative inlays.

Carpenters use a snap line with string when they need to mark a straight line. In general they tend to use a blue chalk to mark their lines. This chalk, supplied as a very fine powder, mixes well with epoxy resin to make a coloured filling for grooves and recesses. It has an excellent colour and costs very little.

It also comes in black, white, red, orange and yellow, and, with a little mixing of different chalks, even more colours can be made. This could be an alternative to the technique of grinding up pastel sticks.

413 Mock-silver inlays

As an alternative to usings coins, bolections or veneers, lidded boxes can be decorated with inlays of pipe solder. This is an alloy used in the plumbing trade, and has a melting point of 78°C (172°F).

To inlay a flat lid, turn the top to the required shape, then, using a sharp parting tool, cut grooves and recesses at the design points. The grooves should be ⅛in (3mm) deep and undercut in a dovetail shape.

To inlay around the circumference of a turning, the area above the inlay is first turned to the finished diameter, leaving the lower part oversize. A groove is then cut at an angle, using the parting tool, to form a reservoir for the molten alloy.

Next, place a piece of alloy in a small ladle and melt it with a torch flame, then pour the liquid alloy into the cavities. As the alloy has such a low melting point, there is no danger of its hardening before the grooves are filled.

After cooling, the lid or box is returned to the lathe and finished with a scraper to the final shape. Sand and finish as normal. Pewter or dentists' amalgam can also be used, although these cost more.

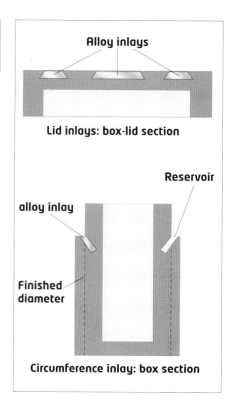

Alloy inlays

Lid inlays: box-lid section

Reservoir

alloy inlay

Finished diameter

Circumference inlay: box section

414 Moulding drawer pulls

The drawer knobs for this jewellery chest are moulded from the same material as the inlay on the top. Inlace is a quick-drying and hard-setting substance available from specialist turners' suppliers.

Divide a section of scrap wood lengthways, face the joint, and then clamp back together. Screw a suitable section of ply or MDF, the same depth as the drawer front, on edge above the joint. Other dimensions are not critical, so long as there is room to access the moulds on both sides. Next, drill a clearance hole for each of the knob fixing screws through the ply and into the scrap, centred on the joint.

Remove the ply and, using the small holes as a guide, drill oversized holes to suit the eventual mouldings.

Place the screws through the ply, add a captive nut to each one, leaving a few threads protruding, and reattach the ply, with the screws dangling *in situ*. Check your measurements at this stage, and make a spare in case of errors.

Overfill the moulds with resin and, when hard, remove the screws and the ply – but not the clamp – and face off the excess resin. After removing the clamp and splitting the scrap, the knobs can be turned to shape on a beheaded screw held in a drill chuck.

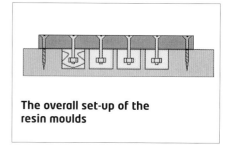

The overall set-up of the resin moulds

Abrasives and finishing

415 Make your own abrasive discs

We all try to save money wherever possible, and one area where considerable savings can be made is when buying abrasives. The price of Velcro-backed discs can be halved if you are prepared to cut them from the sheet yourself.

Hole or wad punches of the size required are very expensive, but here is a way to make your own for next to nothing. What you will need is a holesaw, preferably well used and past its best – but unless you are an electrician or plumber, it's unlikely that you will have one the right size. Fortunately, even if you need to buy the holesaw new, you can still make a 2in or 2³⁄₄in (50 or 70mm) punch for a very reasonable sum.

The first job is to turn a handle: ash or beech is ideal, but any suitable timber will do. The dimensions shown in the diagrams are approximate and can be varied. Fix the holesaw to the handle using a suitable screw and washer. Ensure that the end of the handle is slightly concave or recessed, so that the force of the mallet or hammer blow is directed down the wall of the punch. The spigot does not need to be a tight fit, and should be just less than the thickness of the backplate, to allow the bolt to seat.

With the holesaw securely fixed to the handle, carefully grind away the teeth to leave a flat edge, then grind a bevel at about 15°, and it's complete. Don't try to grind the chamfer before removing the teeth.

Present the holesaw to the grinder at 90° first to remove the teeth all around, and only then proceed to grind the bevel. It is much easier and safer to do this after the holesaw has been fitted to the handle.

Used and worn-out holesaws of any size can be brought back to life and turned into washer or veneer cutters using the same method.

Even the offcuts from the handle need not go to waste: keep them to use – with locking forceps – for sanding inside small boxes.

416 Sanding speed

To allow the abrasive to cut, it is best to use a slow speed when sanding, so set the lathe to about 500-700rpm tops. The abrasive won't wear out so quickly, and the heat generated through friction will be greatly cut down.

417 Sanding in tight corners

With standard cloth-backed abrasives, used in the normal manner, it can be very difficult to get a good finish in awkward areas, such as tightly angled undercuts beneath bowl rims, or in areas of carved or shaped detailing. Using abrasive fixed to or wrapped around bits of wood or plastic may give limited success, but it's still a frustrating business.

The method shown in the drawing is self-explanatory, and should be applicable to any of the well-known brands in use. Normal PVA adhesive gives good results.

The most important thing is that, after gluing and folding, the piece must be cramped very firmly in a vice between two pieces of scrap MDF; a full day may be needed for the glue to set hard. This imparts a stiff springiness in the abrasive which really lasts.

These strips can be used on turnings under power on the lathe, and also for static hand-sanding. They last around six months, and are easily cleaned with an eraser or a nailbrush. They are a pleasure to use, and very effective.

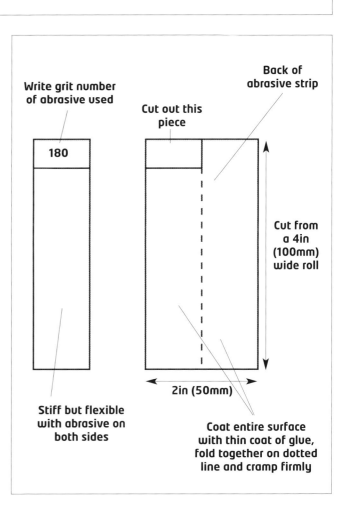

Write grit number of abrasive used

180

Stiff but flexible with abrasive on both sides

Cut out this piece

Back of abrasive strip

Cut from a 4in (100mm) wide roll

2in (50mm)

Coat entire surface with thin coat of glue, fold together on dotted line and cramp firmly

418 Sanding with water

Try using water as a sanding lubricant – provided it cannot get into the electrics of your lathe. Wet the work, then sand, working through the grits. Allow the work to dry off, then rub over the whole thing with very fine abrasive before applying the finish of your choice. This method is great when turning wet woods.

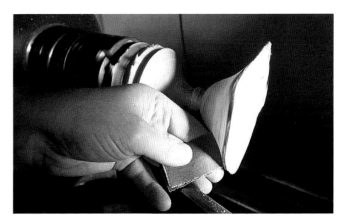

Woodturning tips

419 Sandpaper store

If sanding is an important part of your woodturning, you can spend a lot of time searching for the next piece of sandpaper – and when you find it, it may not be in a usable state. This system began as a way to organize the assorted sizes of sandpaper. Each grit is separated from each other with a file of hardboard, with an extended tab marking the grit, so each sheet of sandpaper stays flat and clean.

The next part of the system is to bring the sandpaper to the lathe in a form that is ready to use. The detachable caddy holds a supply of paper already cut into ⅛-size sheets. It fits inside the main storage box, on top of the uppermost tray. Now, when sanding, you can bring the caddy to sit beside the lathe. As you finish with each grit, put the still-good piece into its cubby-hole and go on to the next.

The caddy is made from ⅛in (3mm) hardboard and covered on the outside with some leftover plastic laminate. The partitions between sizes are simply two layers of laminate, back to back. A comfortable handle of laminated softwood makes it function almost like a basket.

Now the sanding is almost something to enjoy. At least everything is at hand.

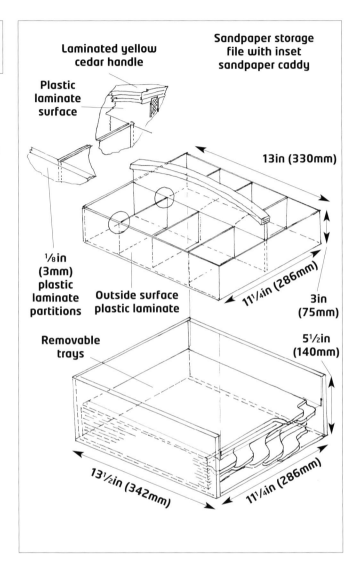

Laminated yellow cedar handle

Sandpaper storage file with inset sandpaper caddy

Plastic laminate surface

13in (330mm)

⅛in (3mm) plastic laminate partitions

Outside surface plastic laminate

11¼in (286mm)

3in (75mm)

Removable trays

5½in (140mm)

13½in (342mm)

11¼in (286mm)

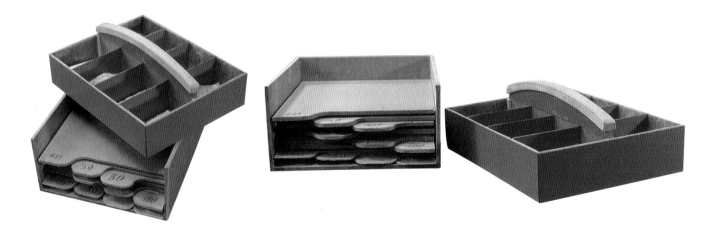

420 Sanding edges

If you are trying to achieve a straight edge on a project and are worried about radiusing off the edge of the profile during sanding, wrap the abrasive around a wooden block. This will ensure that the sanding edge is flat. You should also find it easier to maintain and sand the flat surface.

421 Truing square edges

If you do not have a belt sander to tidy up the square edges on square-edge projects, use spray-mount to glue a strip of abrasive onto your workbench, or to a scrap of ply or MDF. Then, holding the work in your hands, rub it back and forth until the edges are even. You must remember to keep the bowl perpendicular as you do so.

422 Abrasive on a ring

Many turners use strips of abrasive held in spring paper clips, and these appear to work reasonably well. An alernative is to cut strips of half or quarter the width of the abrasive sheet, and hold them in a split ring or on a loop of string.

The hole is punched using an ordinary paper punch. The most difficult part is fixing the sheets onto the ring. They are placed in sequence, coarsest to finest, and are therefore always in the correct order when required.

The ring provides a means of hanging the abrasive on a hook or nail, thus eliminating the need to dig into piles of shavings to find it.

Also, if one or more of the strips wears out sooner than the others, it is not too difficult to insert a fresh strip in the correct place on the ring.

423 Keeping paper dry

On damp days during the winter months it can be difficult to keep sandpaper and Velcro pads dry, especially if your workshop is a garden shed. The solution is to make an MDF box and lid, on top of which is a tin housing for a light-bulb holder. Keep the bulk of your sandpaper in the house, only removing enough for a day's work, and keep this in the box until you need it. The warmth of the bulb – 40W is quite adequate – keeps it nice and dry all day.

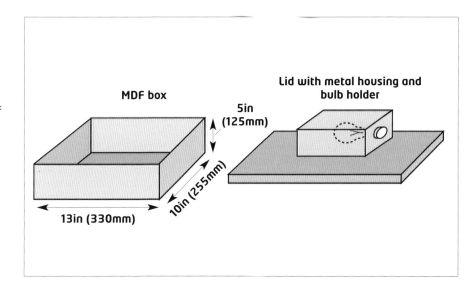

MDF box

Lid with metal housing and bulb holder

5in (125mm)

10in (255mm)

13in (330mm)

Woodturning tips

424 | Making abrasives last longer

Belts for belt sanders can clog up surprisingly quickly, so an abrasive-belt cleaner is a good investment.

Moreoever, if a commercial belt cleaner can lengthen the effectiveness and life of a sanding belt, then in principle it should be possible to achieve the same with any other abrasive format – and indeed you can. Whether using a hand-held or power disc, you can reduce the amount of abrasives you are currently using by something like a factor of four.

First, cut your abrasive-belt cleaner into three lengths: 2in (50mm) long for the fixed cleaner; 3in (75mm) long for the rotary cleaner; and 3¼in (85mm) for use on the belt sander, disc sander or power sander – these can be used for finishing the bases of small vessels and 'weed pots'.

Fixed cleaner

The fixed cleaner is used to clean power-sander discs. Mount a length of cleaner in a convenient place – such as the underside of a shelf adjacent to the lathe – and when you need to clean a disc, simply hold the rotating disc against the cleaner for a few seconds.

Rotary cleaner

The rotary cleaner is for cleaning your normal finishing abrasives. First drill a suitable hole through the 3in (75mm) length of cleaner. A good way of doing this is to hold it in a chuck with O'Donnell jaws, and, at a relatively slow speed, carefully drill a ½in (12mm) hole. You will need to take this slowly, and retract the drill regularly to clear the tacky swarf that is produced. Now mount the drilled section on a suitable bolt, such as a ½in x 5in (M12 x 130mm) coach bolt.

Again you can mount this in the lathe chuck and turn it into a cylinder using a spindle gouge; although you can turn this material with ordinary tools, do not expect any shavings to fly. The waste will in fact stick, so you need to stop the lathe every two or three passes to remove the debris.

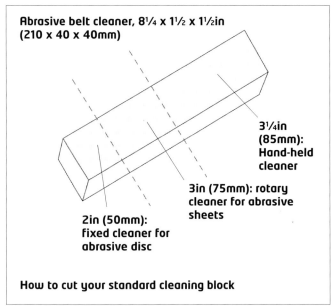

Abrasive belt cleaner, 8¼ x 1½ x 1½in (210 x 40 x 40mm)

3¼in (85mm): Hand-held cleaner

3in (75mm): rotary cleaner for abrasive sheets

2in (50mm): fixed cleaner for abrasive disc

How to cut your standard cleaning block

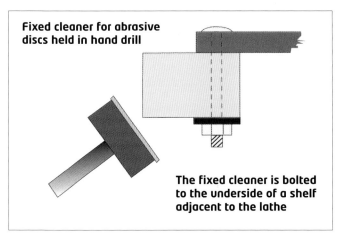

Fixed cleaner for abrasive discs held in hand drill

The fixed cleaner is bolted to the underside of a shelf adjacent to the lathe

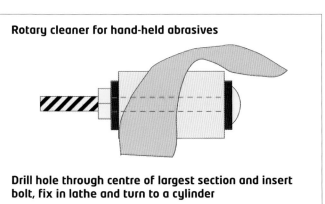

Rotary cleaner for hand-held abrasives

Drill hole through centre of largest section and insert bolt, fix in lathe and turn to a cylinder

Abrasives and finishing

Near right: **Abrasive disc prior to cleaning**

Centre: **Same disc after cleaning**

Far right: **Hand-held abrasives ready for cleaning**

To clean your pieces of hand-held abrasive, rotate the cylinder at a relatively slow speed, and hold the abrasive against the cylinder at about the 7 o'clock position, as if you were sanding a spindle.

It takes less than an hour to make these two items, and they will pay for themselves in no time, as abrasives which would have been discarded will now remain effective up to four times longer.

425	## Home-made drum sander

Here are the details of a simply constructed drum sander. All that is required is a length of polystyrene pipe insulation from your local DIY store.

The insulation is supplied with a slit running along its length, is available in various diameters, and can be easily cut with a sharp knife. For sandpaper 4½in (115mm) wide, a 5½in (140mm) length is required. A dowel is turned from scrap wood, so as to form a tight fit when inserted into the internal bore of the drum. Take just enough sandpaper so that it can be wrapped tightly around the drum body before the ends are tucked into the lengthwise slot.

The sides are glued or taped to the drum so as to be secure during use when revolved between centres. The materials for this technique are very inexpensive, so sanding drums can be made in various diameters and lengths. They can also be adapted for mounting in wood or drill chucks as required.

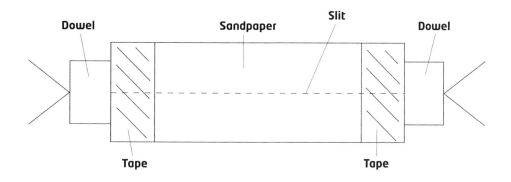

Woodturning tips

 Easier high-speed rotary sanding

When using an electric drill with a rubber sanding disc, or an angle grinder with a 4in (100mm) sanding pad, the weight of the machine makes for an awkward, two-handed job.

Drill a 1in (25mm) hole in the end of an electric motor's shaft, to take a 40in (1m) long flexible drive. Tap a thread for a grub screw to tighten the inner cable, and make a bracket to hold the flanged end of the outer flex. On the other end, use the right-angle drive from an old brush cutter. After fitting the outer flex to one end, build up the inner cable with a bronze brazing alloy, then file it square to fit the square hole in the right-angle drive unit. Drill and tap a ¼in (M6) female thread to the other end of the angle drive.

Rubber sanding discs of 1, 2, 3 and 5in (25, 50, 75 and 125mm), with ¼in (6mm) shafts, male thread, can be spun on and off quickly; Velcro can also be used for fast changing.

This device is a pleasure to use, being very light, and operable with one hand. It gives flexibility of wrist movement which makes it easy to control when sanding convex or concave shapes.

The ½hp motor shown here is from a small, double-ended grinder. A rubber handle allows it to be moved around, or it could be hung overhead. Make sure you get the direction of rotation right!

427 Simple rotary sander

The following tool, constructed from available odds and ends, was devised to sand the surface of a hole through an abstract carving. You need a 4in (100mm) length of mild-steel rod cut from a ½in (12.5mm) diameter bolt, a 4in (100mm) length of ½in (12.5mm) plastic garden hose – the type with a double-helix reinforcement is ideal – abrasive paper or cloth, and a tube of cellulose acetate or other quick-drying adhesive.

The steel rod serves as an arbor to be fitted in the chuck of a power drill. Over this is pushed the first 2in (50mm) of the plastic hose, leaving 2in unsupported. A piece of abrasive sheet cut to a suitable size is then wrapped tightly round the hose with a ³⁄₁₆in (5mm) overlap and secured with a few spots of adhesive; make sure that the overlap is not counter to the direction of rotation. Sanding is best carried out using the unsupported portion of the hose, which is sufficiently flexible to prevent the tool juddering, but stiff enough to enable adequate pressure to be applied.

A number of lengths of hose covered with different grades of abrasive sheet can be made up and quickly interchanged on the arbor to produce a progressively finer finish. The hose should normally be a tight fit on the arbor, but any slippage can be prevented with a jubilee clip around the end nearest the drill chuck.

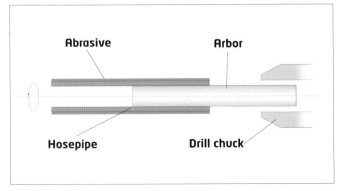

Abrasive   Arbor

Hosepipe   Drill chuck

Abrasives and finishing

428 Save time on polishing

After parting off items from the lathe, it is usually necessary to remove the chuck and fit a Morse-taper polishing mop adapter and mop before bringing up the tailstock for support to finish and polish the parted-off ends of the work. This takes time, so this polishing-mop adapter was devised which takes seconds to fit and remove, without taking the chuck from the lathe. It could easily be adapted to fit a chuck other than the one shown.

The upper photo shows the adapter fitted with an 8 x 1in (200 x 25mm) mop. Note the chamfer and recess for the jaws to lock into.

The bottom right photo shows the whole thing fitted into the lathe jaws. It also shows the retaining washer and ½in (12mm) bolt used to secure the mop to the adapter.

The adapter is made from a section of 2¾in (70mm) diameter mild-steel round bar turned on the metal lathe. The centre is drilled and tapped to accept the ½in (12mm) bolt used to hold the mop in place. The retaining washer is parted off from the end of the adapter before final finishing and drilled out to to provide a little clearance for the unthreaded section of the retaining bolt to pass through. Apply some adhesive to the retaining bolt to ensure that the mop stays in place.

Polishing on the lathe is preferable to using a grinder, because you can control the speed. It also brings the work to an ideal height.

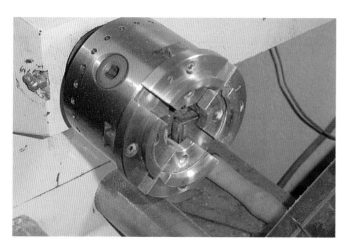

Left: **The adapter fitted with an 8 x 1in (200 x 25mm) mop**

Note the internal curve and recess of the chuck jaws into which the adapter will fit

The whole set-up fitted into the chuck jaws and installed on the lathe

Woodturning tips

429 Sanding discs

Power-sanding discs will sometimes fly off and disappear when the hook-and-loop material loses its grip. There are also times when the appropriate grade of grit is not to hand when you need it. This method allows you to use any grade of grit, and to sand away without risk of the disc breaking free.

By using strips of cloth-backed abrasive the same width as the disc diameter and in length around three times the disc diameter, the sanding pad can be 'clothed' in a strip of abrasive which is folded down the sides of the pad and held in place with an elastic band. To make the abrasive strip conform to the shape of the pad, four small cuts can be made as shown – best not to use good scissors for this.

This method only works on parallel-sided pads. When the area of abrasive becomes worn, the unused ends of the abrasive strip are still useful for hand-sanding. The strip only needs tearing to size, and it is even more convenient if you use rolls in 2in (50mm) width for the most popular 2in pads.

Cloth-backed abrasive used in this way lasts longer than velour-backed discs; but when you do still wish to use a velour disc on the pad, it will work better because the hook surface has had less wear.

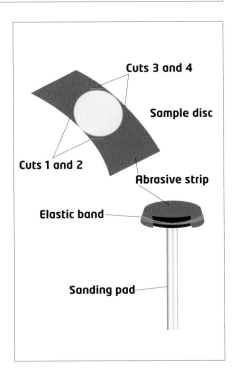

Cuts 3 and 4
Sample disc
Cuts 1 and 2
Abrasive strip
Elastic band
Sanding pad

430 Power-sander extension shaft

With standard power-sanding attachments the shaft tends to be very stubby, leaving no clearance between sander and drill chuck. This severely limits the versatility of the combination.

Extension shafts for flatbits are available from most DIY stores. They consist of a 12in (300mm) steel shaft, ¼in (6mm) in diameter, with a flared end equipped with two Allen screws to take the shaft of a bit. Not only will this extension shaft fit a sanding disc, but it will also take various sanding-disc attachments, including the

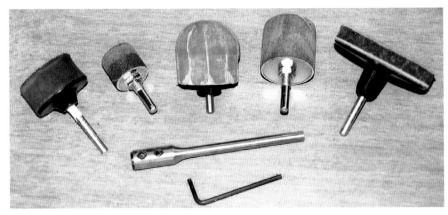

An array of sanding-disc attachments

pneumatic ball-type bowl sander. Power-sanding versatility is increased tenfold. The Kirjes ball-type pneumatic sander is shown

working on the inside of a jagged natural-edge vase – the sort that tends to be especially vicious to unprotected fingers. With the extension shaft in place, however, the sander immediately becomes much more versatile and completely safe to use. The extension shaft is best cut down to around 6in (150mm) long, although this can of course be adjusted to suit individual requirements.

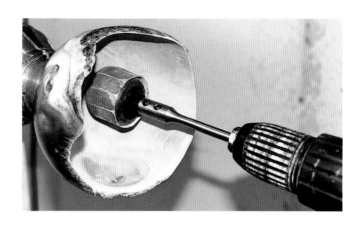

The extension shaft attached to the Kirjes ball-type pneumatic sander

431 Airtight storage

A baby's feeding bottle will keep sealer, varnish, stains, etc. from evaporating.

Cutting off the tip of the teat and pushing a pastry brush through forms an airtight seal. You can push the brush further into the bottle as the level of the contents lowers, always maintaining a good seal.

432 Oil spill

Oil can weep out of the fissures and holes in burrs and other projects for some time after finishing, so never place a newly finished piece directly on a piece of furniture unless there is a place mat underneath it.

433 Grating wax

When making your own beeswax polish, use an old cheese grater on the solid block of wax. The small, thin flakes will dissolve faster in the turpentine or whatever medium you use.

You can also use the grater on a solid block of liquid paraffin wax when melting it to seal the end grain of your timber blanks.

434 Oil better than wax

If you use wax on open-grained burrs, you will end up with wax residue in the fissures, which will take considerable time to clean out. An easier-to-use and more durable finish is oil.

Workshop storage

435 Rust-resisting tool rack

Wiping tools with an oily rag will help prevent rust, but this automatic system saves you the trouble of remembering to do so.

First, make a simple rack by drilling a series of holes, sized to suit your tools, in a length of softwood. Then fit two lengths of brush-type draught excluder underneath the holes, overlapping the brushes by about ¼in (6mm). The rack can be fixed to the end of the bench, made free-standing or screwed to a convenient wall. A few drops of oil or a squirt of spray lubricant in each hole ensures that the tools receive a protective film every time they are put away. A further application of lubricant every week or so ensures rust-free tools, and the slight build-up of sawdust in the holes seems to enhance efficiency. An hour's work has saved days of cleaning.

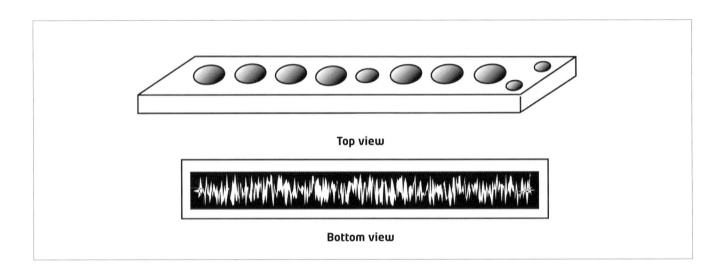

Top view

Bottom view

436 Using magnets

There are some handy magnets on the market that you can use for holding chucks or tools, but a much cheaper option is to get hold of some old radio speakers – the bigger the better – and remove the magnets from them. Old cone-type radio speakers have them at the centre rear, usually behind the speaker transformer.

These magnets are typically about 3in (75mm) outside diameter, about ¼in (6mm) thick, have a 1⅛in (30mm) hole in the centre, and are very strong. Some of them can readily be cut to smaller sizes with a hand-held hacksaw, and they can hold all manner of things, from chuck keys to callipers.

437 | Portability

This 'woodturners' workstation',
designed for club meetings and
demonstrations, combines
portability, stability and security in
one simple system. A very strong
base cabinet, mounted on casters,
replaces the lathe stand. Hinged
blocks at either end swing down to
lift the casters clear of the floor
when the lathe is in use. The space
under the lathe bed is used for
storing movable items such as tools,
chucks and bench grinder. Above all,
the lathe is completely stable in use.

The cabinet top measures 23½ x
51in (597 x 1295mm), with the lathe
bed secured via two wooden blocks
3in (75mm) high. The cabinet top
provides a good-sized work surface
for tools, finishing materials and all
the other bits that might be needed
immediately to hand.

Inside the lockable base cabinet,
one shelf and three deep drawers
provide space for heavyweight
items – including all the movable
lathe parts, such as the toolrest and
tailstock – and such things as
chucks, finishes, polishes, sandpaper
and a few blanks.

The hinged jacking blocks are held
out of the way by magnetic catches,
and it is a simple matter to lift the
whole assembly slightly – one end
at a time – and swing the blocks
down into position.

Woodturning safety

438   Keep the bed clean

One of the least enjoyable aspects of woodturning is cleaning up vast quantities of chips, especially between and under the bed bars. A build-up of chips here can restrict the positioning of the banjo.

Place masonite (or plywood, or heavy cardboard) over the bed to prevent this accumulation. A small rare-earth magnet recessed and epoxied to the underside prevents it slipping. Three covering strips of different lengths will allow for the varying positions of the banjo.

439   Make cleaning child's play

My five-year-old granddaughter called in and caught me clearing up the usual mountain of shavings. Whilst wielding the dustpan with the carefree attitude only available to those of tender years, she came up with such a wonderful suggestion that I immediately promoted her to senior management. Her innocent question was simply: 'Why don't you put the dustbin under the lathe when you are turning, instead of leaving all this mess on the floor?'

On my old bowl-turning lathe, with no bed or tailstock, placing the dustbin (trashcan) in the right place to catch most of the falling debris was simple. It worked! The mountain had turned into a molehill. If you can't fit a bin under your machine, a cardboard box would do just as well.

440   Fire safety

Never leave a scrunched-up oily rag. Failure to dispose of them properly could result in a fire. Oily rags are best placed outside after use, no matter what else you do. Simply lay them out flat or, better still, either open them out and hang them on a clothes line to dry, or soak them in water prior to disposal.

Woodturning safety

Cheap respirator

Shop-bought respirators are quite expensive, but you can make your own. Buy a standard safety helmet, of the kind workmen wear on building sites, from a second-hand shop, and remove the heating element from an electric fan heater. Fix the heater to the workshop wall and use plumbing fittings connected to vacuum-cleaner hose to bring in fresh air from outside the workshop.

Home-made respirator and lathe. The plywood box has half a ton of sand inside to weight it down

Eyecare: removing particles

You may be unfortunate enough to get either metal filings or woodchips in your eyes when turning. You should always wear goggles and a mask, but debris can get in if you wipe your eye with your finger later on. Here are two tips for removing the offending objects. The petroleum jelly method is good for removing foreign bodies from children's eyes as well.

Removing foreign bodies from the eye

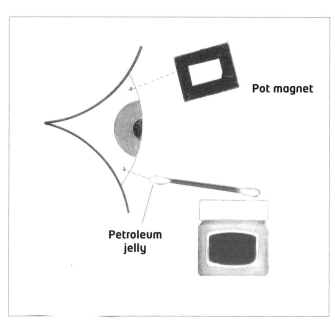

Pot magnet

Petroleum jelly

Eyecare: keeping dust away

I spent nine months in and out of eye clinics after a microscopic amount of dust from some Indian rosewood managed to bite me, despite the very good helmet I was wearing. This following tip came from my experiences and has stood me in good stead ever since.

The talc-like dust from tropical woods can induce eye irritation similar to a stubborn conjunctivitis, resistant to the armoury of lotions and ointments favoured by doctors. Helmets and goggles are not 100% effective in keeping this very fine dust from the rim of the eyelids and the base of the eyelashes. Improved hygiene is the best defence.

After work, wash the face with baby shampoo. Pour a little neat shampoo into the palm of the hand, add warm water and work up a lather – apply to the eyelid area, gently massage with the fingers and rinse in running water. You can do this very thoroughly, as baby shampoo will not sting the eyes, like ordinary soap.

Woodturning tips

444 | Better dust extraction (1)

Over the past few years, woodworkers have generally become increasingly aware of the dangers of inhaling the inevitable dust produced when machining wood and composite materials. This has resulted in manufacturers and tool suppliers offering a wide range of machinery for collecting and extracting dust and shavings.

Most hobby woodturners, for whom space and budget are at a premium, choose one of the smaller, loose-bag models. A common feature of these machines, and indeed many other types of extraction machinery, is that the extracted waste has to pass through the fan unit on its way to the collection bag. To protect the fan against the ingress of woodchips, some form of grid is normally fitted to the fan intake, and a total or partial blockage can quickly occur here, rendering the unit ineffective. This can very easily go unnoticed by the operator, because the fan continues to run and the dustbag normally remains inflated, giving the impression that all is in order.

A simple and very positive solution is to introduce a container, such as a small household dustbin (trashcan), into the flexible suction line. Now anything larger than fine dust will drop out of the airstream, practically eliminating any risk of blockage at the fan. The container can be placed at any point in the suction line – for example, on the negative-pressure side of the fan unit – but should be easily accessible for emptying.

The ideal receptacle is a small household bin with a clamp-on lid. In use, the container will be within the suction system, so it is vital that the lid forms an airtight seal. If necessary, some self-adhesive household door or window draught seal can be used to ensure this.

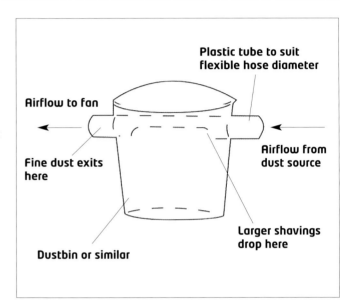

A simple way of providing the necessary inlet and outlet spigots is by using a suitably sized piece of plastic duct tubing, with a central cutout, as shown in the diagram. With the unit in operation, this will cause all but the finest dust to drop from the airstream and into the container. The tube can be effectively fixed and sealed to holes cut in the container sides using a flexible silicone bathroom sealer.

With extraction systems of this type it is important to check that the filter bag is suitable for dust extraction; some have a coarse weave and are only suitable for chip collection.

Where possible, the whole unit is best sited outside the working environment. A small cupboard or box-type housing can be built in the workshop. Alternatively, an internal sealed housing unit with ventilation to the outside is suitable.

445 | Better dust extraction (2)

Some further improvements will dramatically increase the effectiveness of the tip shown opposite.

The diagram shows the pipe passing perpendicularly through the container. However, if the inlet is mounted tangentially on the upper part of the container and the outlet is fixed to the very centre of the lid, any size of woodchip and coarser dust will be forced against the wall of the vessel, losing speed through friction against that wall and ultimately dropping to the bottom of the bin. Only the very fine dust will escape through the central outlet. The photograph illustrates the simplicity of this cyclone system.

The vessel shown holds 20 litres (4.5 gallons), and cost very little. The size of the tubes in this instance is 2in (50mm) to fit the dust extractor used, the dust bag of which needs emptying only twice a year. Because of the vacuum there is no need to use a clamp for the lid. The system has been working satisfactorily for years.

For dust extraction from machines, it is best to use the type of fan unit described on the opposite page, but with the cyclone system already built in. Apart from removing the grids, one other modification is worthwhile: replace the lower, plastic recipient bag with the same-sized fabric upper bag to collect the fine dust. The net result is an almost doubling of the airflow.

Further improvements to the workshop dust extractor

446 | Handling superglue safely

Many turners are apprehensive about using cyanoacrylate (superglue) to fix barrels into drilled pen blanks. It's all too easy to fix your finger to the blank or, through nervousness, end up with a brass barrel stuck halfway.

Look for a stubby screwdriver with a ¼in (6mm) diameter blade about 1⅝in (40mm) long, with a pozidrive or Phillips point. Slip a metal washer over the blade and glue it to the handle. To use it, simply slide the brass barrel onto the blade, run the superglue into the blank and then just pop the barrel into the blank using the screwdriver. Slip the screwdriver out, and the barrel is left in place, with no risk to your fingers.

Washer

Brass tube

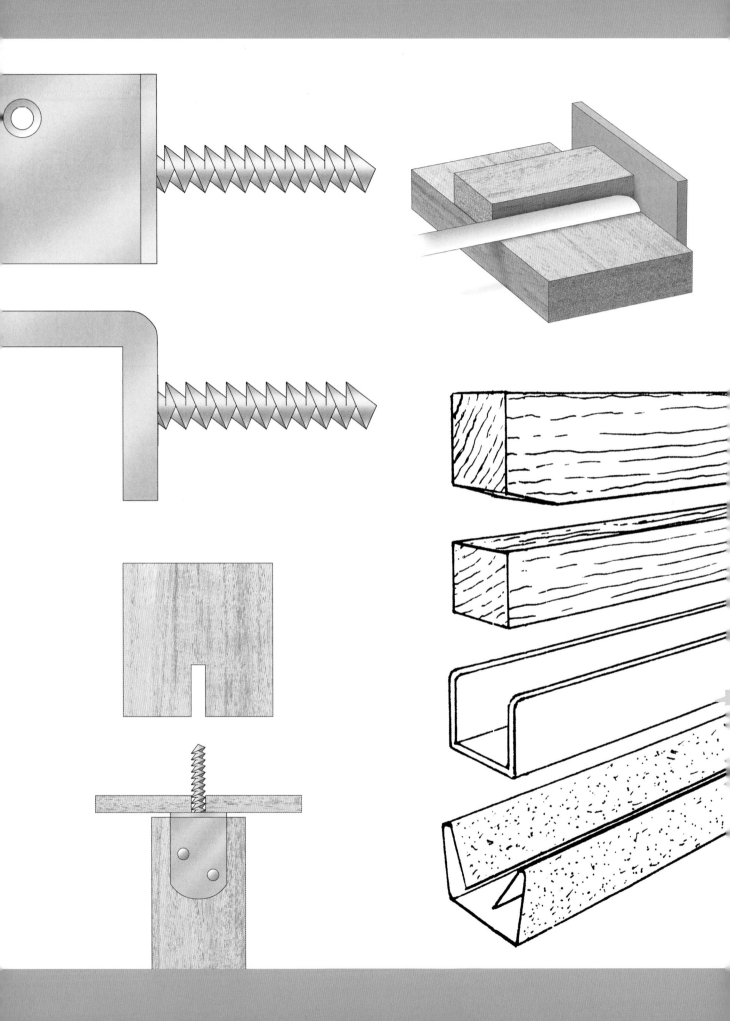

Woodcarving tips

447-464

447 Make a drawknife

An old, abandoned pair of ice skates came in useful when I started a new carving that needed a drawknife. The blades were removed with a flat-head screwdriver. Retain the anchoring bolts, as they will later be used to secure the drawknife handles to the blade.

Use a belt sander with a 220-grit belt, or a bench grinder, to clean off any rust on the blade. Then mark a reference line ⅛in (3mm) from the unsharpened edge of the blade.

Using a 50-grit belt on the front roller of the sander, grind off the two small areas indicated by the dotted lines in the drawing; these extend from the centre of each bolt hole ¾in (20mm) in towards the centre of the blade. Then, with the same belt, start to reduce the thickness of what will become the cutting edge, using your ⅛in (3mm) reference line as a guide.

When you've removed most of the material necessary, change to an 80-grit belt and remove the remainder of the waste, leaving only about ¹⁄₃₂in (0.8mm) thickness at the cutting edge. Change the belt to a 120-grit, then carefully remove the remaining thickness of steel until a semi-sharp cutting edge is established. Now change to a 220-grit belt and continue to remove stock until you have a sharp cutting edge.

Use hand-held waterstones or oilstones for the final grinding, sharpening and honing. Starting with 100-grit, progress through to 2000 or 4000-grit to obtain as fine a cutting edge as possible.

The handles should be made of a closed-pore hardwood such as birch, maple, aspen or walnut. Depending upon personal preference and hand size, a dowel between 20mm and 32mm (¾ and 1¼in) diameter should be used: the length should be 5½-6in (140-150mm). A slot to receive the skate blade must be cut in one end of the dowel, ⅛in (3mm) wide, at a 30° angle, and deep enough – about 1in (25mm) – to accept the blade and the securing bolts. Two holes need to be drilled: one is a counterbore ½in (13mm) in diameter by ⅜in (10mm) deep, the other a through hole ⁵⁄₁₆in (8mm)

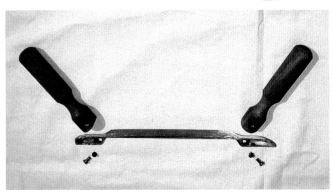

in diameter. To harden and strengthen the wood around the holes, use cyanocacrylate (superglue). Round over the top and bottom of the handles on the belt sander. Give the handles a coat of walnut oil, or other suitable oil, and affix the handles to the blade. Test the blade, and if there are any blunt spots, sharpen as required.

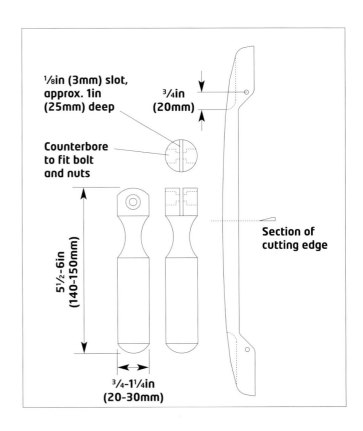

⅛in (3mm) slot, approx. 1in (25mm) deep

¾in (20mm)

Counterbore to fit bolt and nuts

5½-6in (140-150mm)

¾-1¼in (20-30mm)

Section of cutting edge

448 Identifying tools

Even experienced woodcarvers sometimes pick up the wrong chisel. You can overcome the problem by using a set of number punches to stamp the information on four sides of the octagonal handle (so you will always be able to see at least one marking) and filling in the imprint using a felt-tip pen. It's of particular help when choosing, say, a 7/4, 5/3, 9/5 from your small chisels. Those who are gluttons for punishment could even carve the information onto the handle.

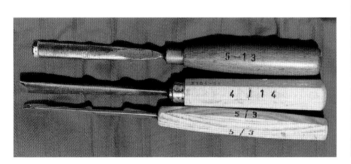

449 Squaring gouges

Here is a simple jig to square off the ends of gouges. Simply fix a batten 1in (25mm) wide by ½in (13mm) and 4in (100mm) long, at right angles across the top of a piece of 4 x 2in (100 x 50mm). Hold the gouge against the batten, flat on the block. Place a grinding flat against the vertical face of the block, and move it backwards and forwards along the block. This will square off the gouge ready for reprofiling.

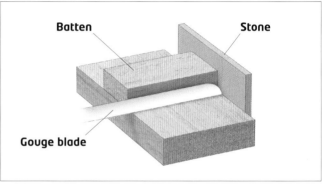

450 Power stropping

A cheap and easy way to make a powered leather strop for your carving chisels is to take an old leather belt, cut it to length and glue it to a sanding drum to fit into your drill press. Feather the cut edges where they join, and arrange them so that the end 'trails' and cannot catch the edge of the tool.

452 Protecting switches

Fine sawdust can find its way into the on–off switch of a power-carving tool and clog it up. You can cure this by cutting a wide band of tyre inner-tube and slipping it over the machine, covering the switch, which can still be operated easily.

451 Honing V-tools

Some manufacturers still sell V-tools with side and bottom bevels of equal length. As the thickness of metal at the apex of the V is often much greater than at the sides, an equal-length bevel will result in an unequal bevel angle, causing the tool to jam.

The answer is to ensure both sides and the bottom are sharpened at the same angle by rotating the tool at a constant angle as you hone it – in effect treating it as two chisels joined by a very small gouge. The resulting bevel will be much longer underneath, where the metal is thicker, than at the sides.

This method works equally well whether using traditional stones or rotary sharpeners. An advantage of using hard felt wheels on a rotary sharpener is that no burr is formed on the inside, thus obviating the need for slipstones.

Workholding

453 Cam clamp

Here is a simple, quick-release way of holding an irregular-shaped, small and fragile piece of work on a chipboard backing board so you can move it around while carving.

You could use double-sided sticky tape, but this would not give much manoeuvrability, and there would be a danger of breaking the carving when prising it off the backing.

In this cam clamp, the workpiece is located with four short pieces of ½in (12mm) dowel, each shorter than the depth of the workpiece. The dowel pieces are screwed to the backing board with chipboard screws countersunk below the top surface of the dowels. The dowel rods can be moved to accommodate any shape of carving, and can even be placed inside a pierced carving. The cam lever is secured to the backing board with a chipboard screw and washer, tightened just pinch-tight. The shape of the cam lever means a workpiece can be quickly and easily secured and released as needed.

454 Sandbags

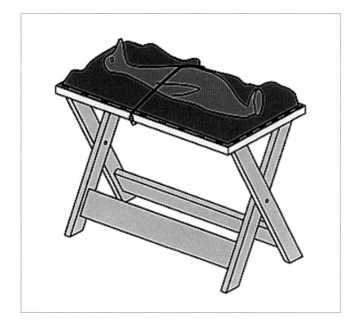

A free-standing carving can be difficult to hold steady once the initial rounding is done. One solution is to use thick polythene bags, filled loosely with sand and taped up.

Staple the bags to a suitable-sized piece of chipboard before covering them loosely with a thick piece of canvas. The whole thing can then be clamped to a bench or Workmate.

Put the carving on the canvas and push the sandbags into position so they hug the carving. The carving can be held securely in position with an elastic bungee cord.

455 Close-up clamp

Those of us whose eyesight is not as good as it used to be sometimes need to have the work close up when standing to carve. This heavy-duty, height-adjustable clamp is made from lengths of bright metal bar. The size of bar is not crucial, but those shown are 1½ x ¼in (38 x 6mm) and 3½ x ⅜in (90 x 10mm). A garage may be able to help with cutting the bars, tapping the threads and welding the parts together. The arms are each 3¾ x 1½ x ¼in (95 x 38 x 6mm), and the end brackets 1½ x 1½ x ¼in (38 x 38 x 6mm). The baseplate is 3½ x 3½ x ⅜in (90 x 90 x 10mm), and the upright tongue underneath is 4 x 3½ x ⅜in (100 x 90 x 10mm).

The clamp is held in a 24 x 2¾ x 2¾in (610 x 70 x 70mm) wooden post. Radius the end and cut a slot to take the metal tongue, then drill a hole through to take a bolt and butterfly nut.

The bottom end of the post can be clamped to the bench or held in a vice as preferred.

The smaller faceplate shown below the screw clamp is useful for holding smaller pieces. This comprises a top plate of 3½ x 3½ x ⅜in (90 x 90 x 10mm), with a 4 x 3½ x ⅜in (100 x 90 x 10mm) tongue welded underneath.

In both cases the tongue has a hole drilled through to take the fixing bolt that secures it to the wooden post. The faceplate has several holes drilled through and countersunk from beneath so wood can be screwed on from below.

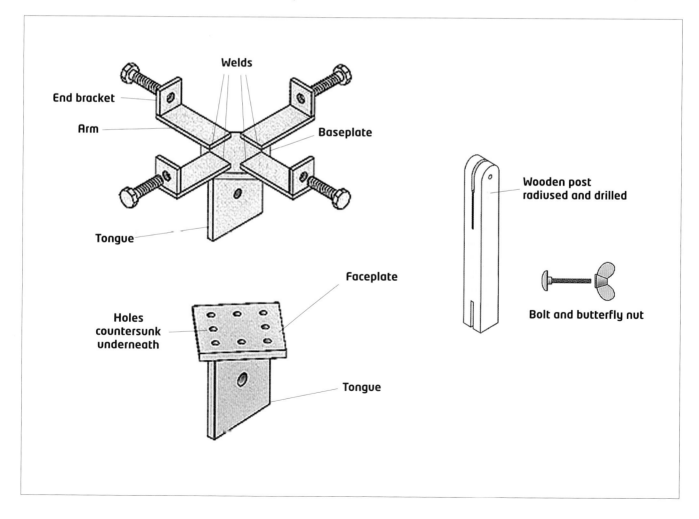

Welds

End bracket

Arm

Baseplate

Tongue

Wooden post radiused and drilled

Bolt and butterfly nut

Faceplate

Holes countersunk underneath

Tongue

Woodcarving tips

456 | Cheap screw clamps

There are some very expensive devices available for holding wood to be carved, but they are not always necessary. Here are some cheap and handy alternatives.

You need a fixing bracket for garden fences. This is a sturdy, corrosion-resistant steel bracket, with a coarse screw welded into one face, and it costs next to nothing.

To make a screw clamp, fit the bracket to a 3 x 3in (75 x 75mm) section of timber with sturdy screws. Take a piece of ¼in (6mm) ply and drill it so that it fits over the screw to create an oversized washer. It is worth remembering to recess the washer or set the bracket flush with the post, so that the washer locates snugly onto the top of the post. Once fitted, the post can be screwed to a bench, or held in a vice, and the work fitted to it.

Four of these fence brackets can be used to secure a block of wood flat on the bench ready for relief carving.

457 | Carving screw

This commercially made carving vice is good value, but not quite as convenient as the old-fashioned carvers' screw. With this model one must install, and later loosen, three fixing screws to change projects (or alternatively, buy more stems and faceplates).

One possibility is to drill and tap a hole in the centre of the faceplate to accommodate a simple hanger bolt. File a couple of flats on the bolt so a spanner can be used to remove it from the workpiece when necessary.

For a deluxe accessory, take a 5in (125mm) length of 1in (25mm) diameter Acme-threaded studding, with a nut to fit, to your local high-street metalworker. Have him remove all but 1in (25mm) of the thread and turn the other 4in (100mm) down to a ⅝in (16mm) diameter stem. Drill and tap a hole in the centre of the end to accept a hanger bolt; a hole depth of about ¾in (20mm) should be enough. Finally, ask him to weld a couple of wings onto the nut to make a wing nut.

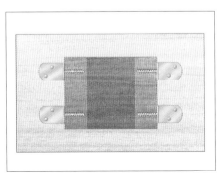
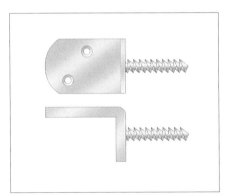

Left
Fence bracket

Below
Screw clamp

Below left
Block secured with four brackets

Above
Bolt tapped into faceplate

Left
The bits and pieces that make the carvers' screw

Above left
The carvers' screw in use

458 Carving horse

This carving horse, which can be folded for ease of transport, is made from readily available materials, including a number of 3in (75mm) door hinges.

It consists of six pieces of wood, of which the jib and strut take the main load. The prototype shown here took about two hours to make. Note that the hinge end of the strut is angled at 107° to restrict the hinge movement, and the footrest is attached by three hefty 3in (75mm) no. 14 woodscrews to withstand considerable twisting stress.

The jib extends beyond the hinge so that a carving vice can be attached: this can be whatever model is available.

The carving horse has proved to be solid and very comfortable (provided a cushion is used), and is now used for routine work.

Smaller wood sections could be used to reduce weight and size; mortising the footrest will also reduce size. Some padding could be added, and dimensions can be adjusted to suit the user.

Remember to keep hands away from hinges at all times, and before sitting on the carving horse, ensure that the stay is securely located in one of the notches.

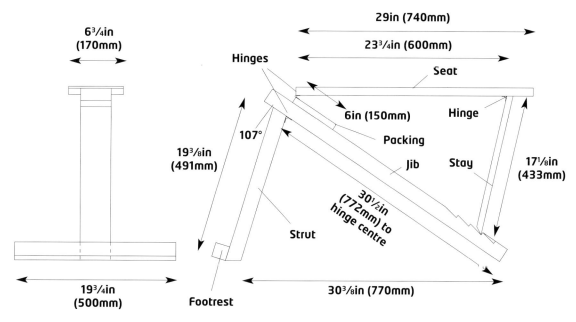

Sanding solutions

459 Custom sanding blocks

An easy way to make small sanding blocks without folding abrasive paper round a piece of wood is to use some extruded aluminium channel from a hardware shop. This device both holds the abrasive paper securely and allows it to be easily changed.

Cut the channel into lengths that measure half the length of a sheet of abrasive paper. For those blocks that are to be used like a file, cut a piece of wood twice the length of the channel, half of which will be used as a handle. Halve a sheet of abrasive paper and cut a piece wide enough to fold around the channel and tuck down into it. Push the wooden handle down into the channel. If it's a fairly firm fit it will tighten the paper as you push it in. If the wood seems a bit loose it can be fixed by wrapping a couple of pieces of masking tape around it before pushing it in. You will need to adjust the thickness of the wood to fit the grit size of the paper.

You can also make useful sanding blocks without handles. These are usually held between thumb and

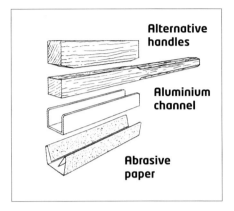

Alternative handles

Aluminium channel

Abrasive paper

fingers, but they are easier to use if the wood is about ¼in (6mm) proud of the channel. You need to slope each end of the wood that goes into the channel so that you can lever it out when the time comes to change the paper.

460 Flexible sanders

Woodcarving requires files that can get into narrow gaps and awkward places. Even with a good selection of files you often find that you don't have the right one. Here is a simple solution.

You need a piece of ¹⁄₃₂ x 4 x 4in (0.8 x 100 x 100mm) aluminium alloy or tin, a similar-sized piece of abrasive paper, and double-sided tape or wood glue.

Using either glue or tape, stick the paper to the aluminium alloy. Cut the alloy into strips of ¼in (6mm), ³⁄₈in (10mm), ½in (12mm), or whatever size you require. These strips can now be bent or twisted to whatever shape you need.

461 Instant sanding stick

Emery boards are handy for cleaning details on a carving. They're not quite as good as a dedicated file or micro-rasp, but just the job if you need something right there and then.

462 Drawing with light

Making preparatory sketches for a carving should be about seeing and understanding rather than creating a beautiful picture, but all too often people who feel that they can't draw are discouraged by their efforts. I know because I was one of them.

After some expert tuition, I found that by drawing on a medium- or dark-toned paper with light and dark mediums such as chalk and charcoal, the results were much better. You are, in effect, 'drawing the light' rather than the shadows and outline. The paper surface can become one of the dark tones. This approach to drawing enables the viewer to understand the three-dimensional form of the subject more easily.

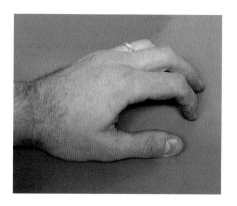

463 Spot repairs

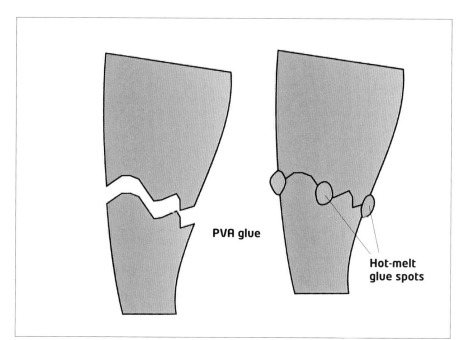

PVA glue

Hot-melt glue spots

Carvings sometimes get broken, and usually in awkward places where it is difficult or impossible to use a clamp to hold the pieces together while the glue sets.

Use a few spots of hot-melt glue around the broken area to hold the pieces in place. This can be scraped off when the main glue joint has set.

464 Using dyes

When staining carvings with water-based dyes, it is easy to get patchy areas where the dye is not soaking into the surface of the carving equally, even when allowance is made for the greater absorption of the end grain.

It is often the natural oils of the wood that are preventing water penetration, in which case adding one or two drops of washing-up liquid to the dye will improve the take-up of the dye considerably.

After applying the dye to your carving with a brush to make sure that all parts are covered, finish with a dry brush to even out the colour before it dries. When the carving is completely dry, it can be polished as required.

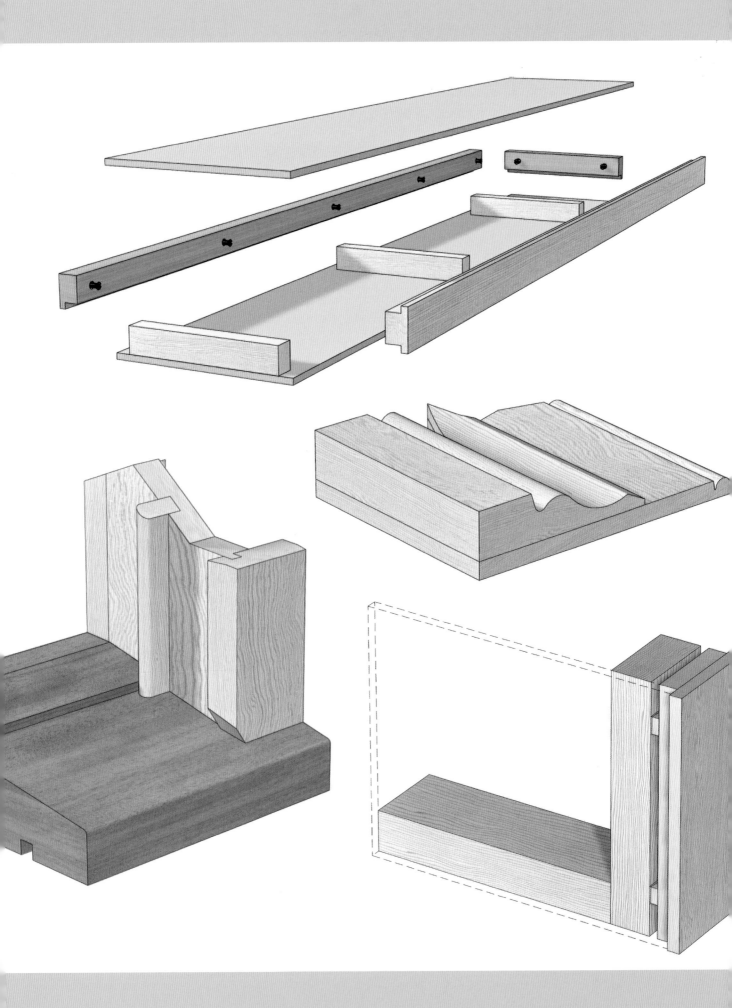

Do-it-yourself tips

465-500

Doors and doorways

465 Hanging a new door in an old frame

Here is the best approach to hanging new doors in old frames. Remove the door stops in preparation for fitting replacements once the door is hung; this is almost always necessary to achieve a high-quality result.

Check the frame for square using some corner offcuts from an 8 x 4ft (2240 x 1220mm) sheet. Record the angles in relation to these sheet corners, or with a sliding bevel, before trimming the height and angle of the top and bottom of the door accordingly. Be sure you take into account any width reductions you may have to make. Be aware of the floor level in the path of the door; if you have a sloping floor or a thick carpet, rising butts may be a better option than ordinary hinges. You can use your corner offcuts to check the floor in relation to the lining.

Allow a 5/64–1/8in (2–3mm) gap around the door (a coin of suitable thickness can be used as a guide; in the UK this would be a 2p piece). Plane or cut the door to width, equally on both sides if you are removing more than 3/8in (10mm). Remember that you may later need to add a bevel or chamfer to the leading edge of the door so that it closes without brushing the lining.

Positioning new hinges in old recesses almost always produces an unsound and untidy job; it is always best to fill the old recesses and then reposition the new hinges accordingly.

Cut the hinge recesses into the door, 10in (254mm) from the bottom and 7in (178mm) from the top. Middle hinges should be positioned in the middle of the door, taking into account the advice above. Attach the butts to the door before carefully marking the lining. It is easy to mess up a perfectly prepared door at this stage by being careless when transferring the hinge heights.

Hang the door from the lining and make any fine adjustments necessary. It is at this stage that you should bevel or chamfer the leading edge of the closing door.

466 Marking hinge recesses

It is easy to mark the depth of a hinge recess in a bare door lining with a gauge, but if the architrave has already been fitted it becomes necessary to take a different approach.

Use a combination square and a utility knife, cutting in about 5/64in (2mm) in two or three passes. Providing you take care with an initial light cut, you will achieve a perfectly crisp line.

467 Making wedges

In order to fit the perfect door lining you need to cut near-perfect folding wedges. The only quick and reliable way to do this is with this simple tablesaw jig.

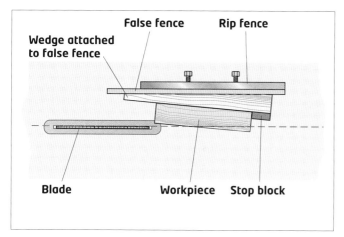

False fence **Rip fence**

Wedge attached to false fence

Blade **Workpiece** **Stop block**

468 Managing without wedges

If you're hanging a door or fitting door furniture and don't have any wedges for the door, use a chisel with a screwdriver or a piece of scrap underneath.

469 Trimming a door

If you need to plane the bottom edge of a door which has already been hung, there is no need to take it off.

A Surform blade or similar, still attached to the card on which it was supplied, will fit underneath the door, and works almost as well as a plane.

470 Budget architrave

Instead of ripping out your plain architrave, fix lengths of dowelling around the edges and run a line of decorative filler between the new and old timbers. This gives the impression of a one-piece moulding of a much more expensive type.

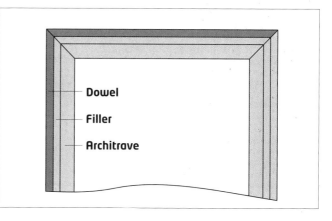

Dowel

Filler

Architrave

Do-it-yourself tips

471 Making door linings

Fitting door linings and hanging doors can be easy if you've done your preparation well. If you don't do it every day, making linings and fitting furniture on site can be difficult to get right, so a quiet afternoon in the workshop, with the doors to be hung on hand, produces the best results.

472 Fitting a narrow door

If you have a door frame that needs filling and an awkwardly undersized door that needs a home, adding a suitably thicknessed board to one or both sides of the lining may be enough to make the door fit.

473 DIY architraves

An easy way of faking expensive period architrave is to fix a standard ogee moulding onto a timber or MDF board with a bead mould along one edge. However, this wide moulding will require fixing into the studwork or block wall as well as into the door lining or frame.

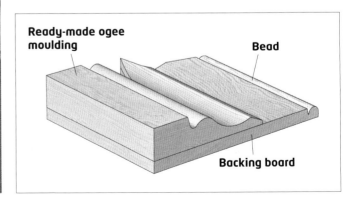

Ready-made ogee moulding

Bead

Backing board

474 Frames without architraves

If you are building a new wall (to be plastered) and want contemporary-style door and cupboard openings without architrave, consider this method.

Make an initial door lining from boards that are the same width as the blockwork or stud frame, and fit this in the opening in the usual way. If you are working on a stud or dry wall, fit this initial lining before fixing the plasterboard, which will run over the initial lining and butt up to the inner lining.

Within this initial frame, securely (to avoid cupping) fix a presentable lining, ½in (12mm) thick and butted, rebated or mitred. If the plaster is thick it may be necessary to increase the inner lining's thickness so that it can receive hinge screws by itself. The width of the inner lining's boards should be equal to the finished thickness of your wall, including plaster (consult the plasterer first to establish this all-important dimension).

Glue the inner lining's joints with water-resistant PVA or polyurethane. Once dry, the plasterer can skim flush to the edge of the lining.

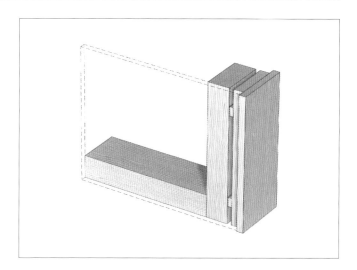

The cutting of the hinge recesses is best done with a router, since the vibration of a struck chisel often produces a crack between plaster and lining. A fine crack will always appear somewhere along the joint line once the plaster is dry and a door is hung, but this is easy to cover up with filler.

475 Cutting and fixing architraves

When applying architrave to a door lining it is best to work as follows. If your frame is not totally square you will need to halve its angles to produce the mitres.

1 Decide how far back the architrave will sit from the face of the lining, and mark the lines at the bottom of the sides and where the lines converge on the top corners of the lining.

2 Making sure that the bottom end of your first left-hand vertical is cut squarely, place it in position and mark on its edge the height of the horizontal offset line. Cut this mitre using your chosen method, and nail it to the lining.

3 Cut the top piece of architrave overlength and cut a mitre at its left-hand end.

4 Offer up this mitre to the one previously cut before marking the length to the vertical offset line on the opposite side. Cut this mitre and then nail it horizontally to the lining.

5 Offer up an overlength right-hand vertical and mark off the top edge line from the horizontal piece. Cut the mitre and nail into position.

Sash windows

One day I was away from the workshop to re-cord some sash windows in a house belonging to the company estate. I was only just into my apprenticeship, and I was busily making a bit of a mess out of it when an elderly man stopped by to watch. It turned out that he was a retired carpenter, and in the course of the conversation which ensued he passed on several valuable tips. Over the years I have made use of these many times. The method of working that he taught me considerably speeded up the time that it took to carry out repairs and, furthermore, enabled me to work single-handed.

476 Pulley wedges

Carry several small wedges in your bag so that they can be used to wedge the cord in the pulley when the weight is lifted into the correct position, allowing the cord to be cut to the right length. The wedges mean that an assistant is not needed.

477 Cord lengths

The required cord lengths must be marked on the pulley stiles, ensuring that the weight neither bottoms on the sill nor fouls the pulley when the sash is in the fully open or fully closed positions. An allowance must also be made for the knot.

A weight is attached to the end of the cord, the weight pushed into the pocket and the cord pulled until the weight rises to just below the pulley.

The cord can then be firmly wedged into place with a small wooden wedge, allowing the cord to be cut to the mark at the pulley stile. This process is then repeated for the other three cords.

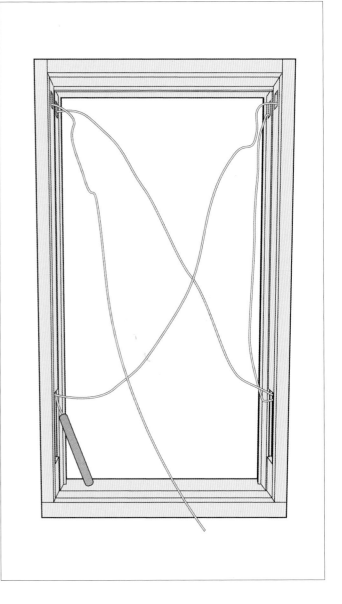

Threading new sash cord economically and quickly

478 Threading the cord

Threading the cord through the pulleys, down and out through the pockets, is done using a 'mouse' – a length of builder's line with a thin piece of lead wrapped around one end, the free end being attached to the sash cord. The method looks very complicated but is really quite simple.

Starting at one of the inner pulleys, the cord is threaded through and out through the pocket. Next it is taken up and through the opposite inner pocket, and again down and out of the pocket. The threading is now continued by repeating the same for the outer pulleys, the cord now ending up exiting from a pocket. A weight can then be attached.

At this stage all four cords are ready to be attached to the sashes, starting with the top sash.

With that done, the pockets can be replaced and the parting beads put back. With the same treatment for the bottom sash, and the staff beads replaced, the job is done.

479 Traditional joinery principles

Some of the very important principles of joinery work were to keep exposure of joints to the weather to a minimum, to avoid moisture traps, and to conceal end grain, which is particularly vulnerable, and is where rot most commonly starts.

The old-style sash windows had the outer lining running down into the sill, leaving a nasty little water trap where the rot usually began, and necessitating splices being made to the outer lining and the pulley stile.

All our new frames and repairs had a small piece cut out which allows any water to run out.

We also painted all surfaces of joints with a mixture of red and white lead – now forbidden. Will modern preservatives preserve for as long?

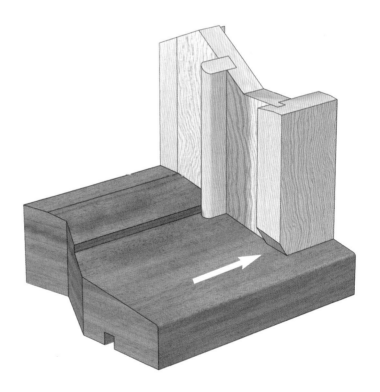

All water traps should be avoided

Skirtings (baseboards)

480 Home-made period skirting

It can be difficult to find wide skirting boards to match period originals, but you can make a plausible match using off-the-shelf mouldings and timber. A ¼in (6mm) coving cutter can be used to add a moulding to the top corner of the ¼in (6mm) MDF and to the main board; an additional cove machined in the archtrave completes the period effect.

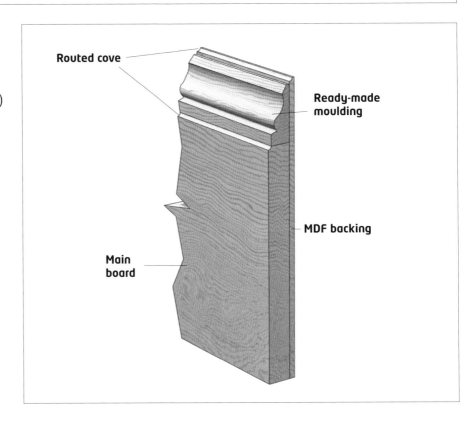

Routed cove

Ready-made moulding

MDF backing

Main board

481 Concealing cables

A good way of hiding cables is to machine a fascia board for your skirtings with a rebate on the bottom inside edge.

Skirtings (baseboards)

482 Covering gaps and pipes

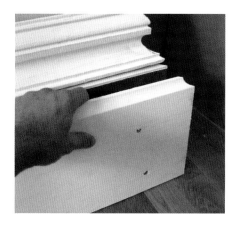  

If you are fitting a laminate or engineered floor but don't want to use a small angle bead to cover the gap around the edge, an alternative is to build out your skirting by fixing an additional board to the front.

When you encounter radiator pipes, build out the skirting to just in front of the pipes (with a gap to accommodate the pipes) before adding a thin ply or MDF facing.

483 Removing skirting board

The following method is the best way of removing a length of skirting that is 'captured' at both ends.

Prise out the skirt from the wall about 5/8in (15mm) or more, using a claw hammer or wrecking bar bearing against a piece of hardboard. If you have a stud wall, make sure that you lever against a stud.

Hammer in two flat wedges 5/8-3/4in (15-20mm) thick, about 12in (300mm) apart; then, using the tip of a handsaw, saw down through the skirting between the wedges, cutting at a shallow angle to increase the length of the stroke.

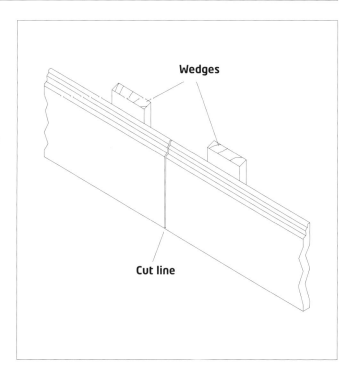

Wedges

Cut line

Do-it-yourself tips

484 Making accurate mitres

Here is a tip for working accurate mitre angles around non-standard corners, as when fitting beading around laminate flooring.

First, take a pad of sticky notelets and tear off two sheets. Then lay these parallel with the two pieces of wall, skirting, or whatever you are working around. Measure the angle with a protractor and divide this by two (for example, 88° divided by 2 = 44°).

If you have a mitre saw with pre-measured angles, swing this to 44°, cut one angle, then swing to 44° on the other side and cut the opposing angle. If you do not have a mitre saw, you can draw around the sticky note onto a piece of paper, cut along this line, then fold the paper in half, giving you a paper wedge of the angle required to transpose onto the wood.

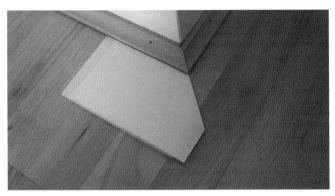

Above right: **Put sticky notelets around the skirting**

Right: **Fold them together to get the required angle**

485 Planning scribed joints

When fitting skirting boards it is always a good idea to consider how the room will be most commonly viewed, as this should determine the direction in which the scribed-ended sections of skirt should run. Gaps will be less conspicuous if they run *away* from the usual viewpoint. This type of consideration should also apply to which quality timber goes where on site – if you are working on more than one room, select the best timber for the rooms where the client (or you) will spend the most time observing the work.

Skirtings (baseboards)

486 Make painting easier

When fitting architraving or skirting to carpeted rooms, it is helpful to rest the timber on thin card. This creates a gap which becomes invisible, but is essential for easy and disaster-free decorating at a later date.

487 Bathroom tip

When working in the bathroom, always make a point of putting the plugs in the basin and the bath – plugholes are a magnet for dropped screws and other small bits and pieces. It may be worth closing the toilet seat too.

488 Temporary fixing

Use decorator's sealant to fix skirting boards; it does not 'grab' as much as the heavy-duty flooring adhesives, making it much easier to remove the wood at a later date. It tends to take just the paint off a wall, rather than a lump of plaster.

Ceilings, floors, partitions

489   Repairing a sagging ceiling

Lath-and-plaster ceilings in older buildings are prone to sagging in the centre. The cost and mess of taking the ceiling down and replacing it with similar materials can be considerable. A cheaper option is to board over the ceiling, pulling it up to the line of the joists above – which may also sag.

The basic technique is to use screws and washers to pull the boards up. A few related tips (see below) may be of interest to anyone facing a similar job.

Do make sure that your eyes and lungs are fully protected when working with either plasterboard or plaster.

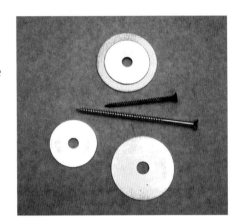

490   Scaffold tower versus board lifter

Board-lifting 'machines' available from hire shops may not be sufficient for major jobs, but for boarding over a smaller, less distorted and more modern ceiling, a board lifter would probably be the most suitable work aid.

A scaffold tower enables you to apply the pressure (with your shoulders and T-shaped props) needed to raise the ceiling. For a low ceiling you could simply stand on a table. If you can afford it, hire a board lifter as well; this will at least make it easier to get the boards up onto the platform.

491   Setting out screw positions

In order to lay out the board grid, you first need to find the joists. A cheap stud detector is quite good at locating them, and by drilling quite a few test holes you should be able to set out the fixing grid.

Used a chalk line to mark along the length of the joists, but be aware that these may wander off the straight lines. Drill more test holes as necessary to correct your fixing grid.

The grid makes it relatively easy to position the fixing screws correctly when you are balancing a board on your head. It is best to stagger the joints in the plasterboard, say by 24in (600mm).

492   Applying pressure

Make your T-props 2in (50mm) longer than the required final position, and use these to prop up the ceiling to almost the right height. However, you may also need to use your head and shoulders – a cushion is a must for your head!

493   Long then short screws and washers

Use 6-10 large-diameter washers and no. 14 pozidrive screws to pull up the 3/8in (9mm) plasterboard and old plaster up to the joists. Once fixed, secure the board properly with 2 3/8in (60mm) drywall screws. Then remove the large screws and washers, and move on to the next board.

494 Planning roof windows

Many roof windows are positioned so high that anyone sitting down in the room can't see anything other than sky. Modesty is normally the excuse, but it is surely better to fit these windows lower than the norm. The bottom pane of glass should meet the frame at between 39 and 43in (1000–1100mm).

Of course, there are safety concerns with lower window positions, but as long as you add safety devices that restrict the opening of the frames, then children and inebriated relatives will be safe.

495 Drilling into carpet

Never drill through a carpet with any sort of drill bit, since it is possible that the fibres will catch or even melt onto the bit, causing very apparent damage. Use a 4in (100mm) wire nail to work in a hole before carefully drilling within it. It is possible to avoid cutting through any fibres with this technique, so a cover-up at a later date requires nothing more than a roughing-up of the pile.

496 Supporting a floating floor

A laminate floor often has areas that dip underfoot. The remedy is to inject a gap-filling adhesive through a drilled hole; however, this only works if you have laid a thin acoustic foam of expanded polypropylene underneath.

Presumably, because the gap-filler sits on top of the foam there is enough movement to avoid binding the floor to anything solid. Fill the drilled holes with wood filler, slicing the surface flush with a utility blade before the filler is completely set.

497 Fixing partitions to floating floors

It is not always possible or desirable for a partition to extend all the way up to the ceiling. It is therefore very important to achieve a good fixing to the floor.

In the case of an engineered floor floated over floorboards, you need to allow for about 3⁄8in (10mm) movement. Drill 1in (25mm) holes in the floor plate of the partition's studwork, then fix 2¼in (60mm) screws through 1½in (40mm) washers and into the floor. Do not fully tighten the screws, so that when the floor expands and contracts the partition can stay in position.

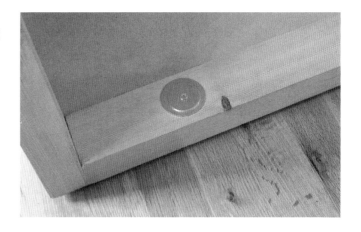

Shelves and worktops

498 | Torsion-box shelves

These simple-to-make box-style shelves are designed to be painted, but should you desire a wood finish, the construction process is almost exactly the same.

A nail-gun is the ideal tool for much of the assembly, particularly if you are working by yourself – although a heavier, air-powered gun will be easier to use than an ordinary electric stapler/nailer.

Providing that you don't skimp on the glue and that all of your timber is accurately thicknessed, this torsion-box construction can take a surprising amount of weight. However, unless you have one or both ends supported by an alcove side, it does not have enough strength to be filled with heavy books. Ply instead of MDF facings would add a little strength.

1 Dimension all of your timber in one go before routing.

2 It is critical that the protruding part of the wall support bearer is exactly the same thickness as the spacing battens. Likewise, the protruding part of the facing piece must be of the same dimension. Both can be *slightly* undersized, but not oversized. Offering one piece up to another will give you a clear indication.

3 Mark out the underside of the top facing board and rub-glue the spacing battens to the surface. Leave for an hour or more before carefully gluing and screwing this onto the spacing battens, using pre-drilled holes. For exposed shelf ends, the last spacing batten becomes the end piece. If you want to preserve the timber facing strip, wait until the support battens have dried before gluing and pinning the spacing strip on.

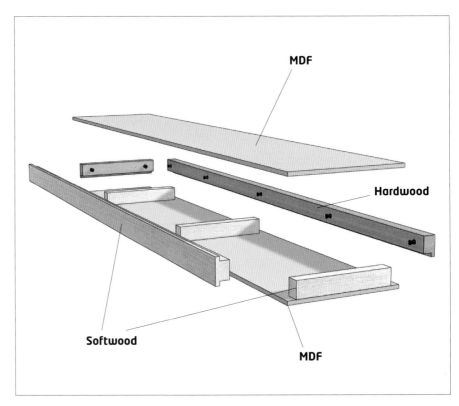

4 Once this initial assembly is dry, you can glue and pin the bottom facing board. To maximize the strength of these pins, slightly skew them in various directions as you insert them into the support battens and the front facing strip. In order to add strength to the underside, turn over the construction and pin into the support battens and front facing strip.

5 Fix the hardwood wall bearer and any alcove support bearers that may be necessary. Don't forget that if your walls are not straight you will need to pack out the wall bearers in order to get a decent fixing through the facing board.

6 Pre-drill every 1½in (40mm) and carefully countersink (no more than necessary) the top facing board along its back edge. Push the box construction onto the wall bearer(s), support it level with a couple of bearers down to the floor, and screw in a couple of temporary fixings. Drill the screw holes into the wall bearer and fix. Add some further screws to the bottom facing board into the wall bearer.

Section of torsion-box shelf

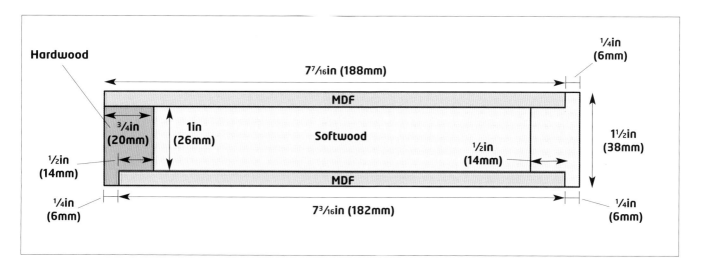

Hardwood

7⁷⁄₁₆in (188mm)

¼in (6mm)

MDF

³⁄₄in (20mm)

1in (26mm)

Softwood

½in (14mm)

1½in (38mm)

½in (14mm)

MDF

¼in (6mm)

7³⁄₁₆in (182mm)

¼in (6mm)

499 Alcove shelf brackets

A simple way to make some elegant shelf brackets is to cut a suitable shape from ¼-½in (6-12mm) MDF and screw them to each side of an alcove. The screw heads are then filled and the whole bracket painted over before a shelf is rested in place.

500 Using silicone sealant

The best way to achieve a truly professional-looking silicone bead around a worktop or similar is with masking tape.

Tape one or both surfaces, apply the silicone and then smooth the bead with a wet finger, making sure that the silicone thins to nothing over the edge of the tape.

Remove the tape immediately, pulling at about 10° away from the bead. Do not touch it until it's dried.

Credits

Bob Abbott 254
Tony Abbs 331
Tom Addison 133
Michael Andersen 346
George Anson 399
Stan Armitage 098
G. H. Arnold 381
Bill Aspell 214

Anthony Bailey 198
Bill Baker 390
Mark Baker 383, 401, 403, 416, 418, 420, 421, 432, 434, 440
Norm Baker 426
George H. Baldock 143
T. Banks 310
Mike Barkwith 360
John Barr 217, 255
Ian Barras-Smith 413
Jack Barron 032
Mike Bates 193
J. A. Beart 167
J. E. Bedlington 164
Derek Bennett 317
Peter Benson 451
Michael Berriman 140
Bob Bert 309
Arthur Biggins 234
Jonathan Bishop 123
Tom Bishop 361
R. C. Black 499
Bernard Blain 125
Ted Bond 323
Alan Boulter 127
Dennis Bowen 427
J. Bowerbank 266
A. D. Boynton 496
William Brock 338
Frank Brolly 105
James Brolly 076, 132, 178, 296, 343
Irwin Brown 025, 138
A. Buckley 078
Henry Burek 243, 262
B. Burns 371
Ian C. Burton 015, 049
Harry Butler 408, 430, 444

Bill Cain 114, 209, 294
Adrian Caldwell 022
Gordon Cargill 291
Sean C. Carter 215
Mark Cass 057, 158, 166
Eugene Chadbourne 238
K. Chandler 146
Edward Charles 020
J. Chatfield 287
John Cheetham 072
Clive Childing 142
Bryan Clarke 437
Gavin Clarke 106
Terry Clover 411
Ray Cochrane 366
Ashley Cockburn 300
Jim Collis 046
Alfie Conn 179
Colin Consanduras 306
Bernard S. Cooper 007
T. Corns 330
Dennis Cotton 386
John Coward 325
Bert Cowdrey 111
H. E. Cox 458
Stan Cox 175, 190
Martin Croft 073
Wallace Culverhouse-Renton 059
Ian Curry 286

Julian Curtis 324
M. A. Cuthbert 223

C. Davies 005
Robert Davis 388, 438
Tim Davison 387
J. Dawes 355
W. Day 124
Tony Dean 004, 033
Chris Denham 356
Peter Dobson 061
Richard Downes 463
Jim Doyle 376
Tim Drake 484
Andrew Dugley 079
Peter Dulley 394
B. Duncan 423
Peter Dunstall 236
John E. Dury 334
Henry Dyer 019

Colin Eden-Eadon 239, 311
David S. Edgar 406
Jon Edge 011
Jesse Edwards 187
Julie Edwards 156
Sid Edwards 276
G. Elliot 315
Laurence Eustace 211
D. Evans 365
Duncan Evans 370, 373
Ray Everest 203, 275
Steven Eyre 144

John Farrow 115
Bill Fellowes 185
Terry Fielding 348
Albert R. Findlay 112
Ian Fisher 372
S. E. Fisher 199
Alex Forester 016
Ron Fox 197, 213, 295, 353, 354, 357
Carl Fraser 086
W. Frobisher 241

Mitchell Gates 084
S. Geehan 002
D. Gibson 261
Barney Glover 177
Alan Gomm 409
Bradley Good 157
Alan Goodsell 195
Kim Gordon 102
Terry Grace 188, 359
Brian Grantham-Hill 030, 184
Mohammed Green 257
Bob Greenshields 395
Basil Gridley 374
Grant Griffiths 278

David Hallam 135
Michael Halstead 189
Sebastian Halton 128
Malcolm Hannah 129
Charles Hansford 248
A. C. Hardman 031
Ian Harman 149
David Harris 419
Mark Harris 091
Bryan Harrison 302
Kevin Harrison 271
Brian Harroun 447
Danny Harvey 337
Lou Harvey 181
Matt Hasler 151
Alan Hastings 170
Peter Hawkins 070
D. Hawksworth 014

Tony Headley 071
Brian Hepworth 274
D. B. Hoare 107
Rob Hodson 389
Phil Honey 435, 439
Bruce Hoover 378
Gerald Horley 068
Chris Hotrod 380
D. Houseman 196
Jan Hovens 410

Tony Ingraham 412

A. Jackson 224
M. N. Jackson 341
Ruben Jamieson 299
Torgny Jansson 385
Frank Johnson 242
Gareth Johnston 083
R. E. Jones 425

Bob Kelland 307
Baz Kemp 045
Don Kenney 462
Bill Kinsman 443
J. H. Kiss 117
Trevor Knowles 035

Tom Lack 397
Andrew Laurillard 039
W. Law 009, 036
Stuart Lawson 028, 204, 208, 226, 263, 268, 272, 277, 465, 466, 489-93
Andrew Lawton 264
Steven Leegrove 058
Neil Linderbrins 096
Terry Lock 064
Ken Loder 131
John from London 090
Andy Lords 069
Iain Lowe 066, 221
Simon Lunt 171
Martin Lyons 041, 316, 329, 335, 345

M & M Tools 352
D. MacCarthy 231
Andy Maclair 500
Winston Majendie 227
W. R. Markham 453
Kevin Marks 113
Ted Marple 104
John Marshall 219
P. Martin 259
Eric D. Martinson 013
G. Marvin 200
Wes Matthews 006
Dave Maunder 349
Andrew Maxwell 082
Raymond Mayo 402
John McCarthy 459
Bob McCartney 333
David McDonald 087
A. McGibbon 055
John McHugh 319
Brian McIntosh 429
Jim McMannus 202
Ian McVickers 428
Julian Meadows 134
Ian Melhuish 461
N. Meller 273
Nick Mellor 358
Pedro Menedez 094
Adam Metcalf 080
Doug Midgley 436
A. A. Miller 027
Charles G. Miller 457
Eric Miller 269

Trevor Mills 454
Wilf Milton 074, 328
Kenneth Moore 043, 165
Thurston Moore 283
Maurice Morgan 141
R. Morgan 153
Bruce Morten 488
Bob Moss 017, 152
Tony Motion 093
Rolf Moulton 225
C. Murray 267
Bob Musgrave 363

Daniel Nazareth 062
Al Neri 265
A. Neves 229
M. Ninham 452
Terry Norton 210

Tim O'Donnell 308
Sean O'Hennessey 053
Wallace Olar 148
Maurice Olsen 042
John Owen 433

Tony Page 377, 407
Richard Pain 405, 417
Russell Paldon 183
A. Palfreeman 313
Richard Palmice 290
N. Pantelides 460
E. Parfitt 205
Frank Parker 154
Ian Parkes 332
Ken Payne 169, 391
Derek Pearce 442
Mike Pearson 368
Martin Pentangely 321
M. Peters 136
Bob Petithomme 375
Daniel Phillips 052
G. M. Pilling 023
Martin Pinner 161
S. Piper 362
Randy Plankton 282
Derek Potter 398
T. Potts 251
Adrian Powell 250
James Powell 037
Mike Powers 012
Wilmott Powers 207
Gary Prestwick 256
Clive Price 448
W. D. Proctor 340
Chris Puttick 174

Gary Ramsbottom 147
Adam Rawat 218
Richard Rawling 067
Rufus Rawlings 095
Doug Rayment 237, 495
B. M. Redgrave 233
Chris Reid 415
Ellis P. Ressado 246
Rupert Restuccia 292
Andrew Revis 201
Brian Reynolds 384
Ernie Richardson 441
Paul Richardson 206, 240
Bob Riches 176
Henry Riddell 108
Stephen Ridgeon 344
Graham Rix 481, 482
Dave Roberts 109
Ievan H. Roberts 392
Rodney Roberts 228
B. Robinson 280
James A. Rodgers 018, 089
William Rodman 116

J. V. Rogers 270
A. M. Roper 455
Alan Roscoe 347
Bernard Rothschilde 314
Adam Rowat 305
M. Rowland 054
K. Rowlands 232

Aled C. Savage 220
N. M. Sayine 026
R. Schofield 162
B. Sedgley 099
Ivor Set 312
Thomas Sharp 088
Victor Sheppard 056
Richard Shock 400
Clifford Shortall 342
Peter Simpson 119
B. Simson 247
Ian Sinclair 230
Tom Skeels 120
Donovan Skeils 475
Jason Smart 118
Henk Smit 445
R. Smith 456
Ray Smith 008
R. Snowdon 422
Bob Southgate 322, 446
Brian Squires 063
Ron H. Standwell 024
Bill Stanton 044
Tom Staples 279
Richard Stapley 040
Roy Stapley 424
A. Steele 075
Jim Stevens 163
Cranley Stokes 150
Keith Stott 077
F. A. Suarez 155
Peter Symonds 249

Wes Tams 085
Peter Tapp 318
Phillip Tattaglia 301
A. R. Taylor 101, 339
K. Telfer 320
J. Thomas 245
Mark Thompson 244
Andrew Thorne 097
James Todd 431
Trend Routing Technology 191, 222, 285, 288, 351
Andy Truman 010
S. A. Tuck 382
Aaron Turner 121
J. Tybjerg 449

C. Vaughan 103

N. Waldron 168
Bruce Walker-George 021
N. Wallis 051
Grant Warnock 258
Peter Watthey 326
B. Wayne 172
J. Weald 034
Bob Wearing 182, 192, 364
Scott Welby 180
John West 350
Andrew H. White 130
Andrew J. White 126
Roger Whitely 003
Richard Williams 186
Derek Willis 092, 159
Ray Willis 476-9
J. Willy 464
Roy Wood 414
Joseph Woodward 281

Index

GMC Publications,
Castle Place, 166 High Street, Lewes, East Sussex BN7 1XU, United Kingdom
Tel: 01273 488005 Fax: 01273 402866 E-mail: pubs@thegmcgroup.com Website: www.gmcbooks.com

Contact us for a complete catalogue, or visit our website. Orders by credit card are accepted.